Praise

Blood Is Thicke.

"This book perfectly encompasses the true story of a remarkable woman who transforms from a struggling/hopeless alcoholic to the most genuine, open, and honest individual who has not only helped hundreds of clients in treatment, but also inspired numerous colleagues alike. Janine has played an integral part of my passion to specialize in addiction in my private practice. In this book and in her day-to-day life, her honest vulnerability is so contagious that I personally strive to conform with her magnitude of transparency and veracity."

—Allie Levy-Akoka, M.S. LMFT, Licensed Marriage and Family Therapist

"Janine's memoir tells the story of a young woman battling bulimia and alcoholism after fleeing her dysfunctional/alcoholic home. Despite great pains, obstacles and setbacks she courageously gets sober and in turn helps countless addicts and alcoholics. In the telling of her miraculous story, she is able to heal a contentious relationship with her eldest daughter. As a clinician, it was an honor to work alongside Janine and observe her transparency, authenticity, vulnerability, and sense of humor, allowing her to reach the most difficult clients. Janine is a gifted storyteller. Her story is a gift for anyone who is seeking change."

—Robin Toland Krieger, MFT, Licensed Marriage and Family Therapist

"T.S. Elliot wrote, 'Success is relative, it is what we make of the mess we have made of things.' Winston Churchill wrote, 'Success is not final, failure is not fatal, it is the courage to continue that counts.' Janine's life is the perfect example of transforming chaos to the miracle of change. Janine reminds me of the great truth, that nothing changes until it is real. If you know Janine, you have witnessed her authenticity and genuine love and care for her clients. I have had the honor of practicing addiction medicine for the past forty years and twenty of those years I have worked with Janine. I am truly grateful and blessed to have teamed with a healing professional addiction counselor of her stature in the field of substance and alcohol use disorders. Janine's book is a testament and inspiration to the miracle of transformation and hope. It is a journey of love and demonstrates that recovery is possible."

—Walter Thomas, M.D, A.S.A.M., F.A.A.F.P.

Blood Is Thicker than VODKA

Wisdom
Editions
Minneapolis

Second Edition December 2022

10 9 8 7 6 5 4 3 2
ISBN: 978-1-959770-36-7

Cover art by Eric Adrian Lee
Book design by Gary Lindberg

This book is dedicated to all those who know the suffering of addiction.

Janine Fox

Blood Is Thicker than VODKA

A memoir by
JANINE FOX
with her daughter KATIE FOX

Wisdom
Editions
Minneapolis

Janine's Prologue— A Mother's Perspective

In 2005, a client at Serenity House, the rehab where I was interning, suggested I write a book. Every time I saw Vince, he asked me the same question, "Have you started writing your book yet?" Vince was a screenwriter and so I told him the truth: that I couldn't write. He dismissed my excuse, "If you can tell a story, you can write it. Just start with a timeline, Janine." He really liked stories about my family, especially the one's about my mother. One of his favorites was when my mum showed up at my prestigious boarding school with only one eye made up. The other completely devoid of make-up.

In 2009, Katie and I were talking over lunch one afternoon, when she made a proposition: "Mum, why don't I help you write your book? Maybe email me stories that you want to tell, and I'll format them into a memoir for you." She had taken creative writing in college, and I knew she had a secret dream to write a book one day. I said "okay" before I had time to really think about the concept of sharing my personal life story with my eldest child.

The next morning, I woke up in a panic, realizing there was no way I could safely share my history with Katie. I knew I would be held back by shame, and I was sure it would create even more distance and hostility between us. We didn't get along since the divorce from my husband when she was fifteen. However, I decided I had to at least make an attempt to face my fears. So, with all the courage I could muster, I wrote my first vignette about meeting my second husband in California while visiting my mother. Katie emailed me back one short sentence, "Where was I when all this was going on?" I had a panic attack that was so severe I spiraled into a vortex of shame for two days. I had to tell her the truth or we would not be able to continue.

After obsessing over the situation for another couple of days, I emailed her.

"The truth to your question is, I don't know where you were Katie, you spent a lot of time with my mother so you were probably with her."

I went on to tell her that I couldn't write my stories if she was going to make them about her, it brought up too much guilt and shame for me. I was surprised when Katie said she understood. She kept to her word and never asked questions about herself again, unless they were relative to the story.

After a couple of weeks of exchanging emails, we decided the long-distance approach was not working. We finally agreed on a schedule where I would go to her apartment every Sunday for a five-hour block of time and we would write together. Mind you, I had not spent more than an hour or two in the company of my daughter since she was fifteen, so I was anxious about how this compromise would work out. To ease my anxiety, I took my dog Molly; Katie had her dog Gizzy lying beside her during our marathon writing sessions (perhaps to ease her anxiety too). Our process was laborious. I wrote a chapter at a time, which I then forwarded to her. It was her responsibility to correct my grammar and add more specific description and flavor to each story.

When I was fourteen, I ran away from home. A man in his thirties stopped to give me a ride and let me stay at his house with his two children while his wife was away on a business trip. I thought I was safe, but he forced himself on me during the night. I didn't even know how to begin writing this scene. We were only thirty-five pages into the book and I was stuck. Katie said, "Mum, I can write the scene." The thought of my daughter writing about a stranger raping me was terrifying. "I can't let you do that Katie. It will be too psychologically harmful."

"No mum," she said, "I can compartmentalize it. I can make it so that I'm not writing about you, I'm just writing about a fourteen-year-old girl and what happened to her." I had to trust my daughter.

From that moment, little by little every memory of my life came back. My daughter helped me uncover the missing sequence of events of my life. My initial concerns turned into excitement as the book began to take on a life of its own.

As my confidence and my trust in her grew, I found myself writing whenever there was the opportunity. The book became my safe place where time didn't matter. The stories, shared with my daughter, absorbed my shame and guilt and my past became my greatest asset.

Then one day I had to put my faith in her to the test.

In 1996, I was arrested for possession and being under the influence of cocaine. Because I was not bailed out of jail, I was transported to Twin Towers in Los Angeles. I never shared with anyone the details of that week in dehumanizing conditions.

My two daughters Katie and Samantha (whom we all called Sam) knew I had been to jail, but never asked me questions. I could not bring myself to write about this experience for Katie to read. I was so afraid of her judgement that I was sure this would be the end of our project. I told her about my fear and we decided I would write about the incident and then read it to her.

As I read, my voice caught in my throat several times. I felt so much self-loathing sharing the details of my jail experience with my daughter, who taught at a prestigious private school. How would she ever understand this?

I finally reached the end and looked up at her face. I expected to see shock and disgust. Instead, tears streamed down her cheeks. She patted the seat next to her on the couch and I got up feeling as if she were the mother and I was the child in need of forgiveness. I sat down next to her and she wrapped her arms around me drawing me close. "I'm so sorry all of this happened to you," she said softly. "I don't know how you made it through, I would never have been able to."

I put my head on her shoulder and we sat in stillness for the longest time. I could never have imagined feeling so close to her as I did at that moment.

Then it was her turn to take a risk.

"Mum, there's something I've never told you."

I told myself to breathe, just breathe through whatever she was about to tell me.

"You told me one time that you hated me and that you wished I had never been born. I always felt you loved Sam more than you loved me. Is that true mum?"

I wanted to tell her she was lying. I would never have said such a thing. Maybe she thought it, but there was no way I ever uttered those words to her. It was always so easy with Sam. Sam was just a baby; I didn't see judgement in her eyes, but I didn't lie to her the way I lied to Katie. I had always felt Katie saw right through me and it killed me every time. She was the one who had to call her father and tell him to come home because I was passed out. She was the one who had to give Sam a bath, get her ready for bed, and then get her up for school in the morning. Katie was the one who found alcohol hidden in the house when her mother was supposed to be sober.

Now I looked at her and saw her pain, really saw it for the first time. I told her I must have been in an alcohol blackout when I said those terrible words. I told her that I felt so shameful all the time and that's why I avoided her. Her feelings were valid. I didn't defend myself. I loved her so much that loving her was painful.

We both cried and held each other for the longest time. Decades of cold, hard resentments and hurt started to melt away with the warmth of forgiveness.

I knew the book was just the beginning for us.

Katie's Prologue—
A Daughter's Perspective

"Where was I when this was happening?"

An innocent question posed to my mother out of genuine curiosity rather than judgement. The minute I heard her response, I knew the question was a mistake. I was the one who had convinced her to write this memoir with me, and if we were going to make it through to the other side, I had to find a way to detach myself and allow her to tell her story.

Secrecy shrouded my childhood. I knew my mom came from a tumultuous upbringing and the odds had been stacked against her from the beginning, but there was so much of our past together that I sought answers to. Maybe helping her write this book could be therapeutic for both of us. She could release all of the demons that still lurked deep down inside of her, and I could approach my search for answers as a reader would. I didn't understand why we were so distant. She and my sister Sam seemed to have such a different relationship. I was too scared to ever ask her why, but I hoped that her past might help me uncover an explanation.

I remembered a story she once told me about losing control of her bicycle when she was a child and plummeting down a hill—a ride that began with the notion of freedom and happiness, as she pedaled along the cobblestone streets, and ended with a literal rock bottom and almost the loss of her life. To me, this was where her story needed to begin. This would prove to be a metaphor for most of her adult life:

the continual chase for sobriety, the longing for escape, but with one false turn, it all comes crashing down, and there you are, trapped again in that bottle.

I sat down on her bed one day with a pencil and paper and drafted this scene. It was strange at first to write about my mom from her perspective as a child, but I wanted to prove to her that I could do it. I wanted her to be proud of me, and I thought if I could get her excited about a beginning, then maybe we could really make this happen.

She then began emailing me stories here and there, and I would create scenes and add dialogue, while trying to make them flow together. This became much easier when we transitioned to writing sessions where the two of us would work together in the same room. I would make us tea, and the two of us would sit with our dogs and write all afternoon.

Listening to her stories and writing them from her perspective allowed me to gain a deeper sense of empathy for the person she was when I was a child. I began to understand why she used alcohol as an escape, and I truly felt her loneliness and desperation. By the time we got to the end, I was amazed that any human being endured what she did and completely forgot about myself. I saw my mother as someone I had not known before. She was strong, determined, and she never gave up in her fight for sobriety.

A scene that has stuck with me to this day is learning about the time she was out in the pasture with a shotgun trying to take her own life but was too drunk to pull the trigger. My mom wrote that scene on her own, and of course, it was something I knew nothing about. Knowing that my sister and I were somewhere in our big, lonely house while this was happening right outside shocked me. It was terrifying, and sad, and unbelievable; but there it was, right in front of me on paper. It was the truth, and as much as I wanted to deny it, to tell her she made it up, that she couldn't or wouldn't have done something like that, I reminded myself: this was her story. Her struggle. If there were ever a moment where I could say, "God, I'm glad she was drunk." it was that one. Reflecting back on that moment reveals how much we had to trust one another in order to do this. She had to trust me to set aside all judgements and not to ask questions like why or how could you? I had to trust that she would truly let all of her guard down and not sway from the truth in an effort to protect herself or my feelings.

If you had told me that writing a book together would have brought us to this point in our lives, I would have laughed. Before the book, we barely spoke to one another. With so much unsaid between the two of us, it was impossible to have a real relationship. Word by word, story by story, we pieced together our voice. This book allowed us to talk to one another as we never had before. It was a safe space in which the two of us could explore our past together.

I found the answers I had been seeking for so many years.

She found closure and forgiveness for herself. The two of us found each other again.

August 2010

She was wearing turquoise sweatpants, the ever-present wad of paper towel shoved down the side of her waistband and a purple Christmas hoodie; perfect attire for a sweltering summer afternoon in Southern California. I flashed back to the time she had greeted me at the door leaning on her walker and wearing nothing but a pair of Depends. This was definitely a step up.

I winced as I took in her appearance. Her hair looked unwashed, the gray roots blending into the orange of her last self-administered dye job. It was thin and wispy, and clumsily held back by a large, garish hairclip in the shape of a giant sunflower. I could see that she'd attempted to give it some volume by hair spraying her bangs away from her forehead, but what she'd succeeded in doing was revealing most of her scalp.

"Hello, Nini darling!" She smiled, extending her arms for an embrace.

"Hi, Mum." I tensed as her arms wrapped around me and held my neck at a rigid angle to ensure her clammy cheek would not touch mine.

"I'm so excited we're going out to lunch. I'm all dressed and ready."

I forced a smile, still breathing through my mouth. The smell of chemicals and cleaning products used to mask the odor of urine and feces permeated the narrow hallway.

As she locked the door behind her, she began to cough and clear her throat. Pulling the paper towel out of her waistband, she opened it and spat the loosened phlegm inside, then refolded the napkin and tucked it safely back inside her waistband.

I matched her tortoise-like pace as we made our way down the dingy corridor. Dark stains covered the tattered, pale blue carpeting.

Standing outside of the drab, brown building waiting for her to exit, I reflected upon the numerous times I had made this trip in the past. It had been many years since I had come here seeking relief from my pain.

I tensed as she teetered over the threshold, fearful that any moment she might lose her balance and tumble onto the sidewalk.

Once we were safely inside the car, she turned to me and smiled. "I'm trying out some new patches!"

My mother was on a continual search to medicate pain caused by her fibromyalgia.

I felt an old twist of yearning in my gut and quickly pushed aside any curiosity.

"Really?" I responded.

"Yes, the morphine goes straight through your skin and right into your bloodstream! I stuck one on right before you came to pick me up. I hope it will help me get through our lunch."

"Me too."

I felt a strong urge to use and gripped the steering wheel tightly as I pulled into a parking space outside the Chinese restaurant. As I helped her out of the car, I noticed that she was beginning to sweat profusely and her mascara was smeared underneath her eyes. The hairspray had lost its hold, and her bangs now plastered to her forehead.

Once settled at our table, we ordered. As usual, she held the waiter captive with her stories of when she used to work as a chef.

"Mum, let him go," I said, embarrassed for the waiter.

I pretended to listen as she gave me a rundown of her latest ailments. There wasn't a medical condition anyone had been diagnosed with that my mother couldn't match.

"Here comes the food!" I said, thankful to cut her off.

"Oooh, I'm so excited to have some shrimp," she said, rubbing her hands together with childlike glee.

The waiter set down our dishes and serving spoons, making a quick getaway before my mother could trap him again.

I then watched, transfixed, as she spooned her shrimp dish directly onto the tablecloth, missing her plate by a good six inches.

"Mum! What *are* you doing?" I said, surprising her out of her reverie. "You're not putting your food on your plate!"

"Oh dear," she said, absently picking the sauce covered shrimp off the table with her fingers and dropping them onto her plate. "I don't know why they give you such small plates these days."

Having relocated her shrimp, she leaned across the table dipping her fingers into her water glass and swirling them around to wash off the sticky sauce. I tried to detach myself mentally as I had so many times in the past.

"Come on, Mum," I said, encouraging her to hurry. "I have to get back home soon."

I endured the rest of the meal as she went into descriptive detail of the demise of her latest relationship.

"Did I tell you Wally and I broke up?"

She had met Wally at one of her Alcoholics Anonymous (AA) meetings. He had a handlebar mustache that he proudly gelled into place with toothpaste. He was in his late seventies and always wore a black leather vest and smelled like an ashtray. The two of them had been inseparable for the past few months.

"Really?" I asked, feigning interest. "What happened?"

"Oh you, know," she said waving her hands dismissively, "men and their bloody tempers."

"So, you two had a fight?"

"Let's just say he had a little obsession that I wasn't very fond of."

"An obsession for what?" I asked, and immediately wished I hadn't.

"Well, he liked to watch his pornos." My mother paused for a moment as if lost in thought.

"Every time I came over he'd put one on, and I just got sick and tired of it."

"He would watch with you *there*?" I asked, incredulous.

"Oh yes, and he was into *everything*. Even men having sex with other men."

"Why would he want to watch *that* with *you*?"

"He always wanted to watch them with me," she answered matter-of-factly.

"The last time I was at his place we had a big argument. He wanted to watch another one of his movies in the living room, and I wanted to watch *Law and Order*."

I imagined a couple of geriatrics, fighting over whether they were going to spend their evening watching gay porn or a crime drama.

"I told him if he wanted to watch his pornos, he could go into his bedroom and watch them on the computer. He refused, and said that it was his house, and he'd watch whatever he damn well pleased wherever he damn well pleased. Then he turned the volume all the way up."

"What did you do?" I was now completely sucked in by the drama.

"I was fed up," she said with a snort. "I grabbed all of my things and told him to call me a cab. I will not put up with that nonsense." My mother declared self-righteously. "Frankly, I have no idea why he was always so starved for sex. It's not like I didn't give it to him whenever he wanted it."

I squirmed in my seat.

"I'm still pretty good in the sack," she added. "Even at eighty."

With that, I summoned the waiter.

"What are you doing?" She asked. "I haven't finished my shrimp."

"You can take the rest with you." I said, a little too sharply.

After paying, I waited as she arduously pulled herself out from between the table and the bench. When she'd finally reached a standing position, I watched in amazement as she leaned over the table, picked up her murky water glass, and drank from it.

"That's better," she sighed replacing the glass and picking up her small box of shrimp.

Her side of the table resembled the eating area of a toddler in the early stages of hand to mouth coordination.

* * *

After I took her back to her apartment and I was driving home, I called Katie. I often called her after a few hours with my mother. I knew she would understand.

"I know how you feel." Katie said sympathetically as I told her about our lunch. "Grandma does the weirdest things. I can't believe we're in the same gene pool as her." We laughed and I immediately felt better.

Living in close proximity to my mother, Katie had become her main caretaker. I finally stepped up after Katie found her grandmother lying helpless on the bedroom floor of her apartment a few years previously. My mother had fallen out of her bed and been laying, unable to move for over twenty-four hours. My daughter, concerned because my mother wasn't answering her phone, went to her apartment to check on her. After that upsetting incident, Katie told me she couldn't do it anymore; the responsibility of caring for her grandmother was too overwhelming and distressing. My mother had been deteriorating following a hip replacement and was falling more often. In a moment of clarity, I was able to hear what my daughter was telling me, and realize how selfish I had been. Katie had gently confronted me, telling me the reason she felt I avoided my mother was because I couldn't let go of the past. I felt guilty that for years I had allowed my daughter to do what I should have been doing.

I now made time to check on my mother daily and take her out to lunch every couple of weeks.

I had a deep-rooted fear that one day I would become like her.

Chapter One
1966

I pedaled my bicycle through the streets of Chesham, wheels spinning hurriedly, hair blowing behind me, rain soaked terrace houses rushing by in a dreary blur. I had always been accident-prone. Perhaps it was because I was always in a hurry and had no impulse control, or perhaps at eight years of age, I had already been programmed with a subconscious urge to flee.

Longing for the sense of freedom to overwhelm me entirely, I pumped my legs faster and faster, desperately wanting to lose myself in this moment. A sliver of sunshine penetrated the gloomy sky that loomed overhead. I squinted upward for a brief moment and furrowed my brow; I could have sworn I heard a faint voice in the distance calling my name, screaming at me to slow down, but the whirring of the bicycle tires against the damp, cobblestone pavement muffled their cries. Then, like the wheels in a clock suddenly gone haywire, the pedals began to spin madly as I plummeted down the hill. I fumbled to reconnect my feet as the handlebar jerked unexpectedly to the right. Yanking it back in the opposite direction, I felt myself lose all control. I sucked in a deep breath, preparing for impact, and then everything went black.

* * *

As I struggled to regain consciousness, I could feel something awkward and heavy weighing me down. I tried pushing it aside, but it was hard to move the metal made cumbersome and slippery from the rain. I couldn't get a good hold on it, so I rolled onto my side and pushed it off me. A searing pain shot across my hip and I looked down to see the brake handle lodged in my groin, blood surging from the gaping hole and quickly forming a pool beneath me. The sensation felt oddly comforting.

My eyes fluttered and for a moment, I thought I saw my best friend Nanette and her mother running toward me, but the figure of a man blotted out their images. The stranger leaned down and reached one of his arms around my waist, as if to share an intimate secret. I closed my eyes to listen and was shocked back into full consciousness as he pressed his thumb into the hole in my groin, plugging the blood flow of my severed artery, and keeping my life from spilling into the street on that cold and rainy day.

Had I known at the time that this uncontrollable desire to flee would shape my entire existence, perhaps I would have kindly pushed this stranger's thumb aside, denying him the satisfaction of saving my life. But I was only a child and quite unaware of what life had in store for me.

* * *

When I was nine, I was sent to my first boarding school. Nanette was going to come with me, but her parents decided that boarding school might be too brutal for her. Apparently, this failed to deter mine. In our family tradition, if you had the money, you sent your child to boarding school. This form of schooling worked two-fold for parents. It enabled them to get their children out of the house, while at the same time giving off the appearance of great financial success to others. In my case, both reasons rang true. My mother was married to her second husband, Samuel Howard Everard Davey, who had his own bio-chemical company where he patented a formula for mechanics to use on their hands, preventing dermatitis.

My parents owned a massive estate called Blackwell Hall, endowed with stables, tennis courts, servants, and a nanny. Samuel Davey was twenty-five years older than my mother and it was obvious she hadn't married him for his looks; he was short and stocky with gray thinning hair that he combed over the top of his head in an attempt to cover his baldness. I hated the thick moustache that scratched my face whenever he kissed me. My mother was thirty years old and an elegant five feet nine inches tall. She wore her dark hair bobbed in the current style and she always carried a pair of soft gloves that coordinated with her outfit. When I was seven my mother confided in me that the only reason she had married Sam was so I could have a father. She also disclosed that he had adopted me shortly after they married.

"Sam is your real father. Your biological father was just a sperm donor. Why, he didn't even contest Sam adopting you when you were four, as he would have had to pay child support."

Even after hearing this, I still could not bring myself to acknowledge Sam as my father and I didn't believe what my mother told me about my real dad. I was sure she probably forced the situation and didn't give him any choice.

* * *

I hated boarding school. The girls ranged in age from thirteen to eighteen and seemed to have their own little cliques. I was one of the few nine- year-olds. I felt lost. The nights were the worst; I lay in my narrow cot listening to the other girls in the dorm whisper to each other and giggle. I was sure they were talking about me. I had always had trouble sleeping and given the circumstances I tossed and turned most of the night.

My mother once told me a story that she believed justified my insomnia. Apparently, when I got too big for my crib, she used to have to tie me to my bed.

"You were terrible," she said, shaking her head. "You'd get up in the middle of the night and wander all around the apartment. We didn't know what to do with you."

"Doctor Greenborough suggested we use your walking harness and tie you to the bed to keep you safe." Doctor Greenborough had also given my mother diet pills, and told her to put a little whiskey in my nighttime bottle to help me sleep.

I remembered the harness. It was yellow and had a little lamb etched on the breastplate. As I got older, I no longer had to wear it to sleep. Instead, my stepfather sat on the end of my bed at night and told me stories about goblins that patrolled the hallway outside my bedroom door.

"They only come out at night," he whispered, moving up the bed, his face getting closer to mine, "and they would love to grab a little blonde blue eyed girl like...*you*!" His eyes suddenly opened wide and I scooted back to the headboard.

If I woke during the night, I would lie in my bed paralyzed with fear the goblins knew I was awake. I wondered if there were also goblins in the hallways of the big, creaky old school that was now my new home.

Lying in my unfamiliar cot, I pulled the thin blankets up over my head so the other girls couldn't hear me crying. "Please," I whispered between sobs, "Please Mummy. Come back and get me. I hate it here."

This would not be the first prayer of mine that went unanswered. A definitive silence forever met my pleas for help, challenged my belief that anyone cared, and forced me to take matters into my own hands.

* * *

As time went on and I remained at boarding school, a part of me wanted to shrivel up and hide, whereas another part wanted to be the girl that everyone liked. It was here that I told my first serious lie, an innocent lie produced with the intention of making new friends. I informed all five of my classmates I had a horse that could play tennis.

"If you put a racquet in Sparky's mouth and throw a tennis ball," I explained to them one rainy morning in our dorm, "he can hit the ball back to you."

My classmates were immediately enamored with me and couldn't stop asking questions about my unique pet. It felt good to have their interest and admiration. For days, I continued to boast about my horse and his myriad talents.

* * *

This story blew up in my face one afternoon when my mother came to pick me up for a weekend pass.

A silk, paisley handkerchief kept her newly colored red hair in place, and enormous tortoise shell sunglasses sat perched on the end of her nose, like a glass placed precariously on the edge of a table. White-gloved hands gripped the leather steering wheel of her red convertible MG sports car as she swiftly pulled up to the school's main entrance, carelessly spraying gravel from her tires.

The girls were anxious for the opportunity to meet my mother and ask her all about my tennis-playing horse. I tried to make it to the car before they could say anything, but they pushed past me, screaming excitedly, and ambushed her before she'd even had a chance to park. Her window slowly descended and I watched helplessly as my classmates began questioning her.

"How's Janine's tennis playing horse?" one of them yelled as they approached her car.

"Can we come and see him?"

"Pleeease," a third pleaded.

My mother only shook her head and laughed, as I hurried around to the passenger side.

"What *are* they going on about?" she asked, eyeing me suspiciously through the window.

"Hey, Mum," I scrambled. "They just want to come over and see Sparky and some of the things he can do." I desperately tried opening the car door, but it was locked.

"Like what," she scoffed. "Bite you on your bottom when you bend over to clean his hooves?" My mother threw her head back, laughing at her own joke. My new friends looked on awkwardly.

"You'd do best not to believe any of the rubbish this one tells you," she said jerking a gloved thumb in my direction. "We call her Pinocchio at home because she's always telling lies. Aren't you, Janine?"

Removing her oversized glasses, she turned her head and gave me a curt, satisfied smile. I was crushed and angry.

How dare she not go along with my lie and why wouldn't she open the door?

I could feel my face burning with shame and I wished the earth would open up and swallow me whole.

Finally, she reached over and unlocked the passenger door and I jumped in, slamming it behind me.

"Just go!" I shouted at her, my eyes welling with tears.

At that moment, I hated her and I hated them. I didn't want to go home with her and I didn't want to ever go back to that stupid school and see any of their faces again.

I tried to focus my attention on something else as we made the long drive home, but it was next to impossible with my three-year-old brother Pete screaming in the backseat.

My mother and stepfather had adopted Peter a couple of years earlier. It was a private adoption as my stepfather was out of the desirable age bracket. I had gone with my parents to a village a couple hour's drive from Blackwell Hall. A middle-aged woman with gray hair pulled back in a bun ushered us in to her terrace house and had us wait in a small living-room, returning a short while later with a blond, blue-eyed boy and a black girl who looked about six years old, was painfully shy and wearing thick spectacles that were too large for her tiny face. The girl tried to hide behind the woman's skirt as the boy wriggled and cried in her arms.

"This is Peter, and he's fifteen months old," the woman said, trying to pry his chubby little fingers from around her neck as she passed him to my mother.

* * *

The next thing I knew we were driving home, my parents talking excitedly while I held the wiggling, crying baby on my lap. My mother was telling my stepfather she wished she could have taken the little black girl as well and she was sure "the poor child had been over-looked for any white baby that came along." I was afraid to ask her what she meant by that.

"What do you think of your new brother, Nini?" She took off her sunglasses and turned to look at me over the back of the passenger seat. "Didn't you always want a baby brother?"

"Not really," I muttered under my breath as I struggled to hold onto him.

"Pardon?"

"Yes, Mum. He's great. Just what I always wanted."

At that moment, the baby whimpered and vomited his lunch in my lap.

* * *

Peter came into our lives to give my parents a son. My stepfather had never had children and my mother had lost her baby boy Matthew three years previously. He had died when he was seven days old due to "medical complications" that were always a mystery in our family. My mother often lay on her bed for hours, ignoring me and staring up at the large gold cupid chandelier she named Matthew.

I felt she desperately wanted to replace Mathew. Peter even had the same blond hair and blue eyes.

"She was taking a lot of pills when she was pregnant." My grandmother confided when I was older. My mother once disclosed that my father pushed her down the stairs when she was eight months pregnant and she was convinced *that* was when the baby had been "damaged."

I didn't know what the truth was.

It didn't take long for the novelty of Peter to start to wear off, as things often did. He cried a lot and was a difficult child to feed. My mother became easily frustrated as he rejected the meals she offered. He hoarded meat in his cheeks like a chipmunk, refusing to swallow. Finally, she would have to force his mouth open and pry the dry chewed meat out with her fingers.

One morning Pete was sitting in his highchair, a bowl of Weetabix cereal placed untouched in front of him. I was at the kitchen table immersed in my new *Black Beauty* novel. Saturated for so long by milk, Pete's cereal was a glutinous mound in his bowl. I watched absently as my mother tried to coax him to eat.

"Come on, Pete! Through the teeth, round the gums, look out tummy here it comes."

She raised a spoonful to his mouth and he turned his head in defiance. This happened a few times until she suddenly and unexpectedly threw the spoon down, got up from her chair, and forcefully pushed his face down into the bowl. I sat there paralyzed, my book still open on the table as his little arms thrashed around helplessly. He blubbered into his Weetabix, spraying cereal all over my mother's chest. She didn't seem to care.

"Next time you'll think twice before you do that again," she snapped as she released him, turned, and marched out of the kitchen.

Pete sat in his high chair screaming, his face caked with soggy cereal, the bowl finally emptied of its contents. I got up robotically, wet a dishtowel, and gently wiped the cereal out of his eyes and ears as he continued to bawl.

* * *

Two and a half years later Pete was dressed in a uniform and sent off to boarding school, the red blazer voluminous on his tiny frame. I watched from my bedroom window as he climbed into the backseat of the car, holding the nanny's hand.

A few days later, I too returned to mine. With memories of my mother shaming me in front of my friends still fresh in my mind, I decided to keep my distance from all of them. I told myself I didn't care. Who needs friends anyhow?

* * *

One Sunday afternoon I was using my free time to explore the grounds surrounding my school when I stumbled upon a bird's nest in a tree. The nest was just low enough that I was able to reach inside and feel the warm bodies of three tiny fledglings. I gently dislodged the nest from the branch and placed it in a safe area on the ground.

"Well hello little ones! Where's your mummy?" I whispered to them softly. "Are you all alone?"

I stroked their tiny, bald heads with the tip of my finger and decided that from now on I would come here every afternoon and feed them until they were old enough to fly. I would be their new mother. I covered the nest with some undergrowth, and satisfied that it was well hidden, went back to the school in time for the dinner bell.

* * *

Not long after, I had gone on my daily visit to the fledgling's nest, the headmistress called me into her office. I nervously entered the room, where she stood authoritatively behind her desk, wearing a knee-length tweed skirt and button-down white blouse. She was a tall, skinny old woman with a long nose and a tight perm. Her Borzoi dog, Henry, came careening out of the corner of her office, paws flailing on the wood parquet floor. He skidded to a stop in front of me and immediately shoved his long, wet nose underneath my skirt. I pushed the dog's face away, at the same time noticing how similar he looked to his owner. They even had matching hunchbacks. As nervous as I was, I felt like giggling at the resemblance. I quickly looked down so Mrs. Basher couldn't see me smiling.

She pointed to the chair across from her mahogany desk and instructed me to sit down.

"I suppose you know why you're here, child?" she said coldly.

I hadn't the slightest idea.

"No, Mrs. Basher." I pushed her dog's nose out of my lap.

"Well, Janine, it has been brought to my attention that you have relocated some baby birds in the school grounds."

"How did you—" I blurted.

She squinted at me, her long, thin nose pointing in my direction like an accusatory finger.

"No, I haven't, Mrs. Basher. I just go down there to visit them."

"Is that so?" She sneered. "So, you've never touched them then?"

"Well, no...I mean, yes. Well, kind of."

"Which one is it then, child?"

"Well, I *have* stroked them a little bit, but mostly I just like to watch them."

"And do you know what happens to baby birds when they're touched by human hands?"

I started to panic. "N-n-no, Mrs. Basher," I stammered.

"Their mother can smell the scent you've left on them, and she instantly rejects them. She'll no longer come to the nest and feed them. Because of you, we'll have to drown those poor birds."

"What? *Drown them*? But why?"

"*Why*?" she shot back rhetorically. "Because you have taken it upon yourself to disrupt that nest and now their mother will never come back and look after them."

"But I can look after them," I mumbled through tears.

"Pardon? Speak up, girl!"

"I said I can be their mother."

"Don't be ridiculous," she snorted. "It is because of *you* that those baby birds will have to be killed. Now, I would like for you to leave my office at once and think about what you have done."

I stood up, my head hung low. Henry scrambled up from beneath my feet and emphatically shoved his nose back underneath my skirt again. I wanted to kick him. Instead, I pushed his ugly face away and walked silently out of Mrs. Basher's office, baffled by the exchange. All I had wanted to do was take care of the baby birds, and now she was telling me that I would be responsible for their deaths. I was ten years old and I was a murderer. It didn't take long for the news to spread around the school.

"She's the girl who murdered those sweet little baby birds," girls whispered. "Can you believe someone would do such a terrible thing?"

I felt misunderstood and exposed as a freak. My lonely life became even lonelier, and I was relieved when the school closed down less than a year later.

I could start over somewhere else; become a new person.

This time people would like me.

Chapter Two

During the summer of 1968, my encounters with exposure took on a literal connotation. My stepfather owned a house in Provence in the south of France. We travelled by ferry and car to a village named Bormes-les-Mimosas to stay for three months each summer during school break. Because my mother and Sam liked to relax, they brought along our nanny to watch Pete and me while they sunned themselves on the beach or drank pastis with their friends.

Sam owned a sailboat and cabin cruiser and we would cross the Mar Ligure to Corsica, a mostly uninhabited island off the southern coast between France and Italy. He and my mother particularly loved nudist beaches. They set up a family size tent at their favorite spot and everyone walked around naked, except me. I insisted on keeping my bikini bottoms on, although Pete was ecstatic to be free of clothing. He had always thwarted any attempts to be dressed, alternately crossing his arms over his chest, or kicking his little legs.

"I've never known a child to be so difficult," my mother complained the few times she tried to dress him.

Seeing my stepfather's penis dangle to and fro as he strolled casually along the shore made my face burn with embarrassment. The fact that he was twenty-five years older than my mother didn't make seeing him naked any less disturbing. Everyone at the nudist beach was either old, overweight, or both. Geriatric men with pale skin and sagging buttocks walked hand in hand with their heavyset wives as they waded into the Mediterranean. Even my mother's body had lost the firmness of youth as she substituted self-care for drinking with my stepfather.

Sam stood out from other campers with his expensive camera hanging loosely around his neck. When he thought I wasn't looking, he suggested my mother bend over and smell a flower as he adjusted the zoom. One time he had her climb a small tree and straddle one of the branches as I watched from behind a bush.

"That's it!" I heard him yell up at her. "Now open your legs as you reach for another branch."

I wondered why I never saw any of these pictures in our albums, alongside family events or holidays.

Most afternoons we walked as a family down to the local café, my stepfather's flaccid penis leading the way, and my mother's bare, pendulous breasts flopping from side to side as she brought up the rear. We sat at a bank of tables on the patio, overlooking the white sandy beach. The ocean shimmered in the afternoon sunlight while small children chased its returning current up and down the shore. They laughed and shrieked as the water rushed around their ankles and swallowed up their tiny feet. I hadn't made any friends as the kids were all more Pete's age.

Sadly, this juxtaposition was inadvertently overshadowed by the view of my naked family huddled around me as we ate lunch. My stepfather always coerced me to order more food, oblivious to the fact that my appetite wasn't exactly at its peak while I was sitting across from my mother's spaghetti sauce splattered breasts, listening to her slurp mounds of noodles into her mouth. Things typically deteriorated after she'd had a few drinks and would then strike up a conversation with a nearby table. It was only a matter of minutes before the couple were invited to join us, and I would be squashed in between naked strangers as I attempted to force down the rest of my lunch.

* * *

I often complained of stomachaches. My mother loved it if I had any ailments, as she fancied herself an amateur chemist and kept combinations of different elixirs and medications in her bag, always ready to offer the perfect solution to any medical problem. Her solution to my indigestion was in the form of a suppository. She was a great believer in the little glycerin bullets.

"Why take a pill when the suppository hits your bloodstream much faster, and doesn't upset your stomach?" she reasoned with me as if she were a doctor. "Up your bottom is a far safer method."

She positioned me on the bed on all fours, my bottom up in the air. I bit down on my clenched fist in anticipation as she began the preamble.

"In a big field, full of the sweetest, greenest grass, lived a little bunny called Hop-a-long." My mother's singsong voice lulled me into a false sense of security, and I would start to relax.

"One day," she continued, "the farmer came into the field carrying his shotgun. Hop-a-long saw him and hopped as fast as he could to his burrow on the other side of the field. All of a sudden there was a loud *BANG!*"

I had fallen for her trick once again, even though I knew it was coming. The glycerin bullet shot into me at the very same moment Hop-a-long met his sudden death.

* * *

During mealtimes, the nanny watched over Pete as he napped. My stepfather believed children should only join adults for meals if their table manners were met to his expectations. I wondered then why my mother didn't also have to stay back with the nanny.

It had taken them a while to secure a nanny who would be willing to join our family on a nudist vacation.

"I've finally found the right girl!" My mother announced to Pete and myself as we were watching *Bonanza* one evening. "Her name is Cherise, and she sounds like a lot of fun. I think you'll both like her."

Cherise had told my mother that she had an equal love for both children and nudity. She had been truthful about the nudity, but it was soon discovered Cherise wasn't very fond of children.

A woman sitting on the beach apparently saw Cherise and Pete struggling in the ocean one afternoon. The observer noticed the nanny pushing the little boy's head under the water, and each time he popped to the surface coughing, she'd push his head under again. The concerned woman came to our tent to report the incident to my mother.

When confronted, Cherise explained she had been frustrated trying to teach Pete to swim. "He was afraid of his face going under the water, so I was just trying to get him used to it."

Despite her pleas for another chance, my stepfather took her by boat to the mainland and let her find her own way back to England.

"I could have strangled her," my mother later said. "She was supposed to look after the child, not kill him."

Pete hadn't told anyone what Cherise was doing to him because at four years of age he still hadn't started talking.

When I asked my mother why Pete didn't talk, her logical explanation was not to worry; boys always took longer than girls with vocabulary.

By the end of summer, I was longing to put on one of my ridiculous and uncomfortable school uniforms again.

Chapter Three

The next boarding school I attended was Hampden House. The manor house once belonged to John Hampden, a famous cavalier during the reign of King Charles I. Mystery shrouded the story of Hampden having been arrested by Cromwell's men and his wife and children locked in a room in the house and left to die. Older girls would excitedly whisper into a new girl's ear that the ghosts of Mrs. Hampden and the two children roamed the halls of the school.

True or not, this was very thrilling and terrifying for us young girls. The school was impressive. The interior walls were oak-paneled and replicas from the original Renaissance paintings hung from the walls. The grounds were breathtaking, bright green fields that seemed to stretch on forever. The school even had its own church. For Sunday mass, we had to dress in one of my least favorite uniforms: pale blue sundresses with white gloves and straw brimmed hats. It was around this time noticed that I was chubbier than most of the girls my age, somehow my uniform never quite fit me the way theirs did. Food was becoming the one consistency in my life; I lived for mealtimes, the anticipation of greasy chips and the pudding of the day covered in thick yellow custard helped me endure the rest of the monotony of school. At the beginning of each term, my mother gave me money for extras; most of this was used to buy chocolate, fudge, and cakes from the school shop. Here, instead of feeding baby birds, I resorted to feeding myself. Some girls teased me, calling me names like "Ten Ton Tessie" or "Thunder Thighs." I started hating my body, noticing how different it was from the others. Of course, I only compared myself to the petite, small-framed girls in the school, wishing I could look like them. Food had become the only joy in my life.

* * *

We were allowed to bring our pets with us, but only if they were caged, such as mice, guinea pigs, and rabbits. That's what initially sold my mother on the school: I could take my pets with me and she wouldn't have to care for them. I brought along my two mice and a black and white rabbit named Jemima. The schoolgirls kept their pets in a freestanding building on the grounds. A few times during the day, I visited my little menagerie, bringing them treats from the lunch table.

On one of these visits, curiosity compelled me to switch around some of the animals. There was no one else in the building at the time, and I hesitantly pulled some mice from different cages and put them in with others. I had never witnessed sex before, and I was transfixed watching the male chase the female around, until he had her trapped and had his way with her.

I'm not even sure that I knew what was going on, but it made my heart beat faster and my face blush. I thought I heard someone outside, so I scrambled to return the animals to their appropriate cages, and hurried from the building flushed and excited, nervous about my little secret.

I was shocked when, a few weeks later, some of the mice were giving birth. There was chaos and an investigation as to how female animals alone in their cages were miraculously having babies. I was never exposed as the culprit. I was scared and excited about having got away with something so big.

My mother signed me up for riding lessons; this was the only extra-curricular activity I got to do. Riding was a status symbol. Any girl that came from the right family background knew how to ride a horse. I enjoyed the lessons and being connected to a strong beast that could take off at any moment. I loved the smell of horses, and burying my fingers in their thick manes. The only downfall was we had to wear standard jodhpurs, riding boots, and jackets. My

28

jodhpurs, being tight, strained at the inseam, and I always had the greatest difficulty pulling the riding boots up over my thick calves. One day after an energetic trot, I looked down to see that the entire jodhpur seam had split. My thigh fat bulged out of the tear like stuffing pouring out of a swollen turkey. I tried several times to push the fat back, horrified that someone might see when I dismounted. Once back at the stable, I took off my jacket, and holding it in front of me, ran back to my dorm to change.

The more I ate the fatter I got, and the fatter I became the more I hated myself. I failed to make friends at this school too. Brains and beauty appeared to be held in high esteem, and I felt I lacked both. I yearned for Nanette and the weekends spent at her house with her loving parents and brothers. Even after being at the school for two years, I still felt rejected by the popular girls I admired.

I went home one weekend a month. As I waited by the main entrance of the school with my overnight bag between my feet, I strained into the distance for a flash of red that would signify my mother's sports car. Sometimes she would forget. She would be consumed with her own affairs and forget that I was waiting for her. I waited so long once that day turned into night, and eventually a staff member had to come and shepherd me back inside.

* * *

In July 1970, I came home for the summer holidays. Something had happened while I'd been at school, but I didn't know what it was and no one bothered to explain it to me. I was twelve years old and grown-up stuff had shaken the foundation of everything that was familiar. All the pets had been given away and belongings packed into a Land Rover and fifteen-foot trailer. There were strangers coming and going, and chaos everywhere.

I ran up to my mother. "What's going on? Where's Mandy, I can't find her anywhere!" Mandy was my blonde, rough-haired Dachshund whom I loved with all my heart. I was always more excited to see her when I got home from school than I was to see anyone else. I was frantic that she had gone missing.

29

"Calm down," my mother said. "We are very busy here and there's a lot to do. Don't worry about Mandy. Uncle George is going to look after her for you."

Uncle George was my mother's brother and my favorite uncle. He had a wicked sense of humor and greatly appreciated practical jokes. George lived with his wife Anita in a beautiful restored monastery in the countryside. I knew Mandy would be well taken care of there, but didn't understand why we were leaving everything behind. My mother assured me that we were just going on an extended trip to the south of France. Normally someone from the village stayed at our house and looked after the pets when we went to France, so it didn't make sense that Mandy had to go and live with Uncle George.

With my stepfather behind the wheel, my mother, Pete, and I piled into the Land Rover and began what was to be our last journey to Le Lavandou. I wondered if they had told my best friend Nanette and her parents that we were leaving.

We stayed with Sam's friends Mimi and Fanny. He had known them before he ever met my mother. I giggled whenever anyone said Fanny's name. Mimi had an outboard engine shop, and every now and again Fanny would be sporting a black eye or a bruised lip. They had two daughters, Martine and Danielle. The girls were quite a bit older but that didn't stop me tagging along everywhere they went. By then I spoke French pretty fluently and, to their chagrin, pretended to be their little sister. No one explained why we were staying in a little trailer outside Mimi and Fanny's house, and no one had an answer to what had happened to Sam's boats or the house we had owned nestled in the rugged hillside of Bormes-les-Mimosas. This was nothing like the three month holidays I was used to.

* * *

"When are we going back to England?" I asked my mother.

"Not for a while," she answered.

"Well, how much longer? You said we were just going for a holiday," I whined.

"I don't know," she said, getting angry. "Don't keep asking me that."

My mother, who up until this point had been the key player in my stepfather's business, now had a job as a chef in a local seaside hotel. My stepfather, who was used to comfort and security, now sat in the trailer and drank wine or pastis all day. Pete and I did not go to school. We played on the beach and amused ourselves in the nearby town.

Sam and my mother's relationship was always volatile, but now they each blamed the other for their dismal situation. I found out later that his heavy drinking was what led to the collapse of his business, and that when we got to France she had to work in a hotel kitchen to support us all.

As the months passed, resentments fueled by alcohol began tearing them apart. They became verbally abusive and violent when drinking and now fought all the time. The trailer was so small it rocked from side to side as the fights became more intense and frightening. Sometimes they were so fierce that there was blood—blood on my mother and screaming rage on my stepfather's face. One time it was so frightening that I grabbed Pete and we ran outside and hid in the bushes. We waited, shivering in our pajamas until it was finally quiet enough to go back inside.

I felt very small and afraid a lot of the time. There was no one for me to talk to, no one to ask advice. I could see from Fanny's cuts and bruises that she was afraid to stand up to her husband Mimi. She often came to the trailer and talked to my mother over a glass or two of pastis. My stepfather would sit outside the trailer on his folding beach chair chain-smoking Gauloises and staring off into the distance. Every day was depressing with unpredictable outbursts of anger.

* * *

One afternoon as I walked along a deserted stretch of beach, a black cat approached me, meowing pitifully. I knelt down and ran my hand over its emaciated body. I watched sadly as clumps of fur fell from my hand onto the dirt.

"You poor little kitty," I whispered. "Don't you have a home or a Mummy to look after you?"

I had finally found a friend, someone who was lost and lonely like me. I felt a surge of love for the abandoned cat and knew I needed to care of it.

The cat looked up at me, her large green eyes caked with infection. I picked her up and felt her frail little body vibrate like an idling engine against my chest.

"I'll call you Minou," I said, holding her weightless body so that her face was level with mine. Minou was French for kitty, and I felt it suited her perfectly.

I couldn't take her to a vet so I cleaned her eyes three times a day with cotton balls and warm water. Looking after her gave me a sense of purpose and her love for me replaced what was lacking from my parents. Within weeks, Minou's body filled out and her fur gained a shiny black luster.

One afternoon as I sat on my bed in the cramped quarters of the trailer, Minou climbed back and forth over my legs purring and rubbing her chin against my shoulder. My mother was out somewhere with Pete, and I was alone with my stepfather. I thought he was taking his afternoon siesta, but then he unexpectedly staggered up to my bed, swaying as if he were on a ship's deck. I held my breath as he attempted to walk over to me, never knowing anymore in what sort of mood he would be. As he got close, the acrid stench of alcohol and cigarettes seemed to be seeping from his pores and through his knit sweater. It was barely noon, but it was evident he'd already been at the bottle for the better part of the morning.

He started taunting me, something he seemed to enjoy doing when he was drunk. Minou, sensing danger, immediately jumped off my lap and took cover underneath the bed.

"That cat is no good," he slurred at me. "Why do you even keep it?"

I sat silently on the edge of my bed, staring at my flip-flops.

"Cat's a waste of money, if you ask me. Serves no good purpose, just costs us money to feed."

My breath caught in my throat.

"Come here kitty," he sneered in a singsong voice, unsteadily bending down and thrusting his hand underneath my bed. Minou tried to dart out, but he managed to grab her by the tail.

"Try to get away from me? You good-for-nothing cat!"

He roughly pulled the cat out from under the bed by her tail and then swung her toward the trailer door. He was so drunk he almost lost his balance. I sat frozen on the edge of my bed. In my mind, I jumped up and snatched Minou away from him, but instead I just sat there, paralyzed. I closed my eyes tightly as I heard the sickening thud of her head colliding with the side of the dresser, the same dresser that was already stained with my mother's dried blood from a week ago. My stepfather then dropped her to the ground like a discarded sack of groceries, and stumbled out of the trailer.

I jumped off the bed, knelt down by the motionless cat, and lifted her warm limp body into my arms. I buried my face in her fur, tears running down my cheeks. She hadn't done any harm to anyone. I cried even harder, realizing I was responsible for her death. I had brought her into this hell. Then I was crying for myself, abandoned in this craziness, left to rot with a drunk of a mother and sadistic stepfather.

Wasn't there anyone out there who could save me?

I knew that somehow I had to get away from this place, back to England, and away from the madness.

Chapter Four

I was now thirteen years old and hadn't been to school in over a year. I spent my days in the wretched trailer that had neither heat nor air-conditioning. When it became too unbearable on summer afternoons, I would walk down the dusty trail that led to the beach. There was a cove at the bottom where tide pools gathered and little crabs hastily sidestepped across the hardened sand. I often passed my time watching them, envying their ability to disappear into tiny holes in the earth when they felt threatened or afraid.

My brother seemed quite content, but then he was only seven. He sat on the beach for hours alone with his bucket and shovel, his sole focus on building sandcastles. When his castle was finished, he would leap to his feet, stomp all over it and then start the process again. I wished I could join him, but I was too worried about what was going to happen to me. I was going crazy. I couldn't stand being cooped up like this any longer.

Mimi and Fanny's two daughters were not interested in having me tag along anymore now that they both had boyfriends. I felt so ignored that I just had to do something to get the attention I craved and make my mother realize how truly insane my stepfather had become. Hopefully she would tell him to leave if she knew he had hurt me. Using a paring knife one afternoon, I held my breath and cut the back of my hand. I watched as tiny, crimson beads of blood surfaced and began to travel down to my wrist. I opened my stepfather's dresser drawer and pulled out one of his large, white handkerchiefs that I wrapped loosely around the wound, wanting to be sure that it kept bleeding through the cloth.

Looking through the grimy little window, I saw my mother weaving her way home after her lunch shift at the restaurant. She staggered up the steps of the trailer, oblivious as her chef's hat was knocked off her head by the low doorframe.

"Look!" I cried, as I thrust out my hand. "Dad attacked me with a knife."

I slowly peeled back the now blood-soaked handkerchief to show her the half-inch-long gash on the back of my hand.

She tried to focus on my face for a moment, and then looked down at my hand.

"Well, knowing you, you probably did something to provoke him."

She brushed past me and collapsed onto the bed.

Resigned that my plan had not had the expected outcome, I dressed the wound myself with some gauze I found in the medicine cabinet.

When I had told her what he did to Minou, she had responded by saying that the cat was in a better place now, up in heaven with Mr. God.

* * *

My mother did finally make some effort by enrolling me in the local school. My first day was a nightmare. The French children giggled and pointed at "La Petite fille Anglais." I was terrified of the classes. I could speak French but I wasn't literate. I knew the teasing would get really bad once it was discovered I couldn't read or write in French. I didn't know what I was going to do other than just pretend I was going, but not show up. It seemed the only solution.

My mother worked all day at the restaurant, other than the couple of hours she came back to the trailer for a nap between shifts. I figured she wouldn't notice if I never went back to the school.

I spent my days at a bar café on the seafront. The jukebox was always on and I could watch the old men playing boules in the sandlot across the street. It was here that I met Havre. He approached my table and asked if he could sit with me and buy me a drink. In areas close to Marseilles, the Moroccans and Algerians had a bad name. They were viewed as drug dealers and predators of tourists and young French girls. I could see that he was either Moroccan or Algerian, but he was nicely dressed and he looked like a student. I reckoned he was somewhere in his early twenties; he seemed safe so I told him I'd like an Orangina.

As I sucked the cold, sweet sparkling liquid through a straw, I studied him a bit more closely. He had fine features and thick, wavy dark hair parted on the side, and long and dark eyelashes accentuating hazel eyes. He leaned forward with a questioning look on his face. "Why do you come here, to this bar alone? You should be having fun playing with your friends," he said, picking up his beer.

I told him how unhappy I was living in a trailer with my parents. I told him how we had to leave England and no one ever explained why. I told him how I missed my friend, my home, even my school. He listened empathetically, shaking his head every now and then.

I was so relieved that someone finally wanted to hear my story that I leaned forward and whispered, "I just want to be able to escape and go back to England to my grandmother's house."

He leaned in toward me as if we were engaged in some sort of conspiracy, "What you would do if you went to your grandmother's?" he asked in his broken English.

I thought for a moment, "Well, she was always the one who cared when there was no one else, so I know she'd let me stay with her and my grandfather."

I grew quiet as I thought about my mother's mother, who always spoiled me. I had lived with her the first six weeks of my life while my mother remained hospitalized to recover from a severe infection following my birth. My grandmother and I felt that time together was when we bonded. The happiest times of my life were when I was with her. Her house had the feeling of love, normalcy and consistency that I craved. I started crying as I thought about Granny and how much I missed her.

The young Moroccan passed me a napkin.

"Shhhhh, no crying, maybe I can help you to get back to your grandmother."

I looked at him quizzically. He then went on to tell me about a friend of his who was going to Dieppe.

"He leave tomorrow morning, very early, and he drive his car. I tell him come and pick you up from my apartment. You don't needing any money. He is good friend of mine."

We talked some more, and I figured from Dieppe I could get the ferry across to England. The idea of an escape plan made my heart race and thoughts rush through my mind. He pushed his empty glass back and got up from his chair.

"I go and call him now. His name is Eric."

I watched as my savior walked back into the bar.

Can I do this? Do I dare run away and leave them all?

The more I thought about the plan, the more logical it became. By the time I saw him walking back to my table, I had made the decision that I would go.

"Okay," he said, smiling down at me. "My friend said he take you, he come at two in the morning to my place. I pick you up tonight, you will be safe. I get you at midnight."

He looked at me with genuine concern, "You want still to go, yes?"

He glanced down at his watch. "It is one o'clock now, you have plenty time."

I nodded and said I did. I drew him a map to the entrance of the parking lot on one of the napkins. I realized I didn't even know his name.

He took the napkin, clasped it in his hands and raised his eyes to the sky. "I feel that God send me here to help you. I am Havre by the way."

"Janine," I said shaking his hand.

I had nothing to lose. Once I was back with Granny, everything would be all right again. I knew she would understand why I had to run away.

I walked home from the beachside bar feeling excited and scared. Nobody was home, and I could see Pete playing with another kid his age at the far end of the parking lot. The rest of the day, I kept the curtains in the trailer open so that I could see if someone approached. I started to search through all of the drawers until I found my passport, and then I found some cash in one of my mother's coat pockets. I hid the passport and money under my pillow and decided I wouldn't bother taking clothes, other than a couple of changes of underwear, socks, and some T-shirts that I could just put in a plastic bag. I needed to travel light.

I was lying on my bed pretending to read when my stepfather came back from the bar. He was whistling as he walked up the steps and it sounded like he was in a good mood. I was sure Mimi had probably bought him a couple of drinks. I cringed as I pictured the two wife-beaters making small talk over a bottle of red wine.

"How's my little girl?" he asked, putting items away from the local mini-mart.

"Just reading." I hoped he wouldn't come any closer.

I was in the room I shared with Pete, the kitchen and dining area separated us from my parent's bedroom. We may as well have all been in one big room, such was the lack of privacy.

When I heard Edith Piaf's rich guttural voice fill the trailer, I knew he was pouring himself another drink. It wouldn't be long now before he passed out. My mother would be home by eleven.

I felt myself drifting in and out of a dream world, waking constantly to check the time on the clock. I was afraid I wouldn't wake up, and I couldn't set the alarm because then someone else might hear it. I woke up again at eleven-thirty and decided to stay up. My heart was pounding.

No going back now.

I pushed the covers back and quietly climbed out of bed, I was already dressed in street clothes. My brother was out cold on the small bed beside me. I could hear my stepfather's loud snoring, accompanied by my mother's heavy breathing at the other end of the trailer. I tiptoed to the only door, and gingerly pushed it open. The hinge creaked and I held my breath, but nobody stirred. Outside in the dark, I was even more afraid. In the silence of the night, I heard only the chirping of crickets. I began thinking that perhaps this wasn't such a good idea after all. Then

I saw headlights appear at the top of the driveway. They flashed once. I carefully closed the door behind me and walked toward the lights, trying as best as I could not to make crunching sounds on the gravel.

I opened the passenger door of the small Fiat and the Moroccan turned to me and smiled, "Come on little girl, we go now."

I hadn't noticed before, but now I saw that he had a gold tooth. For a moment, I wondered if I was making a big mistake, but the moment passed and he handed me a large mug sealed with a plastic lid.

"Hot chocolate help you to stay awake. Come, we must hurry, my friend is coming soon."

He smiled again and this time I couldn't see the gold tooth. *Had I imagined it?*

We drove into town in silence. I warmed my hands on the mug while sipping the sweet hot chocolate. After what seemed like forever, we pulled up alongside a large brick building. It looked like an old mansion converted into apartments. I glanced around and saw a few cars parked on the dimly lit street, but there was no sign of life other than a mangy looking cat hunting around some garbage cans.

"Come," he said. "We go up, is no good to stay here in the car."

I followed him up the staircase of the apartment building, the lighting so dim I could hardly see. I felt light-headed and dizzy and had to concentrate on not tripping over the uneven steps. Once on the second floor we went through a door and into a hallway. I held my breath to avoid the heavy aroma of cardamom, cumin, clove and other cooking spices permeating the air of the equally badly lit hallway. I was in his apartment, but everything was hazy and shapeless. I had difficulty keeping my eyes open, and just wanted to lie down somewhere and sleep.

* * *

He kept me in a sparse and dirty room. The dripping of the faucet from the sink underneath the window lulled me into a hypnotic state…drip… drip…drip. Heavy drapes hid the only barred window. It was always dark. No friend ever came to take me to Dieppe. It was all a lie, and I was the fly caught helplessly in the spider's well-camouflaged web.

Havre, if that was his real name, came and went and I had no idea of time. There was no clock anywhere in the room. When he left, he locked the door behind him, the oversized iron key clanked like that of a prison cell. He told me he had to go and make phone calls or to get us some food. He gave me more of the hot chocolate he had given me the first night. By now, I figured the drinks were drugged with something, but it didn't matter, they made me sleepy and when I was sleepy, I wasn't afraid. I remembered Martine and Danielle telling me that the Moroccans would steal young blond girls off the streets because they could get a good price for them. I wondered if he was planning to sell me to some rich old man in Morocco or Algeria. I hoped that perhaps he wasn't allowed to have sex with me if he was going to sell me.

Unfortunately, this wasn't the case. On the second night, he roughly pulled down my jeans and underwear. I didn't fight or say anything, not wanting to anger him. I could smell beer on his breath as I lay immobilized staring up at the dull dirty bulb hanging from the gray ceiling. He never said a word, and I gave up my body because I didn't know what else I was supposed to do.

After he left I carefully pulled back one of the drapes and looked out through the bars to the alley below. I watched the stray cats jump in and out of the garbage cans as a wino in his disheveled, dirty clothes, bottle in hand, yelled at them. There was no one to call out to for help.

On the third day, my captor took me with him. He told me that he wanted me to meet someone. As we walked along the sidewalk, I could feel the painful pressure of his fingers digging into my arm. If I were ever going to make a break for it, it would have to be now. I looked around and noticed a gendarme on the other side of the street giving someone directions. Fight or flight kicked in, and with all the courage and strength I could muster in that moment, I yanked my arm back and broke free from his grip.

"Help me! Help me!" I yelled, running across the street.

I dared not look back to see if he was chasing me. I ran up to the officer, crying hysterically. Through my broken French I told him what had happened. We looked all around us but the Moroccan was gone.

A few minutes later, I was in the back of a little blue and white police car heading to the town gendarmerie. There, two stern-looking detectives questioned me. The room was small and scant of furniture other than a table, three chairs, and a light hanging above us. I couldn't stop crying. They wanted to know what he had done to me, but I was too embarrassed to tell them he had sex with me. I just wanted to go home. I now wished I had never tried to run away. I sat at the interrogation table for what seemed like forever, too uncomfortable to answer their questions.

The detective sitting across from me smiled empathetically. "We call your mother at the restaurant, she is coming soon," he explained in his best English.

Then I heard shouting coming from the hallway outside the room. The door opened and there *he* was, gripped between two gendarmes, his face covered with red marks and a split bottom lip.

I turned to the detective across from me. "That's him!" I said, afraid to look at my captor again.

I had told the police his first name and the general location of the building where I had been held captive. My kidnapper must have gone back to the apartment. The police had unleashed their vengeance on him; it was an opportunity for them to act on their prejudices and get away with it.

Shortly thereafter, my mother arrived.

"Where's my daughter? Where is she?" I could hear her shrill voice from down the hallway.

I knew immediately that she had been drinking. I felt my face burn with shame—shame on top of shame. The detective went to calm her down and suggested she take me to the local doctor to be checked for any sexually transmitted diseases.

I followed her out of the gendarmerie to her little gray Citroen 2CV. As soon as we got into the car, she turned to face me.

"How dare you! I knew you weren't going to school."

I leaned back against the door thinking she was going to slap my face.

"I lost two days of work because of all this, and now I have to take you to a doctor. You cause nothing but trouble!"

With that, she started the car, and we bounced out of the parking lot and onto the street.

The medical examination was humiliating. I lay on the table trying to cover myself from the elderly doctor's cold, calloused hands. By the time it was over, he confirmed that I had been sexually assaulted, but he didn't know to what extent. I wouldn't answer any of his questions because I was too ashamed by them. He eyed my mother, and I could tell from his look of disgust that he knew she was drunk. He curtly recommended she take me home after the nurse gave me a shot of an antibiotic.

I was now back at the trailer I had tried so desperately to get away from. This would be the last time my stepfather ever spoke to me. My mother later told me that he couldn't deal with the fact that I had been raped. I was to be put on a plane as soon as possible and sent to live with my grandmother in Brighton. My mother reached out to my godmother Patsy. I hadn't seen her since I was a little girl but remembered she used to send me gifts for my birthdays and Christmas. Patsy stepped up and wired my mother money to help get her goddaughter back to England.

My victory felt empty. I had romanticized the drive to Dieppe, the ferry, and then the train to Brighton. I had planned to show up on my grandmother's doorstep, knowing how happy she would be to see me. But that wasn't how it turned out. I'm sure my mother had already called her, briefing her on the horrible things that had happened, and how they felt it had all been my fault.

My mother told me that my kidnapper had been deported back to his country, but there was no trial, no testimony, and no closure to what had happened to me. My last week in Le Lavandou was hell. My stepfather ignored me and he and my mother fought more than ever. "She's your little whore." I heard him say to her during one of their arguments.

* * *

A few years later my stepfather would die a homeless drunk on the streets of Bristol, England. To me he had died the night I came home from the police station.

Chapter Five

The naïve little girl who lived in the English countryside playing cowboys and Indians had gone, and in her place was an angry adolescent.

As I had anticipated, my mother told my grandmother about the incident in France. On the drive back from the airport, my grandmother informed me that if I was going to live with her, I wasn't to discuss it. She didn't want anyone else in the family to know either, so I needed to sweep it all under the rug and get on with adapting to my new life. There was a lot to do, including getting me enrolled in school.

My grandmother lived a simple life in a flat in Brighton with my grandfather, who was now in poor health with diabetes. It was very different from the trailer in France. Conservative florals, beiges, and burgundies decorated their modest flat; with rich pieces of furniture adorning rooms, always smelling of fresh lemon wax. China and cut glass, heirlooms from my great-grandmother, generously filled cabinets. Everything had been just so—until I arrived. The first thing Granny did was to enroll me in a nearby Catholic school, walking distance from her flat—my sixth school, if I counted the awful one in France that I attended for one day. I felt I couldn't once again go through the routine of trying to fit in. As usual, the school semester had already started; the girls had formed their cliques, and were not interested in getting to know a new girl.

At thirteen, I had developed breasts and started to notice the way men looked at me. My period began the year before on the Sealink ferry traversing the channel to France. At that time we were in a dire situation and I was afraid to tell my mother. I had an idea of what a period was because a girl at Hampden House got hers when she was only nine, and I remembered feeling sorry for her that she had to wear huge regulation pads in her underwear. I took care of the problem in the ferry bathroom with the only padding I could find, stuffing my underwear with harsh, non-absorbent sheets of toilet paper.

It didn't take me long to start hanging out after school with students from Sussex University. They were in their early twenties and treated me like a peer. I no longer had any interest in school anyway; my challenge now was how to cut class without being caught. My new friends and I would spend time in pubs, laughing and playing darts. Sometimes someone would buy me a beer or a shandy. This was a lot more fun than doing homework.

We never talked about the bad thing that happened to me in France, which was fine with me. I spent all my free time in the town, just like I did in Le Lavandou. I couldn't wait to get back to my grandparent's after school, change out of my uniform and into my "grown up" clothes and go back out. In the summertime, Brighton was filled with students from all over Europe.

* * *

"Janine darling," my grandmother called to me from the kitchen as I was getting ready one evening.

"Yes, Granny? I can't stop now as I'm meeting a friend to help me with my homework." I walked into the small kitchen. My grandmother was bent over the sink, pink rubber gloves immersed in a bowl of bubbles and dishes. A cigarette dangled delicately from her lips, the inch-long ash trembling as she spoke.

"Oh, there you are dear."

The only time my grandmother smoked cigarettes was when she was at the sink doing the dishes. She turned to look at me, grasping her cigarette between two rubber fingers. She took one last inhale before squashing the cigarette out into the ashtray on the kitchen counter. She blew the smoke out slowly as she looked me over. I bit my bottom lip, anxiously waiting for her response. I was sure, as she stood there looking at me with arched brows, that she must have been wondering what had happened to the little tomboy who used to come and visit her, begging for slices of bread to feed to the sheep in the field across the driveway, and then at the end of the day soiling her white bed sheets with dirty feet.

"Janine darling," she finally said. "Surely you can't go out like that? You'll catch your death of cold."

I looked down at my red hot pants. It had taken me a good half hour to try to cinch them around my waist, and I finally had to be satisfied with getting the zipper nearly halfway up. My plumpness was being strangled by my waistband and was forced to relocate into one giant mass around my midsection. Thankfully, my shirt was long enough to conceal this defect.

"Granny, this is what all the girls are wearing. I promise you I'll keep my jacket on."

I ran my fingers through my peroxide bleached hair and pulled on some boots.

"See you later," I yelled, slamming the front door behind me.

* * *

One day, without warning, my mother came back.

She arrived at my grandmother's flat with my brother and an old leather suitcase. She announced that she had left my stepfather in France in the hopes that the three of us could start a new life together.

"He's a vicious drunk and I'm not going to put up with it anymore! From now on it's you, me and your brother," she said.

I didn't want to leave my grandmother's. I was happy there, or at least as happy as I could be, but my grandmother told my mother it would be best if she took me with her. With my grandfather's failing health and my juvenile delinquency, it was just too much for her to deal with. She was an old lady and couldn't handle the added stress. I didn't even cry. What difference would it make?

My mother found a place for the three of us in a city named Bath and I was once again enrolled in a new school. She had secured a job as the chef in a hotel-restaurant, but for some reason our stay was cut short. We had just settled in a little flat in the center of the old Roman city and I had been at my school less than a week, when she came home one afternoon and told us we needed to pack up our belongings because she had found a better job somewhere else.

Within two days, we were living in another hotel in Basingstoke, Kent. The three of us shared one room with one bed and no television. *This was the better job?*

The furniture was sparse and I kept the drapes closed to obscure the details in shadow. A single bulb covered by a dingy, white lampshade illuminated the room. I sat in an old armchair in the corner of the room one afternoon, picking at the torn upholstery of the seat cushion, when my mother informed me that she would be enrolling me in a school the following morning. I wanted to throw the curtains open and scream, "You mean it gets worse than this?" Instead, I just sat there fingering the spring that I had discovered inside the hole.

I started school the next day and instantly hated it, but mostly I hated living in a crummy hotel room with my brother and mother. She was intoxicated by lunchtime and spent the majority of her nights and weekends unconscious. I have no recollection as to whether or not Pete was enrolled in school at this time. I know he was never taken to see a dentist or a speech therapist. His teeth were crowded and overlapping, and he couldn't pronounce his r's or th's. He also had great trouble reading and writing. Pete was the lost child, overlooked and unnoticed.

Almost immediately I started hanging out with a small band of truants at my new school. I altered my boarding school accent in an attempt to fit in with my new group of friends who carried knives and ditched classes regularly.

Our hotel was located near a US Air Force base and I made friends with an American serviceman. Ted and I struck up conversation when he came to eat at the restaurant. My mother instantly dismissed our age gap and was simply pleased that there was someone to keep me out of her way in the evenings. With her blessing, Ted sometimes came up to our room while she was down in the kitchen making a roux for one of her sauces. Ted played with Pete and asked him questions about himself, which I was sure made my brother feel important. No one really talked to Pete, other than telling him what to do. I felt my mother hoped some man might come along and take me away, she probably hoped he would take Pete too.

It wasn't long before she lost this job as well. The management discovered she had a drinking problem when they found her passed out on the kitchen floor in her chef's uniform, the bowl of roux and whisk still in her hands.

We moved to Brighton: yet another room in another hotel, school number nine, and she was still drinking. Nothing changed except the location. I continued to eat away my frustration and there was no shortage of food where we lived. I could simply go down to the kitchen and eat as much as I wanted. With greasy chips and pastries piled onto my plate, I went back to the room and ate until my mind went numb and I could fall asleep. I couldn't stand it anymore and knew I had to do something. I had always known my biological father was living somewhere with a real family, in a real house, but my mother wouldn't tell me where that was.

"Where does my dad live?" I would constantly ask her.

"I don't know. I lost track of him a long time ago. He never paid me child support, and then he just disappeared. I even took him to court to try to get money out of him to take care of you."

She told me the same story in myriad ways. I knew it was a lie because Sam had adopted me so they must have had some contact with him. I never believed anything she said. I had a feeling my dad probably thought about me as much as I thought about him, he just didn't know how to find me because we moved so much. I knew he had an affair with my mother's friend Audrey and she blamed him for Mathew's death, but I didn't understand what that had to do with me, or why I couldn't see him.

* * *

The week before I was scheduled to start my new school, I made the decision to run away. Maybe if I ran away and threatened to never come back, she would allow me to go and stay with my father. She would see how serious I was. I formulated a plan.

The Sunday before starting my new school, I stole some money out of my mother's purse while she was passed out on the bed. I already had a lightweight bag packed and ready to go under the bed, I had just been waiting for the right moment.

"This is it," I said to myself. "There's no going back now." It seemed this statement had become my motto.

I pulled the bag from its hiding place and turned to my brother who stood by the bed silently watching me. He was eight years old and I decided it was time to tell him the truth.

"I'm running away."

His eyes filled with tears.

"Can you take me wiv you? I don't like it here eiver."

"I can't," I said. "It is a long, hard journey and you aren't old enough."

He hung his head and started to cry.

I was afraid he'd wake her up. "Here, let me show you where I'm going on my map." I unfolded it, spread it flat on the floor, and pointed to London. I had a feeling the police would question him and I didn't want them to discover that my real plan was to go to Edinburgh.

On a map, Edinburgh was the city the furthest distance from Brighton, so I decided this was the place I would go. I guessed it was about four hundred miles north of London. I wanted my mother to know that this time I wasn't joking. I was *really* running away.

"Don't wowwy." Pete's tone was serious. "If anyone asks, I'll just tell vem I don't know where you went." He wrapped his skinny little arms around my neck.

I gave him a hug, and tried to reassure him, "Once I find my dad, maybe he will let you stay with us too." He smiled and gave me back the folded map.

I left a note on the chest for my mother telling her that I was going to catch the bus into Brighton to see a film with a friend. I figured I could have told her that I was moving into Buckingham Palace to live with the Queen. It didn't matter what the note said, she wouldn't even discover it until I was long gone. I knew that Pete would put a blanket over her and gently lift her head, slipping a pillow underneath. He was always gentle and caring, concerned about her well-being. I never understood why he didn't hate her like I did. He had been adopted, only to be mistreated by her and my stepfather. He had been beaten, neglected, kept out of school, and denied any kind of medical care or help for his learning problems. Yet he loved her, and always made sure that her alcohol induced sleep would be as comfortable as possible.

I couldn't risk going out of the front door, so I made my way down the narrow staircase from our room to the hotel kitchen. Avoiding any possible eye contact, I walked quickly past the staff and out of the back door to the garden. They didn't seem to notice me, being preoccupied stacking plates and shouting orders to one another. I nonchalantly swung my bag over my shoulder, walked through the garden, and onto the street.

I was fourteen and I was going to have to be brave. It was fall and already getting dark. I had a long way to go. I knew that once I started this journey, I could no longer turn back.

A Spanish waiter who worked at our hotel had given me twenty pounds. I had confided in him, telling him how much I despised my life and wanted to run away and find my father. His English was so broken he probably thought that I needed the money for something else. Regardless, I used a portion of it to pay for my train ticket from Brighton to Victoria Station.

It felt strange riding the train alone at night, with only my bag for company. I imagined what other girls my age were doing at that very moment, sleeping safely in their beds while their parents slept protectively in a nearby room.

My first night I stayed at a cheap inner-city hotel by the train station. My heart was pounding as I approached the front desk.

"Can I help you, miss?" An old man in a wrinkled button down shirt asked. He rested his elbows on the counter and leaned in close squinting his eyes as he looked me up and down. His breath was stale and a few stray crumbs clung to the hairs of his wispy mustache.

"Yes, please. I'd like a single room for the night," I replied with as much confidence as I could muster.

He eyed me suspiciously. "Just you?"

I looked around, confused by his question. "Yes, just me."

"You look awfully young to be staying in a hotel room all alone."

"Oh, I get that all the time," I replied quickly, forcing a smile. "I'm actually eighteen. Born in 1954."

"That right? Awfully pretty to be staying in a hotel room all by yourself," he said again.   "Perhaps you might like a bit of company," he offered with a perverted wink.

My stomach turned. "Thanks for the offer, but I'm actually quite tired. I'd just like to get a room please and go to sleep."

He slid the registry toward me and gave me a knowing smile, as if to say he knew I'd come around.

"Well, if you change your mind, you know where to find me."

"Right." I said, scribbling down Nanette's name, followed by a fictitious surname. Nanette Kennedy sounded perfect. I slid the registry back toward him and snatched the key out of his liver spotted hand.

That night I lay in the small, uncomfortable single bed and cried. I felt lonely and afraid of what lay ahead. I couldn't go back now, but I didn't know what I was supposed to do next. I tossed and turned most of the night. As soon as the sun came up I couldn't wait to get back on the road.

The following day I walked until my feet hurt and then started to hitchhike once I was out of the city. In my back pocket I carried my crumpled map with bright yellow outlines, where I had highlighted the major towns on the way to Edinburgh. My plan was to ask each driver who stopped if they were going to the next town on my map. I was given a couple of rides before it started getting dark.

The moon loomed overhead and the country road I had traversed all afternoon now seemed to lead to nowhere. The woods surrounded me, and each sound of a snapping twig or the rustling of leaves made my heart skip a beat. I shielded my eyes as cars passed by, ignoring my outstretched thump pointing north, their headlights blinding me in the darkness. I was beginning to panic and felt a strange and unwanted longing for my mother, when at last somebody stopped. The car pulled up alongside me and the window descended. A man perhaps in his thirties looked at me; he seemed concerned.

"Where you headed?" He asked, resting his elbow on the window frame.

"Edinburgh," I replied.

"That so? Well, you're in luck. I'm heading north, but you'll be in need of a few more rides to get you all the way to Edinburgh." He ran his fingers through his dark, wavy hair and flashed me a smile. His teeth were perfect and their brightness flashed in the moonlight.

"Really?" I asked.

Then he glanced down at his watch and grimaced. "Oh dear. You know…. it's actually a bit late for me to take you all the way into town now. I've got a couple of kids waiting for me at home."

"Oh right, that's okay. I understand," I said dejectedly, and turned to leave. "Thanks anyway," I called over my shoulder.

"Well…tell you what," he shouted back. "I feel awful leaving you all alone here. Why don't you come home with me anyway? I'll put you up in our spare room for the evening and you can head out to toward Edinburgh first thing in the morning."

I felt slightly uneasy about his offer to stay the night, but he obviously had a family at home so it sounded safe enough. I glanced back at the woods, briefly considering the alternative before I opened the passenger door and climbed into his car.

It was a nice family sedan equipped with an expensive leather interior and the faint smell of cigarettes. I assured myself if he were a serial killer he wouldn't be driving a nice car like this.

He put the car into gear and steered us back onto the road. Looking straight ahead he asked, "What's a young, pretty girl like you doing all alone out here in the middle of nowhere?"

I looked down at my bitten fingernails.

"I umm…" I stammered. "I finished school and I wanted to go to Edinburgh to see some friends. I didn't have enough money for the train."

"Isn't it a little risky for you to be all alone out here?" His eyes didn't leave the road.

A vague sense of uneasiness rippled in my stomach. I had worked hard for many years to dissociate from fear. I pushed aside any feelings of impending danger I may have had and asked him how far we were from his house. He told me we were less than a mile away and that he had two children who were being cared for by a nanny while his wife was in Denmark on a modeling assignment.

* * *

Once in his house I saw pictures of his wife and children adorning the walls. They seemed like such a happy family and it filled me with a sudden sadness that I couldn't relate to the children's smiling faces as they stood, posed in front of various backdrops. His wife was beautiful, a slender woman with long, dark hair and a tiny mole on her right cheek.

The children were already asleep when we arrived, so he showed me to the guest room and told me to ask if I needed anything. I put my bag on the dresser, removed my shoes, jeans and jacket, and climbed underneath the heavy blankets. It felt so good to have a big, comfortable bed all to myself. I closed my eyes and envisioned that this nice man was my father. That it was *my* mother who was off modeling in Denmark, and my brother and sister who were sleeping soundly in the adjoining room.

I was just drifting off to sleep when I heard the door to my bedroom creak open. I figured he was just coming in to check on me, as any protective father would, so I kept my eyes closed and my back to the door. I heard him approach the bed, wanting to make sure I was asleep, I assumed. I didn't want to disappoint him, so I feigned sleep, breathing slowly and heavily. He leaned over me, so close I could feel his breath, and then for a reason indiscernible to me, the covers were slowly being slid off of my shoulders. The bed groaned as he climbed in beside me.

In a moment his bare skin was against my back and my legs. I knew without looking that he was naked. I felt something hard pushing against me and then it was prodding me as he moaned slightly. My heart was pounding so hard I felt it would burst through my chest. I wanted him to stop but I was frozen in fear. He rolled me onto my back and I squeezed my eyes shut so tightly that tears rolled down the sides of my face and trickled into my ears. I lay motionless as he climbed on top of me. Kissing me, he pulled off my underwear. His tongue was frantic, prodding the inside of my mouth and leaving a cold trail of sticky saliva around my lips as he swept it around the outside of my mouth. I was fourteen and I was fat.

How could he want to have sex with me when he was married to such a beautiful woman?

I didn't understand, but I didn't say anything, praying that it would be over soon. I drew in a sharp breath as he forced his way inside. It hurt and filled me with confusion. A slight whimper escaped my lips as he started to move. It lasted a few minutes, during which time my mind went back to the sordid room with the Moroccan, and then he collapsed on top of me. Not a word had been exchanged between us, and now I was feeling crushed by the weight of his relaxed motionless body. Finally, he lifted himself off me and climbed out of the bed, leaving the room as quietly as he had entered, closing the door behind him.

I lay there in the dark, in a strange room, in a house I didn't know, and it was then that the realization hit me: if a man did *anything* for you, you were to show appreciation by allowing him to have sex with you. My understanding of that silent barter was becoming clearer and clearer. I was laughable; how foolish of me to have the thoughts I had. Was I so naïve to think that this father saw me as a young scared girl and that he just wanted to help?

I would make sure I never deluded myself like that again.

* * *

I woke the next morning from a dream. I had found my father, only he was a king and I was a princess, and he was taking me back to his kingdom on the back of a majestic, white stallion. Then the sharp intrusive memories of the night before flooded back into my consciousness, my stomach turned and for a moment I thought I might have to run to the bathroom and vomit. I wanted to get out of the house without having to see him but I knew I would have to go downstairs to get to the front door.

I cracked open the bedroom door, hearing the sounds of laughter coming from the kitchen. I felt trapped; my heart pounded in my chest and pulsated up to my throat. I pulled on my jeans and quickly ran a brush through my hair. I grabbed my wash bag, opened the door and checked right and left. There was no one in the hallway, so I ran across the landing to the bathroom and locked the door. I thought for a moment of trying to get out of the bathroom window, but realized that it was a foolish idea. The window was way too small. I cleaned myself up the best I could and went downstairs. The kitchen smelled of coffee and bacon and my mouth started to water. I couldn't remember when I last had a cooked meal.

"Hi!" A young woman greeted me, and the children looked up from the table.

I assumed she was their nanny. She was probably in her early twenties and I wondered for a moment if he had done the same to her as he had to me.

"What's your name?"

I was distracted by the little boy's question.

"My name is Nanette," I told him.

"Are you going to be our other nanny?" the little girl asked.

"No," I replied. "Your daddy just let me stay here for the night."

"Would you like some breakfast?" the nanny asked.

"Yes, please, I'm really hungry."

I looked at her gratefully and she pulled out a chair for me.

"Where is...?" I realized I had forgotten his name.

"Oh, Mr. Davis? He already left for work," she assured me.

I breathed a sigh of relief and wondered if she knew that Mr. Davis took advantage of young girls when his wife was away. Once I had eaten enough, I thanked her and said goodbye to the children. I asked her the easiest way to get to the motorway.

"Just wait a moment and we will take you," she said. "It's a couple of miles. Aren't you afraid, hitchhiking alone?" She asked, pulling on a jacket and calling to the children.

"No," I replied. "Most people are really nice."

She dropped me off close to the slip road and I watched as the car disappeared from sight. I felt the loneliness return, knowing that the children were loved and I wondered why I wasn't. I resolutely pulled up my hood and with a deep breath of bravado stuck out my thumb in the direction of Edinburgh.

Chapter Six

Two days later I was in a big town and getting closer to my destination.

I had been given rides by people who could only take me as far as the next town or city, so at night I slept in either a covered bus stop or train station. On those occasions I would take all of my clothes out of my bag and dress in layers to try to keep myself warm. The cold would often keep me awake. Isolation and uncertainty were with me all the time; sometimes I cried because I was so cold and lonely, but without anyone to comfort me, my emotions even felt pointless.

On one of those frigid days I was walking along a street lined with shops, when I stopped in front of a pet shop window. A litter of black puppies were all heaped on top of one another in a plexi-glass container, biting each other's ears and flopping onto their backs.

My breath fogged the window and I wiped it clear with my glove so I could see them better. Watching their joyful play made me yearn for happier times in my life. I impulsively stepped into the shop and was greeted by a blast of warm air. I asked the owner how much the puppies were.

"Five pounds," he answered.

I had exactly five pounds and some change left in my pocket. I didn't even try to think through what I was about to do. I needed a friend.

"Here you are," I said, sliding the money across the counter. "I'd like a girl please." He reached in the container and roughly pulled out one of the puppies.

"Here, this one should do you," he said, handing her to me. "It's a girl, she's a little smaller than the others but she's got spark in her."

I held her close, breathing in her musky scent and felt homesick.

"Do you need any food or supplies?" the man asked me.

I glanced down at my remaining loose change.

"Oh, no thank you," I replied quickly. "We have plenty of food and supplies at my house."

I gave him a reassuring smile and minutes later I was walking out of the store with a little black puppy with dark brown eyes and smooth, pink belly. I named her Rebecca. I didn't know how I was going to feed her, but that didn't worry me too much, I knew I'd figure something out. I wasn't alone anymore and I felt like there was finally something in the world that needed me.

A little way down the street I came to a small grocery store. I pushed Rebecca up under my jacket and hid her from sight. I casually strolled up and down the aisles, pausing at the various pet foods. I took two small cans off of the shelf, and nervously glancing around, put one in each of the deep pockets of my jacket. At the cash register I picked up a small pack of gum to justify being in the store. I paid for my gum, and as I was reaching for the door, I heard a man's voice.

"Excuse me miss, please stop right there."

I froze, my heart skipping a beat. Instantly I could feel the heat rising from my neck up to my cheeks. The man came around to face me.

"I'm sorry miss, but I need you to empty out your coat pockets."

Other shoppers paused to watch.

What was I thinking? I didn't even have a can opener.

I walked back to the cash register and reluctantly pulled a can of dog food out of each pocket, placing them on the counter. I was trying to keep the little dog from dropping to the floor when one of her legs dangled from beneath my jacket. The manager pulled my jacket open and saw Rebecca clutched to my stomach. He shook his head.

"Now get out of my store. I don't ever want to see you in here again."

I ran down the street holding Rebecca tightly so she didn't fall. I wanted to get as far away from the people in the store as I could. I felt more afraid than ever now that I had no money left, but I had no idea how to turn back. I couldn't have come this far for nothing; yet I felt my options were diminishing by the hour.

That night I slept in the waiting room of yet another train station, my little dog the only source of warmth as I held her close.

* * *

The next day I was back on the road again, my thumb pointing north. I held the small dog under my jacket and thought that maybe I should have made a cardboard sign with EDINBURGH written on it. Just then a big truck pulled over and I winced at the sound of the air brakes. Rebecca wriggled in panic and I held her tighter.

" 'Ello, love, where you heading to?"

The truck driver leaned across the cab so I could hear him above the sound of the rig's idling engine.

"I'm going to Edinburgh." I shouted back at him.

"Well, hop on in." he smiled at me. "That's exactly where I'm going."

I swung open the cab door and hoisted myself inside, trying not to drop Rebecca or my canvass bag. We pulled out onto the road and I sat back, relieved at the amount of space between us. The cab smelled of cigarettes and cheap cologne, and a semi-naked island girl swayed her grass skirt back and forth on the dashboard. I pulled Rebecca out of my jacket and kissed the top of her head.

"I'm so glad I have you." I whispered into her ear.

"Who is that?" the driver asked. "Good thing I'm not allergic, isn't it?"

I kept looking out from my elevated view through the cab windshield. I didn't want to talk to him; I just wanted to get to Edinburgh. I still had no idea what I would do when I got there, but then again I really hadn't researched my plan too well. I started thinking about what my mother was doing and if the police were involved yet. I wondered if she had even called them. I'd been gone almost a week and I wanted to know what people were saying about me. For a moment I hoped that my mother thought that I'd been killed; at least then she would be blaming herself and feeling guilty. I wanted her to feel bad, after all, this *was* all her fault, and yet at the same time, I desperately wanted to curl up in the familiar bed with her and Pete.

"Time for a cuppa!" I was startled out of my reverie. The truck driver was exiting the motorway at a Little Chef roadside café for weary travelers. I did fancy a cup of sweet tea and maybe some cake.

I felt self-conscious walking into the dining area with a fat, middle aged trucker.

I think he said his name was Bob; I didn't even care. I listened to him talk about his wife and kids as I thought about my little dog; she didn't have anybody in the whole world—only me, and I had left her out in the truck. I started to feel anxious. I ate my slice of cake quickly, wondering how much weight I had lost; my trousers were getting loose on my hips. I grabbed a handful of creamers and slipped them in my pocket for Rebecca.

"Bob" finally finished his tea and we walked back to the truck. He reached out to hold my hand and I hastily pulled away from him. Once in the cab, he left the keys dangling in the ignition and turned to face me.

"C'mon," he leered. "You don't think I'm going to take you all the way to Edinburgh without getting something in return, do you?"

I tensed, fixated on island girl. She wasn't swaying now. She was just watching me, waiting to see what was going to happen next. I heard a low growl coming from Rebecca. She was only a few months old but she could already perceive that the truck driver was a threat to us.

When he leaned toward me, she lunged at him, sinking her baby teeth into his finger.

"Fucking dog!" he cried, pulling his hand back.

There was a moment's hesitation as he looked down to see if she had broken the skin. I quickly pulled on the handle, pushed the heavy door open, and jumped out of the cab. Rebecca was squashed under my arm and she let out a yelp as my feet hit the ground. I grabbed my bag from the floor and ran across the parking lot.

"Fucking dog!" I heard him scream.

I looked back and saw that he was still in the truck, so I slowed my pace until I found the bathrooms. I sat on the curb outside the ladies' room and waited until I saw his truck pull out and merge back onto the motorway with all the other faceless, nameless drivers.

"What a good girl," I said, kissing Rebecca on the top of her head. "You're the bravest little dog ever!"

She looked up at me with her soft, brown, trusting eyes.

"Come on, let's keep going," I said with courage I wasn't feeling.

I got up and walked across the parking lot toward the motorway. Just then a car pulled up alongside me.

"Do you need a ride anywhere?"

I bent down to look through the open window and nearly jumped for joy when I saw that it was a woman behind the wheel.

"Yes, to Edinburgh," I told her, hoping she was going there too.

"I think I can manage that." she smiled at me. "Come on, get in!"

I walked around and got in the car.

"What a sweet little dog," she said reaching out to pet her.

Rebecca's pink tongue emerged and licked her hand. The woman turned to me with a look of concern.

"It must be so scary for you to hitchhike alone."

"Well...I did just have a close call," I told her, explaining what the truck driver had just tried to do.

"You poor thing," she looked at me sympathetically. "Well, I'll make sure you get to Edinburgh safe and sound."

I settled back in the seat and finally felt secure enough to fall fast asleep.

* * *

That night we arrived in Edinburgh. The woman told me she was staying at her sister's house, but she would give me enough money to spend the night in a hostel. She explained that she couldn't just show up with me at her sister's, but she also didn't want to leave me out on the streets in the dark. We had exited the motorway earlier in the day and found a pet shop. Now Rebecca had food, a little bowl, and a red collar and leash.

"What are you going to do tomorrow?" She asked.

"I don't know. I'll start looking for a job I suppose."

She pulled over and asked a city policeman where the nearest hostel was and he directed us a few streets away.

"You turn right at the Boar's Head and then left at the Dog and Swan."

I found it amusing that even the police gave directions by way of pubs.

As we arrived outside the hostel building, she turned to me, "God bless and be safe."

I thanked her for the ride and the money and said goodbye.

The night shift worker said the day manager would not allow a dog on the premises, but I think he felt sorry for me because he told me he'd let us have a bed as long as we were out by eight the next morning. That night I fell asleep on a narrow metal fold out bed. Holding Rebecca close, I could feel the reassuring rhythm of her heartbeat against my chest and her warm breath on my face.

* * *

Early the next morning, I walked to the central park in Edinburgh and came to the realization that this was where I would have to sleep from now on. I was cold, hungry and getting pretty desperate. I hadn't eaten since the cup of tea and cake, and with the last of my money I had purchased a puppy. I sat dejectedly on a park bench as Rebecca wound her leash around my leg. She finally gave up and settled down to chew on it.

This wasn't the way it was supposed to be.

I had imagined that if I ran away, something might happen to improve my circumstances. Instead I was even worse off, seeing that I didn't even have a roof over my head now.

As I sat feeling sorry for myself, a young man walked up to us. He knelt down and started petting Rebecca.

"What a sweet little puppy," he said smiling at me, "What's her name?"

Rebecca licked his fingers and nibbled at his watch as he stroked her head.

We began talking and I told him that I had just arrived in the city. He asked me where I was staying and I told him that I was supposed to meet friends but they never showed up. I also told him I had run out of money and then I unexpectedly started to cry. Taking pity on me, the stranger told me he shared a house with two other students: another guy and a girl. The guy was in the military and stationed in Germany for two weeks of training. His room was available, but only until he came back. I felt relief flood through me, anything can happen in two weeks.

As we walked back to his house, I learned my rescuer's name was Martin. He studied at Edinburgh University, and was in the Scottish Guards. I thought this all sounded very romantic and on top of that I'd have a place to stay for now.

I slept in his roommate's room for one night before we became lovers. Of course Martin didn't know my real name, or that I was only fourteen years old. During the day, he would go to the University and I would explore the city and play with Rebecca.

One morning, while Martin was in school, I was bored so I snooped in his closet. There I found his army gear, fatigues, and a rifle. I donned the outfit and looked at myself in the mirror. I made a war face and giggled. I opened the bedroom window and balanced the rifle on the sill. Adjusting my cap, I looked down the barrel, imagining I was a sniper.

I honed in on a young woman in a red dress and black heels. She strutted down the street with a confidence that annoyed me. In my mind I pulled the trigger and watched her drop her shopping bags and crumple in a heap onto the pavement.

Satisfied with my imaginary targeting skills, I closed the window and returned the rifle and fatigues to the closet. All of a sudden I felt anxious and confused. A ripple of fear ran through my stomach.

What if I hadn't put everything back exactly where it had been? What if he found out I had been through his closet?

He would probably be furious with me and tell me to leave and I would have no place to go. The rest of the day I paced my room, anxiety coursing through my body, unable to relax until I knew I was safe again.

* * *

Martin came back to the house later that afternoon, but it wasn't the fatigues that caught his attention. It was Rebecca. Unbeknownst to me she had chewed on an antique chair that apparently belonged to his mother. He called me over to where he was kneeling by the chair.

"Look at this!" he exclaimed, looking up at me and pointing down to the mutilated leg.

I didn't know what to say, so I just stared blankly at Rebecca's destruction.

"I'm sorry, this just isn't going to work," he said matter-of-factly. "That dog has already had several accidents and now this. We are not even supposed to have pets here. She's going to have to go."

"Go where?"

"I'll take her to the pound now," Martin said. "She's still a puppy. They shouldn't have any trouble placing her."

It was all happening so fast. I didn't know how to make him change his mind.

He walked out of the room and I heard Rebecca yelp as he picked her up and carried her outside.

My puppy, she was my puppy. He couldn't just take her away from me. She was all I had.

I ran in my room and shut the door. I curled up in a fetal position on the single bed and cried. I couldn't imagine poor little Rebecca in a pound, she would be terrified. The thought of that made me cry more.

The next day was a Saturday and Martin was home all day. He asked if I wanted to go for a drive. I ignored him, sitting on the window seat in the living room, staring vacantly at the street below. I hadn't eaten anything for breakfast and I wouldn't talk to him. This continued throughout the afternoon, until finally I went back to my room and lay on the bed sobbing. I must have fallen asleep because I woke up to a wet tongue and fur all over my face.

"Rebecca!" I screamed, pulling her to me as she continued to frantically lick wherever she could.

"She was still there," Martin said smiling. "I just couldn't leave you like that. I had no idea how it would affect you. I was being selfish."

"Thank you, Martin. Thank you." I wrapped my arms around his neck. "I'll make sure she's really good from now on, I promise."

* * *

The two weeks came and went before I knew it, and I had yet to find a job. I didn't even know how to go about looking for one. The other tenant was coming back soon and I would have nowhere to go. As the day got closer my mind raced, plotting out all the different stories that might work in order for Martin to let me stay. Finally, I was spent and I knew there was nothing I could do except tell the truth. Maybe he would feel sorry for me and find a way for me to stay.

Unfortunately, my intuition was wrong and my reluctant confession was quickly followed by a phone call to my mother. Martin stood next to me as I dialed the number.

"Hello…Mum…it's me, Janine."

She didn't sound upset or shocked; she just asked me where I was. I handed the phone over to Martin and listened helplessly as he told her he would put me on a coach to London the following morning.

That night I told Martin everything. I told him about my mother and stepfather and how unhappy I had been when my grandmother sent me back to live with my mother. He listened sympathetically, but he wouldn't be persuaded. I was sure he must have been afraid that he could get into trouble for harboring a runaway, or worse for having sex with a minor.

* * *

Sitting in my seat on the coach, I held Rebecca tightly. Martin had paid the extra fee so that I could take her with me. He stood out in the drizzle waving as the coach pulled onto the street. I had given him my mother's address and he promised to write to me, and even come visit me.

The coach traveled the long arduous journey to London as I stared blankly out of the window. I couldn't acknowledge the beauty of the green pastured landscape spotted with grazing cows and sheep, as my mind was elsewhere. I thought about my father, and how I would run away again if my mother still wouldn't let me meet him.

* * *

She was waiting at the coach station and we drove back to the hotel in silence. I was relieved not to have to answer any of her questions. My life seemed to have become a predictable routine of sitting in cars, coaches, and trains, staring out of windows, my thoughts lost in the blur of towns, roads, and trees that we passed. I was forever being taken or sent somewhere.

Back at the hotel, the police were waiting to question me. They wanted to know where I had been and what had happened to me. I lied to the female police officer as she looked kindly into my eyes. I told her that I had hitchhiked to Edinburgh, and people or families let me stay in their houses. I denied that anybody tried to hurt me or took advantage of me.

"Do you know you were on the front page of the local paper?" the policewoman asked gently touching my hand. "After a while we thought you might have been killed. Do you realize how you must have scared your poor mother?"

My eyes filled with tears and I wished she was my mother, my "poor" mother already looked pretty sauced by this time. I didn't understand how the police couldn't tell she had been drinking. Satisfied that I was safely back where I was supposed to be, they left.

My mother picked up Rebecca.

"Where are you taking her?" I asked, panic in my voice.

"We can't keep her here. She has to go to the pound, someone will adopt her."

My face contorted in agony as I begged, "Please, oh pleeease don't take her away. Please let me keep her!"

My mother ignored me, walking out of the room with my little dog tucked under her arm. She turned her back on my pleas and that night, I decided to turn my back on her.

I would go and live with my dad and I'd never have to see her again.

Chapter Seven

The only picture we had of my father was one where he was holding my hand sitting on a park bench when I was a toddler. The picture was taken from a distance, his head was turned slightly away from the camera, and looking down at me so it was hard to see his face. My grandmother had a friend whose son knew my dad through a connection in the stock market, and due to that link, initial contact was made. All I knew about my dad was that he was a stockbroker, and that he and my stepmother Audrey had four children. Two were hers from a previous marriage and the other two were my half-sisters. I was excited to have brothers and sisters I had never met.

My grandmother set up the meeting in a pub near our current residence, in a town fittingly named Rottingdean. Our hotel room overlooked the village pond and on the other side of the pond was a quaint nineteenth century pub. My mother was busy working the lunch shift at the hotel, so all I had to do was follow the path to the pub and sit at a table by the entrance. The last thing I wanted was her coming with me.

I waited patiently at a table by the door with a small suitcase at my feet. Sipping my Coke, I watched middle-aged men walk past me and into the pub, waiting for one of them to stop and look at me with some sort of recognition. I was hoping my grandmother had given my father an accurate physical description of me.

When he finally approached, I was disappointed he wasn't more handsome. He was tall and skinny. I was relieved that I had not inherited his nose, and assumed that he must have relied heavily on his charisma to have married my mother *and* been able to charm another beautiful woman at the same time. My father stopped in front of me, peered through squinted eyes and then feigned recognition. I noticed his heavy-lidded blue eyes held a sparkle of humor.

"Oh my God!" he exclaimed, taking his soft plaid cap off his head and pointing a long skinny finger at me. His curly hair was balding at the crown.

"You must be…wait a minute…" He looked up at the sky as if searching for my name.

Then he looked back down at me, his eyes opening wide in recognition.

"I know! It's Janine!" He replaced the cap, adjusted it and slapped the palm of his hand to his forehead in mock surprise. "Are you really my long-lost daughter?"

I felt embarrassed and self-conscious, unsure how to respond to this dramatic production.

"Look at you. You're all grown up!"

He spoke loudly and stayed at a safe distance. People at the outside tables were turning to look at us. I don't know what I expected, but it wasn't this unemotional stage play.

"When I last saw you, you were a little tiny thing," he said, indicating with his hand level at his knee just how small I must have been. I thought about the picture.

"Hi, Dad," I smiled at him. I wanted to get up and hug him, but fear of his judgment held me back.

"Do you want something to eat? We've got a bit of a drive."

"No. I'm okay, thanks."

He turned to walk back to the parking area and I took that as my cue to pick up my suitcase and follow him.

He opened the door to a sky blue Volvo and I hesitated. I wasn't sure whether to sit in the back with my suitcase or put my case on the back seat and get in the front with him. Either way seemed stressful. At the last moment, I chose the latter.

Once in the car he started the ignition and leaned forward to switch on the radio. We exited the parking lot, turning onto the country road that would take us out of Rottingdean toward a little village named Plumpton. My grandmother had told me that much. I wondered if he knew we had been living so close to each other.

I sat in silence and listened to Simon and Garfunkel sing "Bridge over Troubled Water."

"Who else lives with you?" I asked when the song ended.

He turned down the radio. "Well, there's your stepmother and you have two step-brothers and two half-sisters."

"How old are the girls and what are their names?" I asked, curious about my half-siblings.

"Sarah is seven and Emily is about a year old. Sarah's a really good rider. Do you ride?" He asked turning to look at me.

I wasn't sure whether to embellish my riding abilities; I then remembered the incident with my tennis playing horse and how that had backfired.

"I do know how to ride. I used to take lessons in school, and I had a pony when I was eleven called Sparky."

"I'm not that good though," I added as an afterthought.

"That's all right," my father said, reaching forward to turn up the radio again. "Just try not to fall off. Your sister is always falling off."

The rest of the drive was quiet apart from the radio. I felt both excited and scared that I was actually sitting next to my real father. I had dreamt about this moment for years, however now I was nervous about staying in a house full of strangers. I wondered if they were going to be happy to see me.

About forty minutes later we pulled through large iron gates and onto a gravel driveway. I gasped at the sprawling Tudor estate. In the next moment an Irish setter's tongue was flopping at my window.

"That's Molly," my father said as he got out of the car. "And this is Woodlands." He motioned to the house in front of us.

I followed him to the impressive oak front door with Molly trotting by my side. We stepped over the threshold and into a magnificent foyer, only to be greeted by utter chaos. I could hear screaming coming from one of the rooms, and a uniformed nanny ran past us in a state of disarray. A partially dressed chubby baby crawled on the Persian rug in front of me, drool suspended from its mouth as a Cavalier King Charles Spaniel attempted to lick the remnants of lunch from the baby's face.

My father led me through the chaos and into the kitchen. Audrey, my mother's nemesis, turned to greet us.

"My goodness, Janine," She pronounced my name Chah-neen. "How wonderful to see you again." Her face contorted into a smile much like the Cheshire cat in *Alice in Wonderland* and she extended a limp hand to shake mine. "Would you like a drink?"

She was holding what appeared to be a glass of wine, and she motioned toward the bottles on the kitchen counter. "Vincent, why don't you get Chah-neen a drink and you can refill my glass."

My father poured me an orange juice, turned to my stepmother and stated, "I think you've had enough."

With that, he passed me my drink and promptly walked out of the kitchen leaving me alone with her.

Audrey clumsily reached over to the wine bottle and refilled her glass. She was tall and thin, and jewelry dripped from her neck and wrists. I was mesmerized by the opaque rock on one of her fingers. I felt trapped and desperately wanted to get away from her; I wished my father would come back. She turned and looked at me through narrowed eyes.

"So Chah-neen, where do you and your mother live?"

"Oh, we live in Rottingdean," I offered non-committedly. "Is there a toilet I can use?" I asked, hoping to make an escape.

"Yes, let me have Sarah show you." She stumbled through the kitchen doorway. "Sarah!"

A moment later a skinny girl of about seven came running into the room, her long dark hair pulled back in a ponytail. I wondered if she had been the one I heard screaming.

"Sarah, this is your half-sister Chah-neen," she said motioning toward me. "I want you to show her where she's going to be sleeping and the bathroom she can use."

"Oh, hello," my new sister greeted me. She didn't seem surprised and I wondered if she knew I was going to be staying for a while. Granny hadn't told me what the plan was to be, other than my father was going to pay for me to go to a private school again. I followed the girl with the swinging ponytail through luxuriously furnished rooms, each one with a huge fireplace as the central focal point. We passed through a room where a boy about my age was sitting on an antique sofa watching television.

"That's Adam," she turned and whispered. "He's always really mean to me."

She then led me through her room and into a connecting guest room. "You'll be staying in here," she said and skipped out through the door into her room.

* * *

Two weeks later, I felt like I had stepped into a reality show. I learned that my father was the joker, Sarah the caretaker, Adam the hero, Audrey the alcoholic, and it appeared I was the lost child and scapegoat. I was given spare clothes to wear by my father's horse groomer who was close to my size. I discovered that she was carrying on a secret affair with my eldest step-brother, John. They were both fearful that Audrey would find out and she would be fired. I didn't see much of John because he was at university and working. The baby, Emily, was either in her high chair eating or harnessed in her big black carriage and left outside in the back garden. She was cared for by the nanny and Audrey seemed oblivious to her whereabouts. Baby Emily was often left outside for long periods of time.

"Fresh air is good for a baby…see those beautiful rosy cheeks!" Audrey justified her child rearing skills with pride.

Emily had developed a talent of being able to relocate her carriage when left outside. She would pull herself up as far as her restraints allowed, and then plop back down with all her might, leaning forward and grasping the sides of the carriage with her chubby little fingers as if she were executing a ski jump. Even though the brake was on, the carriage would invariably travel, bouncing some distance on its suspension. Eventually, someone looked through a window and noticed baby and carriage on the move. In my opinion baby Emily's cheeks were rosy from all the exertion of her thwarted attempts to escape.

I felt ungainly in my stepmother's presence. She was so beautiful, tall, and slender with wavy red hair that rested softly on her shoulders. She had been a model and everything about her exuded money and style. However, on days when she had consumed a few too many glasses of wine I found myself embarrassed for her.

One night, her cat Doo Doo went missing. My stepmother was convinced he was outside, and demanded everyone search for him before he was eaten by a fox.

I noticed my father's old Santa beard tossed on the arm of a couch. Christmas had long passed but the beard still got used for a laugh.

"Daddy, put on your long white beard," Sarah would plead. She told me he sometimes answered the door wearing the beard.

The white beard matched Doo Doo's coat perfectly. I impulsively grabbed it and stuffed it in my jacket pocket, running outside to join in the search.

Returning to the house some time later, my stepmother was informed that sadly no one could find Doo Doo.

"What could have happened to him?" She asked, looking forlornly at my father.

"I'm sure he'll turn up," he replied, pouring her another glass of wine.

As he went to the kitchen to return the bottle to the fridge and she tilted her head back to swallow the contents of her glass, I pulled the balled-up beard out of my pocket and threw it onto the living room rug.

"There he is," I announced. "I found him lying in the middle of the road."

"Doo Doo!" she screamed, horrified, and dropping her glass to the floor. She crawled over the carpet to the beard and scooped it up into her arms. A look of shock came over her face as she brought the beard slowly up to her chest, confused by its weightlessness. She held it at arm's length and shook it out, her shock quickly transforming to anger.

"Bloody child," she shrieked at me. "What's wrong with you?"

My stepmother tossed the beard back onto the floor, and pulled herself up to a standing position with the aid of a nearby chair. As she staggered out of the room, Sarah turned to me shaking her head. "You know you really shouldn't have done that."

My stepmother's reaction was not what I had hoped, although I wasn't sure what I had expected. I had just wanted to make everyone laugh. I retreated to the guest room confused. How many times had frustrated grown-ups asked "What is wrong with you?"

I wished at that moment I knew exactly what "it" was that was wrong with me. Maybe then "it" could be fixed. I sat sullenly on the edge of the bed; my clothes were still piled in my open suitcase. I had been at Woodlands for over a month now, but I didn't know if I was allowed to put them away in any of the drawers of the vintage chest. Looking at my case, I wished that I could just curl up in it and close the lid. Lucy, my father's horse groomer, had been kind enough to wash my clothes as well as lending me her warm sweaters and jackets whenever I needed them.

I grabbed a crumpled pack of cigarettes out of one of my boots and went over to the bedroom window. I pulled one out, lit it, took in a deep drag and blew the smoke out of the open window. I felt immediately calmer. John could always get cigarettes for Adam and me.

My stepbrothers had their own quarters in a new extension between the living room and the stables. This gave them some privacy and autonomy. Sarah's bedroom was in the original part of the house, painted with pretty lilacs and yellows, and outfitted with her own miniature four-poster bed. An antique rocking horse silently guarded the vast array of toys and collection of European dolls crammed up against the walls.

Woodland's grounds were picturesque. The single-lane roads traversed acres of fields where the local hunt charged its path early on Sunday mornings. From farms to manor houses, and small cottages housing farm workers, Plumpton was a place far removed from the city life, yet under an hour's train ride from London. Woodlands was situated adjunct to Plumpton racetrack and much to my father's delight, we would sometimes watch the point-to-point races from the roof of the house.

Life with Vincent and Audrey was a far cry from my life in a trailer or a hotel bedroom with my mother and Peter. I enjoyed hanging out with Lucy, talking to her as she tacked up the horses and listening to her accounts of the local gossip. As Adam was my age, he introduced me to some of his friends and John would drive us to and from parties. Sarah had her own pony, as I had when I was eleven. His name was Nimble and she spent a lot of time out riding with my father or playing with the neighboring children. Adam had a pony too, which I was allowed to ride from time to time. On the weekends, my father and stepmother drove to the local pub with Sarah, Adam, and myself crammed in the backseat, choking on smoke from Audrey's cigarettes and my father's pipe. The baby stayed back at the house with the nanny. This was our Sunday family outing. The kids all waited in the car outside the pub, munching on bags of crisps and drinking cokes. Every now and again, an adult would come out to the parking lot and give us false hope.

"Only a few more minutes. They're on their last round."

Other families practiced the same ritual, so children often climbed into each other's cars to play and have fun. One little boy once let the hand brake off and a car filled with laughing, screaming children rolled down the hill and into the bushes.

Eventually, parents appeared at the pub door, including my father, always pipe in mouth, cap on his head, laughing and joking with his peers. My stepmother looked as if she had survived a spin cycle in the washing machine, her hair disheveled and runway outfit more off than on her body.

By the time we all got home, the Sunday roast was usually rendered to a burnt offering.

* * *

It was a Saturday evening, raining outside, and we were bored with watching television.

"I dare you to make yourself faint," said Adam. I considered his challenge, wanting to impress him. "Okay," I said feigning fearlessness. "What do I have to do?"

"Great!" Adam said, jumping to his feet excitedly.

"You have to do fifteen squats, and then put your thumb in your mouth and blow as hard as you can."

Easy. There was no way that was going to make me faint.

I got up off of the couch and stood in front of the coffee table. Sarah and Adam watched expectantly.

"One... two... three... four... five... six..." They counted as I dropped to my heels and then pushed back up. "...fifteen!"

I put my thumb in my mouth and blew as hard as I could. The room suddenly swelled as I attempted to focus on Adam and Sarah. Their faces blurred together and then disappeared completely as everything went black.

I opened my eyes to discover I was lying face down on the living room floor. Sarah and Adam were gone and there was a throbbing pain under my chin. I rolled over onto my side and touched the leg of the coffee table in front of me.

I must have hit the corner when I fell.

I slowly reached my fingers up to my chin and felt the warm stickiness. Looking down at my hand I saw it was covered in blood and I began to cry.

Just then Sarah ran back into the living room, followed closely by my dad and Audrey.

Adam was nowhere to be seen.

"Oh my God!" exclaimed my stepmother.

"What the hell did you do?" My father asked, looking down at me.

"I fainted," I said miserably.

"You stupid child! What were you thinking?"

"She needs stitches, Vincent!"

"Sarah! Get Janine a towel!" Audrey commanded the seven-year-old. "Vincent, you can't take her to the hospital, we have to get to the party."

"Oh God," my father said, drawing out the "o" in God. He seemed to be thinking. "I know! We could have Bente take her!"

I felt embarrassed that I was causing such a problem for everyone.

Bente was my stepmother's friend who was visiting from Denmark. I had only just met her that morning.

Sarah came back, gingerly handed me a towel and looked up at her mother for further instruction.

"Now go and fetch Bente. We have to go!" My stepmother pulled my father's arm. "Come on, Vincent! We'll be late!"

It took Bente a good ten minutes to figure out how to turn the lights on in my stepmother's Mini. Navigating the dark country roads, I could feel her anxiety intensifying. I knew she probably wasn't used to driving on the other side of the road.

I pressed the towel to my chin trying to stem the flow of blood.

By the time we found the hospital my entire face was throbbing and the small hand towel was soaked in blood. I struggled not to cry out as the doctor stitched my chin, squeezing Bente's hand tightly as she stroked my forehead.

Driving home, I began to feel the effects of what the doctor had given me for pain. Not only was my chin numb, but I had a tingly sensation in my scalp and a sense of ease and comfort began to spread throughout my body.

By the time we got back to Woodlands, Adam and Sarah had gone to bed and the house was dark and silent.

"Night, Bente," I whispered, giving her a hug and walked unsteadily to my room.

The next morning, I was greeted by a hyper Sarah pouring herself juice in the kitchen.

"Ouch, that looks really bad," she said sympathetically.

My chin was sore, but at least it had stopped throbbing. "Are Dad and your mum still asleep?"

"Yep," she said hopping up and down on one foot.

"They sleep late when they go to parties. Do you want to come and play with me?"

I dejectedly followed her into her bedroom.

My dream of my father being my savior had come to a very unsatisfying conclusion.

Chapter Eight

Soon thereafter it was decided that I should go to boarding school. My father came up with a place in Tunbridge Wells, Kent, which was far enough away from Woodlands that I wouldn't be going home on weekends.

My father gave Lucy some money and directed her to take me clothes shopping. I wouldn't need much as I was going to be wearing school uniforms again.

The Convent of the Sacred Heart had a reputation for turning girls into modest and mild-mannered young women. If I were to be redeemed, it would have to be accomplished in the next four years.

I wondered if this is what my father had in mind when he dropped me off at the school office a couple of days later.

"Don't get into any trouble here or you'll have to go to the dog pound next," he said wagging his finger at me. I was sure he was being serious.

The convent was set in scenic grounds and was headed by the Mother Superior. The rest of the staff consisted of a mixture of nuns and teachers. The teachers were all extremely old and challenged, controlling classrooms full of suppressed girls. Students were made to attend mass every morning, but some of us became adept at avoiding this. One nun we all liked named Sister Sarah was much younger than the others and dressed in regular clothes. She entertained us by playing popular tunes on her guitar in our dorm room at night. The Second Vatican Council had relaxed the strict rules on nun's habits; however,

Sister Sarah was the only nun who took advantage of this change. I never understood why nuns wore habits if it was no longer mandatory. Rumor had it that even when the nuns bathed, they kept their habits on. We school girls sat around giggling as we imagined nuns squatting over a bathtub in their habits as they used a small washcloth to wipe down their privates.

I was only to be at this school for two years and redemption was elusive. I was unused to the discipline and hadn't been in a school for more than a few months in the past two years. The rules and regulations bored me and I felt different from the other girls. The required uniforms were ridiculous: Either a red cardigan or blazer, brown pleated knee-length skirts, tan blouses, and red and white striped ties. I struggled with my tie every day. We were even forced to wear regulation, heavy wool underwear.

It wasn't long before I found a handful of rebellious girls like myself. The only way I could survive the repressive torture was to break rules. I loved practical jokes and could never resist a dare.

"Hey Janine, I dare you to play a trick on Sister Mary!"

Sister Mary was one of the older, more traditional nuns. Her room was located across the hallway from our dorm and it was her job to make sure dorm lights were out by nine at night. Armed with a spool of cotton and a needle, I crept into her room during the dinner period. I then proceeded to stitch up the feet of her black stockings. When everyone came back from dinner I excitedly told my cohorts what I had done.

"Oh my god, Janine! I don't know how you think up these things," Mia said.

Mia was Italian, and her D-cup was the envy of every convent girl.

The next morning a commotion was heard coming from Sister Mary's room as she stumbled around trying to get her feet into her stockings so she could ring the morning bell. Sitting on our beds, we clutched our knees to our chests and rocked in unison as the tears of laughter rolled down our cheeks.

On another occasion, I stole some powerful glue from the janitor's closet and managed to sneak it into the classroom a few minutes before our elderly biology teacher was due to start her class. I coated her chair with a generous amount of the transparent liquid and took my seat as the other girls filed in. Mrs. Shutes arrived shortly after, wearing a thick, knee-length tweed skirt. She made her way to her desk and sat down. Being so old she gave lessons directly from her chair. As soon as class was over and we shut our books, I struggled to maintain my composure as I watched her try to stand up and dismiss us. She looked puzzled as she placed both hands on the armrests and tried to leverage herself out of her chair. Grunting and gasping, she tried again and again, but to no avail. By this point, all of the girls in the classroom were giggling. I opened up my desk and flashed the can of glue to my classmates who began roaring with laughter at the realization of what I'd done. Meanwhile, Mrs. Shutes was now attempting to climb out of her skirt to free herself. After a lot of effort, she emerged, like a butterfly from a cocoon, wearing a large pair of light blue bloomers, and fled from the classroom in tears.

After a trip to the mother superior's office, I was ordered to give Mrs. Shutes both a written and verbal apology, which I did with much reluctance. I was also told that my monthly scholarly allowance would go toward buying her another tweed skirt. I felt the pain of having to cut down on my chocolate consumption, as most of my pocket money was used in the school store, but this was the most fun I had had in a long time and I was thriving on all the attention I was getting.

* * *

When I was fourteen my dorm accommodations changed from being in a room with seven girls, to sharing with just one.

My new dorm buddy Nina and I were too much alike to be good for one another. Either our unruly behavior or our resistance to authority inevitably got us into trouble. We discovered how to sneak out of our room at night; stuffing our beds with pillows, we would ease open the first-story window and easily access the drainage pipe from the window ledge, grabbing hold of the brackets to carefully make our way down to the ground. A boy's reform school was located across the road from the hockey field. It was here in the gym that the two class systems came together. One boy usually brought a guitar and someone else brought a bottle of wine. We hung out, passing the bottle around as the guitar strummed and we smoked cheap cigarettes. It was all quite innocent, but I noticed the way the boys looked at me. Nina would tease me later in our dorm.

"They like your big boobs and juicy lips!"

I wished they liked my eyes. That would have felt safer; they were deep blue and framed by dark lashes. When living with Mimi and Fanny in the South of France, Fanny called me "Petite Nini avec les grandes yeux bleu!"

I yearned for more accolades.

At dawn, Nina and I left our friends, climbed back up the outside of the school building, and in through our narrow dorm window. The nuns were never the wiser, except on one particular night.

Someone must have heard noises in the grounds and phoned the police. The first thing we noticed was a beam of light scanning the school grounds and then we heard the barking.

"Oh my God, I think they called the police!" Nina said, panic in her voice.

She was right; the police arrived with high-powered flashlights and tracker dogs. We all spilled out of the gymnasium and dispersed in different directions. Nina and I managed to hide in a compost heap on the lower hockey field as the boys headed toward the road. It was cold and we huddled together, fearful that our breath would attract attention from the police or their dogs.

"It smells so awful!" Nina whispered.

"Shhh," I elbowed her. "They'll hear you."

We waited for what seemed like hours, our eyes straining into the darkness. We heard voices drifting further and further away, until finally we felt it safe to come out.

"Come on Nina, we can make it back to our room," I encouraged her by grabbing her hand, and together we ran.

Exhausted, we made it back to the building. We assumed the police had followed the boys over the wall by the road. Feeling for footholds, we scaled the pipe and made it back up to our window.

It was still open, just as we'd left it, and I heaved my body over the sill and onto the bed below. Our beds were still stuffed with pillows, untouched.

"Oh, thank God," I sighed. "I don't think anyone even noticed we were gone."

I threw my arms around Nina and hugged her with relief. She pulled away immediately.

"Ughhh," she exclaimed grabbing her nose. "You smell like shit."

"So do you," I retorted, and we both collapsed on our beds in fits of laughter. Still reeking of compost and relieved we hadn't been caught, we pulled up our blankets to await the morning bell.

The next morning, through the pipelines of school gossip, we heard that two of the boys had been apprehended. Luckily, they had not exposed us and for now we were in the clear.

* * *

Once we turned sixteen, the convent allowed us a pass into town on Saturdays, as long as we went in twos and agreed to stay together. We had to stay in our school uniform, attired not only in our repulsive brown skirts and red sweaters, but also wearing mandatory hooded red capes. It didn't take long for Nina and myself to get our first boyfriends.

One afternoon, we decided to ditch classes and meet these boys in a dingy, basement town tavern, aptly named the Hole in the Wall.

During a routine lunch assembly, Nina and I hid under the stage in the school theatre. We carried our street clothes with us in small plastic shopping bags. It had not taken us long to find a way to be rid of our uniforms. As the nuns droned on and on about Our Lord and Savior and what it meant to be well-rounded young ladies and how grateful we should be to have hot meals - we stealthily made our way to one of the windows facing the grounds and climbed outside. With our heads ducked low, we ran along the tree line to the fence that bordered the school. We scaled the fence and landed in the park on the other side, captivity and freedom separated by mere inches. Once in the park, we walked hurriedly to the public bathrooms.

"Let's change our clothes in here." I suggested trying to catch my breath.

"Where do we leave our uniforms?" Nina asked.

"Look," I pointed to a ledge under a high window. "We can fit our bags there."

A few minutes later we emerged from the bathrooms in flared jeans and skimpy T-shirts. At the park gate we called a cab from the pay phone.

"We're going to the Hole in the Wall please," I instructed the driver when he pulled up at the gate.

He eyed us suspiciously, and for a moment I thought he was going to say something, but he didn't. He drove us into town, finally pulling up to an opening in an old wall; one could just make out the fading sign above the door. I thanked the cabbie and gave him his fare. As we walked down the rickety staircase, we saw our friends waving to us from a dimly lit table.

"Hey girls, what'll it be?"

"We'll have two half-pints of scrumpy." I said, turning to Nina who was looking at me nervously.

She had witnessed me on scrumpy a few weeks previously at another bar; one of the guys had ordered it for me and I was hooked immediately. It tasted like apple cider, sweet and refreshing. After downing a half-pint, I was still thirsty so I ordered another. The next thing I knew, I was in the bathroom watching the walls spin. The outing ended with me throwing up all over one of the guys I had a crush on. Nina had to feed me cups of coffee before we could even try to make it back to the convent.

I cringed at the memory and reassured her. "I'll be fine, I'll only have one glass—no more."

"You sure?" she said. "I'd hate a repeat of what happened."

At that moment Nina's boyfriend came up behind her and wrapped his arms around her waist; Dave Botsworth was quite a sight. A heavy, dark beard shrouded his face and he always wore a black cloak and top hat.

I turned to my boyfriend, Hank. Hank lived with his mother and wrote me beautiful poetic letters on blue, scented stationery. He had brown, feathered hair and hazel eyes. Unfortunately, one leg was shorter than the other, so he had to wear a stacked boot under his velour bell-bottoms. His constant companion was a red and green parrot that sat perched on his shoulder and nipped people who tried to pet him. I knew Hank wasn't as good-looking as Nina's guy, but I loved his gentleness and his romantic letters were a welcome distraction from convent life.

As we sat at the table, casually sipping pints with Dave, Hank, and their mates, our chemistry teacher Mr. Roberts descended the staircase.

"Oh no, this can't be happening," I said through clenched teeth as I grabbed Nina's arm.

I pulled her off her chair and under the table with me. The guys noticed what was happening and quickly stood up, blocking us from the stairway. We stayed crouched on the dirty, beer-spattered floor until we were informed he had left. One of the boys pulled a crumpled ten-pound note out of his pocket and told us to get a cab. It was almost dusk by the time we hurried from the main gate to the bathrooms to change back into our uniforms. We then clambered over the fence and back to the safety of the school grounds.

We wanted to believe that Mr. Roberts hadn't seen us, however we both had a feeling of impending doom. That evening, before dinner assembly, a nun came into the television room where I was watching *Top of the Pops*. She informed me that the Mother Superior wanted to see me in her office. When I arrived, Nina was already sitting hunched in an oversized antique armchair, head bowed and eyes transfixed on the ground. She wouldn't even look up at me. I knew at that moment it was all over. I later heard that a part-time teacher had been in a coffee shop across the road from the bar and when she saw us, she called the school to inform the Mother Superior, who sent Mr. Roberts to investigate.

Nina and I were already on suspension at this time. A couple of months earlier we had staged a joint "suicide attempt" in order to get out of our upcoming French test that we both knew we were going to fail. We weren't quite sure how the plan would pan out, but we were desperate. Nina took a handful of her vitamin capsules and I tried to cut one of my wrists with a pair of nail scissors. My wrist was easily fixed with a Band-Aid and Nina threw up the vitamins; however, we both ended up being taken to the psyche unit of the local hospital for evaluation. After talks with our fathers, the Mother Superior reluctantly allowed us back to the school with the understanding that we were on probation. This time she called our fathers' to inform them we were expelled. We were sent to our dorm to pack.

We said nothing to each other as we crammed the last two years of our lives into our respective trunks. I didn't even get a chance to say goodbye to Nina as I was shepherded down to the school entrance.

I was silent as my father drove back to Woodlands, listening to Karen Carpenter sing "We've Only Just Begun," hoping the song would never end and that we would never reach our destination.

Nina's father took her to live with him in Saudi where he worked for an oil company. She was sent to an international school and I wouldn't see her again for six years.

The next few days went by in a blur. My father called my mother to inform her of what had happened. I hadn't seen her since I moved out. He handed me the phone.

"Hello, Mum," I said softly.

"What are we going to do with you Janine?" she said with a heavy sigh. "I suppose you've ruined this for yourself too, haven't you?"

I started crying.

My father took back the phone and told her he had come up with a solution: I was going to work as a nanny in Denmark. Nora was an old friend of my father's and she was willing to do him a favor. She was a divorcee with three children and was in need of a housekeeper and nanny. I was the perfect answer to both their problems. If I completed the job for a year, my father would buy me a plane ticket there and Nora would send me home. There was nothing I could do or say to change the situation. I had been given a chance and I had screwed it up. Being sorry didn't matter either. I had acted out for the last time and would be sent further away than I had ever been sent before.

Chapter Nine

I couldn't speak Danish and I couldn't cook. I couldn't even keep my own bedroom clean. I was sixteen years old and leaving my country for an unfamiliar one where I would live for an entire year in servitude to a stranger. The girls were six, eight, and ten years old. This had to be a joke; I couldn't even take care of myself.

Nora gave me a small bedroom in the back of the house. It was cluttered, but clean and sadly felt more like home than the bedroom in my father's house. I was given the equivalent of ten pounds a week to care for the children, cook, clean the house, and maintain the yard. I had no experience doing any of these things but pretended that I did. I tried to roast a chicken one evening and ended up cremating it and almost burning down the house. After that, Nora helped me in the kitchen, teaching me how to make simple things, like pastas and stews.

The children spoke English as a second language and had a lot of fun teaching me Danish. I was treated like their older sibling. Once again I was in a family system, but I wasn't a part of the family for which I yearned. While the children were in class, I had a lot of free time. As soon as I returned from walking them to school, I headed straight for the kitchen. Taking a loaf out of the bread bin, I would lay out four slices of bread side by side on the countertop and lavishly spread them with butter and strawberry jam containing plump sweet strawberries. I then stacked them onto a plate and took them back to my small bedroom where I devoured them, blissfully numbing my mind as I chewed on the sweet, fluffy, jam-soaked bread. Once again food became my supplement for love.

* * *

Six months had passed and I finally built up the courage to ask Nora to call my dad and ask if I could come home early. I hoped he was feeling guilty for banishing his daughter and might change his mind. However, Nora informed me that he was adamant that I stay the full year. The contract was not to be broken, even if my behavior was exemplary. I was disappointed, hurt, and angry.

I decided, if I could, I would find a way never to go back.

* * *

On weekends I took the bus into Copenhagen and walked around Tivoli Gardens, mingling with the tourists. One day I stopped to watch a street artist. I had seen him before, sitting cross-legged in tattered jeans, painting on the sidewalk. He had thick, brown hair with a full, dark beard and weathered face. I thought he looked like Charles Manson. At boarding school, we had watched the aftermath of the Manson trial on the news. I had been shocked by his demonic deeds and at the same time enthralled by his charisma, especially the power he had over women.

The artist wore a necklace with a turquoise stone that swayed back and forth as he sat hunched over the canvas, engrossed in one of his pieces. A dog patiently lay next to him on an old plaid blanket. I stooped down to pet her as I watched him paint. She was a beautiful brown Doberman Pinscher, and as I stroked her soft fur, the artist and I struck up conversation.

"What's her name?" I asked him in English.

"Her name is Lady," he replied in a heavy accent.

He told me his name was Hans and he was Austrian. I could not speak German and his English was very limited, but we discovered that we could communicate in French. He had been married to a French woman and had lived in France for a few years; my rusty French was coherent enough that we were able to understand each other. He asked me how old I was, threw back his head, and laughed when I told him.

"You are far too young for me, little girl. I am old enough to be your father."

I didn't care what he thought. I was determined to make him mine. After all, he was a far cry from a plate of jam sandwiches. My father had called Nora once to see how things were working out, but other than a couple of letters from my mother, I had no news of home. Suddenly I didn't feel lonely anymore.

Instead of going home as planned at the end of the year, Hans picked me up in his over-sized old car with Lady's head hanging out of the back window. Nora told my father I was planning to leave with a street artist in his thirties rather than coming home. He made no attempt to stop me. Nora relayed that all he said was, "So now she's running off with a middle-aged hippy!"

I hoped he might try to persuade me to change my mind, but in truth he was probably relieved he didn't have to deal with me anymore; the two short years I was in his life was undoubtedly enough for him.

* * *

We packed our whole lives in Hans' car: his artwork, all the clothes that we owned, and the dog. During the day we located the main street in a town that had he most tourist traffic and set up our tables. Over the next few weeks Hans taught me how to make jewelry using silver plated wire, semi-precious stones, leather, and silver dipped horseshoe nails. The wire I used was soft and flexible. I could bend it with pliers, making crisscross patterns to form shapes and threading beads through the wire. I made rings, necklaces, and bracelets, and displayed them on a long portable table draped with a dark blue velour cloth as Hans painted beside me.

Some days were good and we would go to a nice restaurant for dinner and sleep in a four-star hotel. On days we made little to no money, we slept in the car. I could never get warm on those cold nights.

We traveled through Denmark, Sweden, Austria, Luxemburg, and Switzerland from fall to spring. In the summer months, I had the most fun in Italy as we set up on the strand by the beach. Hans had a friend in Pisa, a middle-aged homeless man named Gerard. Gerard was a wino with a scraggly red-gray beard and a missing front row of teeth. He would shuffle along the streets, sleeping bag rolled up on his back, closely followed by his scruffy black-and-white dog as they looked for meals in trash cans. Hans knew that Gerard was always at his favorite bar.

In Pisa, many hours were spent in bars. Hans and Gerard conversed in German and drank red wine, while I sipped my Orangina and contemplated what everyone was doing back in England. At that time in my life, I was unaware of the escape alcohol could offer me. I had tried wine a few times but didn't like the taste. The one time I got drunk on Scrumpy was enough to put me off forever.

I decided alcohol just wasn't for me.

* * *

We made our base at a slum hotel in Pisa. Hans knew the manager, a tall, bald man in his fifties with a cleft lip and a giant scar running from the top of his lip to under his cheekbone. Hans told me he had been imprisoned for fifteen years for killing his wife by hitting her over the head with a chair during a fight. He gave me the creeps and I was afraid to make eye contact. I always made sure I was with Hans when we were in or around the hotel. We had a spacious but sparse bedroom where we kept all our belongings; I liked that the room had a small balcony overlooking the street. The bathroom was in the hallway and shared with other guests. We did have a little sink in our bedroom, which I occasionally had to use as a toilet when I needed to pee during the night. There was no way I was willing to navigate the dark hallway by myself.

Occasionally I would get a letter from my mother addressed to the hotel, saying that she missed me. She would tell me about her new boyfriend or job. I never heard from my dad.

We met up with Hans' German friend Klaus from time to time when they were in the same city. Klaus was also a street artist, but more talented and versatile than Hans. Hans painted generic heads of Christ wearing a crown of thorns, which the Italian Catholics loved.

Even when he painted other people, they still looked like Jesus, just without the crown. I felt Hans was jealous of his younger and more talented friend.

One night as we lay side by side on a dirty mattress in the corner of a good Samaritan's living room, Hans turned to me and said in an accusatory tone, "I see the way you look at Klaus."

"What do you mean?" I asked him, confused.

"You know exactly what I mean," he sneered, propping himself up on one elbow and glaring at me through the darkness.

I laughed uneasily at his intensity. "Don't be stupid," I said. "I have no idea…."

My words were suddenly cut off as he reached out his arm and slapped me cruelly across my face. My eyes filled with tears as I pressed my cool palm against the burning sting of my cheek. With that, I quickly learned not to provoke Hans or give him any reason not to trust me. I lived this way for another year, until I was eighteen.

* * *

Christmas of 1975 was drawing near, and I wanted to go home and visit my mother and brother. I was scared to see my father, and certainly didn't want to hear what my stepmother had to say about the choices I had made. Hans agreed I could go for two weeks.

I traveled by train through France, and then from Dieppe I took the sea-link ferry across the Channel. I arrived late Christmas Eve at Victoria Station. My mother had written me a letter with a phone number to contact her when I got to London. All I knew was she working in a cafeteria and living in an apartment close to Paddington. Exhausted, I set my backpack down at the rail terminal and pulled her folded letter from my back pocket. I called the number from a payphone. It rang and rang, but no one answered. Confused I put the phone back in its cradle, located another payphone and dialed again. This carried on until after midnight. My mother knew I was arriving Christmas Eve. I couldn't understand why she wasn't answering my calls. My anxiety was increasing and I looked around helplessly. I didn't have enough money for a hotel, I was tired and I didn't know what I was going to do.

I saw a policeman and nervously approached him. "Excuse me, please. Can you help me?"

The officer turned his attention to me. "What's the problem?"

"Well, I am supposed to be staying with my mum and I can't find her. I don't know where I am going to sleep tonight and I don't have any money."

He looked up at the terminal's information board and furrowed his brow.

"Seems the train on platform six is in the station until five in the morning. The cleaners usually come about an hour beforehand, so you'll be good until about four, I'd say. You can sleep there."

"Sleep on the train in the station?" I asked.

He assured me it was legal and I would be safe.

"But it's Christmas Eve," I replied meekly.

"Look miss..."

"No, that's fine," I interrupted. "I'll sleep on the train."

Feeling dejected, I made my way to platform six and boarded the train. Transients settling down for the night already claimed many of the seats. I finally found a row of three seats together and made myself as comfortable as I could. I pushed my handbag under my head, afraid that someone might try to steal my passport. I didn't sleep at all that night. Without heat, the train was as cold as it was outside. I curled up as tightly as I could, and pulled my jacket up over my head in an attempt to create warmth from my breath. Self-pity enveloped me like a thick fog. It was now Christmas morning and I had nowhere to go. The next day, I caught the train back to Newhaven. I would go back to Hans, the hotel, and the only life I'd come to know.

* * *

Hans's need to control me and his unpredictable moods and outbursts of anger were wearing on me. I wanted to leave him but had no idea how to make my want a reality. Our transient lifestyle was not as exciting as it had seemed when he rescued me from Nora's house.

We were on the bus to Pisa one morning when I started feeling faint. The bus was cramped and hot. I held onto the overhead bar as we weaved through the city streets, some fat woman's hairy armpit pressed into the side of my face. I could hardly breathe and I felt nauseated and dizzy. By the time we arrived at our stop, I was so weak I could hardly stand. I dropped to my knees on the sidewalk. Hans pulled me up and asked a man passing by for directions to the closest hospital.

Luckily, the hospital building was only a block from the bus stop. I couldn't speak Italian and the hospital staff could not speak English, German, or French. Eventually a doctor was able to explain to me by drawing a diagram that I was pregnant. Hans and I rode back to the hotel in silence. By that evening he had decided there was no way he could support a baby. I would have to go back to England and take care of the problem. I wanted to ask him about the little girl I knew he had in France. He had told me she was seven and her name was Frederique. I wondered if he wanted her mother to get an abortion and that's why he never saw her? I didn't ask because I knew he'd get angry. He reassured me that he would make as much money as he could in the next few weeks and then join me in England. He said he wanted to marry me and he would get a proper job.

* * *

I was able to track down my mother in Brighton this time. She had sent me a letter apologizing for not seeing me Christmas Eve in London, explaining that she had fallen asleep and never heard the phone. She told me that she had quit that job and was now living in a flat with Pete and her new boyfriend Alex. Having safely made the journey to England again, I followed the directions to her new residence, which was at the top of what I was sure to be the steepest hill in Brighton. Finally, I stood breathless in front of the depressing run-down building and pushed the rusted doorbell. I heard the faint trill in the hallway and waited. At last, my mother opened the door.

"What are you doing here?" She slurred, furrowing her brow. She seemed confused and didn't remember our conversation. I hadn't seen her in over two years and it was obvious her drinking had progressed. Booze had distorted her features; the woman who had once been a beautiful socialite was now bloated and unrecognizable. Her mouth was permanently downcast and she was wearing a stained housedress and slippers.

I followed her up the grimy steps to the landing. The odor of boiled cabbage seeped from under her neighbor's door. My mother had been able to secure a low income, one-bedroom flat, which was a step up from the endless hotel rooms she had called home for years. I soon learned that the hallways always smelled of cabbage, and the other tenants, Gladys and George, shared the communal toilet. Gladys was pasty white, flabby, and morbidly obese. George was bony and nervous, hanging onto his wife's every word and anticipating her every need. Gladys's thin red hair never looked washed and clung to her forehead in oily strings. She rarely wore her dentures and I would listen at the door of my mother's apartment for the sound of her shuffling slippers to depart down the hallway before making a dash to the toilet.

My mother proudly told me that she met Alex in the bar across the street. She had noticed him for a week, sitting quietly in the dimly lit corner of the barroom, head bent over his drink. One night they struck up conversation and Alex drunkenly told her his story. He and his wife had been unable to have children and after years of disappointment they went through the process of adoption. Alex thought the baby would lift his wife's depression and make her happy. One day when he came home from work, he found his wife passed out on the bed with an empty bottle of sedatives still clutched in her hand. In the bathroom nearby, the body of his ten-month old adopted son floated lifeless in the bathtub. His wife survived but the baby didn't.

"Oh my God mum, what a horrible story."

She told me she took Alex home that night. I wondered if she in turn had told him her sad story and reason for sitting in the dingy bar night after night, incrementally drowning her life in barley wine?

Alex had the bloodshot eyes and bulbous nose of an alcoholic, burst capillary veins running across it like various routes on a roadmap. He was illiterate and I wondered if this was why he teased me about having been educated in private schools.

"I know your kind," he'd say, leaning in close to my face, his swollen nose threatening to touch the tip of mine, "You think you're better than me because you went to those snobby schools."

I was tempted to tell him that in an alcohol blackout my mother had told me his wife killed their baby. "Did you feel responsible?" I wanted to ask him.

Instead I just walked away.

The entire apartment consisted of two rooms and a kitchen. The bathtub was in the kitchen. If you raised the cheap, teak countertop, the tub was below, usually filled with carrot and potato peelings. If I wanted a bath, I risked Alex spying on me through the hanging beads that served as the only door, so I bathed like a raccoon at the sink, splashing water on my hands and face and quickly washing my underarms with a cloth.

The situation was dismal. Both of them were in the latter stages of chronic alcoholism and Pete was basically looking after himself. He was twelve years old and he wasn't in school. My mother was always too drunk to enroll him, so I did. I also went to a clinic and had the abortion. My mother gave me no guidance, other than sharing with me that she had an illegal abortion when she was nineteen and almost died.

Hans's money paid for the procedure and a cab back to the apartment. He was supposed to come over and join me after the abortion. I remembered him telling me we'd get married, he'd get a proper job, and we'd settle in Brighton.

In the short time I was back in England, I felt blissfully free, despite living in my mother's accommodations; I could come and go as I pleased and not have to constantly check in with a jealous boyfriend. I knew it would be a huge mistake to marry Hans.

Two weeks later, I met Hans at the train station as we had arranged. The plan was to go straight to the courthouse and get married. Surrounded by pedestrians pushing past us on their way to and from the station, I summoned up the courage to tell him the truth.

He stood there shaking his head as I explained why I couldn't marry him. I felt exasperated as he rejected everything I was saying, he kept insisting I was upset because of the abortion.

"No, it's you!" I shouted at him in frustration, "I don't want to be with you anymore!"

I had wanted to say this for a long time but lacked the courage. In Italy I was completely dependent on him; but here, back in my own country, I could finally say the words. He grabbed my arms and told me I couldn't do this to him. He wouldn't let me do this to him.

"Let go," I screamed, as I broke away from his grip and ran. I pushed through people on the sidewalk. As Hans was swallowed up in a sea of human traffic, he shouted, "I'll find you, I'll find you and I'll kill you."

His last words would haunt me for years to come.

Chapter Ten

I ran back to my mother's booze-soaked apartment for refuge.

Now what was I going to do?

I had never finished school or acquired any job. The idea of having to take care of myself terrified me. I wasn't afraid of working, but I had no idea where or how to start looking for a job. I had attempted a typing class at the convent, but while the other students' skills improved as the class progressed, mine remained terrible. I probably typed at best thirty-five words a minute by the time I had finished the course. I had no idea what I was going in order to earn a living.

My mother sobered up long enough to come to an interview for a waitress position at the Metropole Hotel. The Metropole was one of the older, classier hotels on the Brighton seafront. She did all of the talking and I let her sell me.

"Janine has skills in so many areas. She has been used to cooking, cleaning, and taking care of children. Why, she had to take care of an entire household in a foreign country when she was only sixteen!" My mother turned and smiled proudly at me.

I was sitting in a chair next to her and across from the General Manager, unsure of where to look: at my mother, the manager conducting the interview, or my half chewed fingernails? I finally settled on looking out of the window and let my gaze drift off toward the horizon, as my mother's voice droned on endlessly. Thanks to her persuasion, I secured the job.

I was only at the Metropole a short time when I was approached by one of the waitresses. I had seen her on the floor during training but we had never spoken. She introduced herself as Cheryl and told me that she was looking to share her flat.

Later that day, I followed Cheryl down the steps leading to a basement that was only a ten minute walk from the hotel. The place was cold and damp, with only a two-bar electric heater as the sole source of warmth. The heater was in her room and had to be continuously fed coins in order to run. It was depressing, but it was a lot better than continuing to live at my mother's. I told her I could move in the next day.

Cheryl and I sat huddled in front of the little heater in her room for hours after our evening shift, trying to warm ourselves enough to be able to make it to our beds. We were both eighteen and that's all I knew about her. We shared the rent but she kept the main room as her bedroom, and I was assigned a trundle bed in the narrow hallway leading to the bathroom, which I didn't really think was fair. During the night one of Cheryl's male visitors would invariably collide with my bed as they tried to navigate their way to the bathroom in the dark.

To add to my discomfort, she was having an on again off again affair with one of the married managers at the hotel. He would stop by to visit her after his shift. As her bedroom was the main room in the flat, it was the only access to the kitchen and front door. I was confined to my little bed in the hallway waiting until it was appropriate to venture out, the sounds of their lovemaking echoing throughout the tiny room.

Late one night, I'd already gone to bed and was trying to sleep through their lovemaking. The noises finally stopped, and I figured they must have finished. I heard the door open to the narrow hallway and I could feel his presence by my bed. I was facing the wall curled in a fetal position feigning sleep.

Please just go to the bathroom.

I felt his weight as he sat on the edge of my little bed; I froze and held my breath. He gingerly tried to pull the cover down, but I was gripping it tightly still pretending to be asleep. After a couple of tugs, he gave up, got up and went into the bathroom. I put my fingers in my ears so I couldn't hear him urinating.

* * *

One afternoon between shifts, I was walking through the hotel dining room and noticed an elderly man sitting in one of the oversized regal chairs in the foyer. He was dressed in robes and the traditional Arab headdress. He smiled and nodded as I walked past him.

"Do you need anything?" I asked.

"No, no thank you." He shook his head. "Do you like to work here?"

No one had asked me that question, and I stopped and smiled at his bluntness.

As the days passed I learned that his name was Sheik Abdullah Azhazel. His father had been put to death for his political beliefs in Iran, at which time Abdulla and a few followers escaped to Kuwait. Abdullah was a young man and over the years he was able to build himself wealth with a large construction company. If I brought him coffee or a sandwich, he would tip me with a fifty-pound note. This went on for some time, until one day he asked me if I would like to have lunch with him. On my break, we walked along the seafront to a little ethnic restaurant.

Sitting at the table eating hummus and kuboos, Abdullah told me stories of his father and other members of his family, and I found myself being more open with him than I had with anyone else in my life.

As we walked back to the hotel, he turned to me and said, "I wish to help you, and this is how I can." He pressed a bundle of bills into my hand.

I didn't know what to say, nor did I have any idea how much he had given me.

"Thank you," I mumbled under my breath.

"You are welcome," he responded. "You are so kind because you take time to talk to me."

* * *

When I got back to the hotel, I went in the bathroom, shut a stall door and pulled the wad of notes out of my pocket. I sat on the toilet and sifted through the bills, I realized I was holding five hundred pounds in my hands. I had never seen that much money in my life.

In the ensuing weeks, Abdullah and I would have coffee together and walk along the sea front in deep conversation. At the end of the walks and talks he would invariably press money into my hand and tell me to use it to buy things for myself that I needed. I started a savings account with no real plan in mind. Abdullah was interested in my family and asked me questions about my mother, my grandmother, and my father. As I told him about my mother's drinking and my father's disinterest in me, he shook his head clicking his tongue and patting my arm sympathetically. In turn he told me about his wife and daughter in Kuwait that he missed so much, but they didn't want to leave their traditional lifestyle and move to England.

We found solace with one another.

One day I decided to take Abdullah to meet my mother, maybe he could help her too? I warned him of the condition of her apartment as we got out of the cab.

Abdullah lifted the front of his skirts as I led him up the narrow staircase and into the hallway with its familiar smell of boiled cabbage. At the top of the stairs my mother opened the door and Abdullah extended a fifth of first-rate scotch as a greeting.

"This is for a very fine lady," he said graciously as he handed her the bottle.

My mother was used to drinking canned barley wine from the corner off-license and she was impressed with his extravagance. Alex had been missing a few days and I was relieved he wasn't there. When I told my mother that my new wealthy friend would be coming for a cup of tea, she had seemed excited. I noticed that she must have cut back on her drinking with Alex gone. She didn't even open the bottle of scotch, instead proudly placing it on the three-legged armoire as a centerpiece. I also noticed that she had attempted to tidy up the flat, picking clothes up off the chairs, and cleaning up the usual glasses and dirty plates.

She had spent some time on her appearance, trading in her usual stained housecoat for a pair of slacks and a sweater. I pulled up a chair for Abdullah, wincing at the mismatching cups and saucers, and the almost empty packet of stale biscuits on the coffee table. I went in the tiny kitchen to put the kettle on and I could hear Abdullah telling my mother what a difference I had made to his dreary days in Brighton. I was happy that someone was telling her how special I was.

As we sipped our tea, my mother recounted some of her childhood stories; being fourteen years old when Hitler started to bomb England, how she and her five siblings were put on a train and sent to live with family friends in the countryside, as the eldest they made it her responsibility to look after her brothers and sisters. I always wondered if she resented her parents for taking her out of school.

Abdullah listened with interest, paraphrasing her words and making her feel important. I wondered what life would have been like if he were my father. I envied his daughter.

We left the apartment and I wondered if he had slipped her any money while I was in the kitchen washing the permanently tea stained cups. I didn't ask, but I hoped if he had that she'd use it to buy something for Pete.

* * *

My mother called me a week later to tell me that Hans showed up on her doorstep demanding to know where I was living.

"I didn't tell him anything," she assured me. "I don't think he'll come back again."

But I wasn't so sure; I felt the cold grip of fear as I remembered the intensity of his dark eyes when he said that he would find me and kill me. I hadn't thought about him in a while, but now paranoia set in and imagined I caught glimpses of him in various places.

Was that him staring at me out of the bus window? Was that him in the line behind me at the railway station?

One time I was sure I saw him coming out of a cinema. He never did show up again, but every now and again I felt certain that I had just spotted him in a crowd.

* * *

I was setting up the tables for the lunch shift one day when I noticed one of the banquet managers eyeing me. I asked around and found out his name was Clive. I had noticed him staying after hours in the evening, sitting in the restaurant as we waitresses were laying up the tables for breakfast. He towered above the other staff by a good eight inches. His blond, wavy hair was parted at the side and tucked neatly behind one ear. He was as far removed from Hans as a person could be. I liked his aura and sense of stability.

It didn't take long for him to approach me and ask me if I would go for a drink with him after work.

We were sitting at a bar in a hotel on the seafront when Clive admitted that he had been besotted with me for quite some time. He went on to confess he had been watching me from a distance and couldn't get me out of his head. I felt excited and giddy that someone was so smitten with me. I agreed to go out with him again. I had never heard the word "besotted" before, and made a mental note to look it up in Cheryl's dictionary when I got back to the flat that evening.

As we continued spending time together, I realized that although I wasn't attracted to him physically, I was attracted to his intense preoccupation with me and his sense of security. It gave me such a feeling that I no longer needed the greasy chips and the fluffy jam sandwiches. My relationship with my father and stepsiblings had fizzled out when I left for Denmark. Alex was back, so my mother was drunk again. Clive was my new rescuer.

I still loved to visit my grandmother. It made me feel good that she kept my favorite biscuits in the familiar silver container from my childhood. I'd tell her about Clive and his fine upper-class family, knowing this would impress her and convince her that I wasn't completely a lost cause. I was eighteen and Clive was twenty-eight. Before the year was over he had asked me to marry him.

* * *

The wedding service was to take place in a small Catholic church in Brighton. Ongoing bitterness and conflict between my parents left me no other option than to have to choose between my mother and father. I wanted my father to walk me down the aisle, but he wouldn't come without Audrey. When I tried to explain this to my mother, her face contorted with rage,

"I will not be in the same room with that woman. Not on your Nelly!"

Once again I had to endure the story of how Audrey had stolen my father from her and ruined her life after her baby died.

"Do you know that bitch used to send me clippings from lonely heart's clubs?"

As I had only known my dad briefly, I decided I would rather offend him than hurt my mother.

My father's response was to remain uninvolved. I was by now very aware how absent he was when faced with any conflict.

* * *

I wasn't in love with Clive, but I was desperate for my life to change, and I could always pretend.

Clive's parents, brother and sister were to attend our wedding, along with his other relatives and family friends. His father was an attorney and his mother had the luxury of not having to work. She lived an affluent lifestyle with her self-imposed rigid rules and high expectations of others. His parents lived in a large, prestigious house with beautiful wood parquet floors adorned with Persian rugs. The family especially loved to get together on Sundays and sit in the richly furnished living room, sipping tea, and assassinating the characters of most of the people they knew. I wondered if they talked about me when I wasn't there.

Much to my mother's chagrin, the reception was to be held at my Aunt Margaret's house. Margaret was the sibling closest in age to my mother, and their relationship had always been fraught with envy and resentment. Margaret knocked my mother off the pedestal of being the only child when she was born. However, my aunt had graciously offered her home and I was relieved, as she and my uncle were well-to-do, and their house would meet Clive's mother's standards.

The support on my side was conspicuously lacking. My uncle George would take the place of my father and walk me down the aisle. Uncle George had been my advocate in the past. I was grateful for how he had taken me in when my mother first came back from France and was trying to find a place to live. He knew of her drunkenness and he felt sorry for me. He was recently divorced and had never had any children, and I think he saw me as the daughter he never had. My grandmother, my youngest aunt, and her husband completed my family assemblage. My mother's relationships with her siblings had always been at odds. She had been her father's favorite and a star student before she had to leave school at the end of WWII when my grandmother found out she was pregnant again. My mother could not hide her bitterness when she talked about her youngest sister Anita.

"I was the maid and the nanny, and boy did that baby cry!"

I wondered if Pete reminded her of Anita with his constant crying.

My mother's boyfriend, Alex, was not invited. At one time my grandmother, feeling sorry for her eldest outcast daughter, offered to give Alex a job. He was to mount door handles on the front doors of the apartments in a building where she worked part-time showing property to prospective buyers. Alex was inebriated from the time he started the job until he was finished. After he completed the project, my grandmother arrived at work to find all the door handles mounted at various heights and angles; not a single one of them matched another. She had to hire someone to repair Alex's work and didn't want to ever see him again.

* * *

The week before the wedding, I spent hours shopping for an appropriate outfit for my mother. I finally found what I felt was the perfect dress, matching shoes, and a handbag.

The day of the event, a cab deposited her at my aunt's house. She staggered in wearing the new burgundy silk dress that cost me nearly an entire paycheck. I looked at her in horror. Above her right eye was a darkly penciled brow, arched in a look of surprise. Blue eye shadow caked her right lid and mascara clumped the lashes together in a tarantula-like mess. Her left eye was completely nude, her natural eyebrow virtually invisible. In her drunken stupor, she had apparently forgotten to do her other eye. The first to see her, I dragged her into the bathroom to fix her face and fed her cups of coffee until she was sober enough to at least maintain her composure. I later found out that the day after the wedding, she sold the dress and accessories to one of my aunts.

Nanette was my bridesmaid. I was glad that I reached out to her and told her I was going to get married. She stood tall and slender in a pale pink, crepe dress, her thick, blond hair falling below her shoulders. She looked like an angel.

As I stood nervously at the back of the church, I was conscious of my stomach straining against the high cut waistband of my wedding dress. I hadn't been able to spend much money, but found a dress that was simple and to my taste. It was white, lightweight, with a sweeping train that brushed the ground. There was no veil, but instead a white lace hood attached to the back of the dress. For the walk down the aisle, I wore the hood up over the sparse bun on the top of my head. My uncle walked toward me smiling with his arm extended.

I went through the ceremony as if in a daydream.

When it was all over, friends and family members gathered in the living room of my aunt's house. People milled around, sipping cocktails and making small talk; I guessed the strangers among them were friends of Clive's parents. I cringed every time I heard my mother's drunken cackle carry across the room.

My sense of inadequacy was worse around Clive's parents; their expectations and harsh judgments of others made me feel even more insecure. I wondered if they were disappointed Clive had chosen me to be his wife. His entire family were over six feet tall. His mother had the biggest hands and feet I had ever seen on a woman; her jet-black, Jackie-O hairdo framed an angular, arrogant face. Black eyebrows arched like raven's wings over her beady eyes.

I was standing in a corner pouring myself some champagne when Clive's father approached me.

"So…" he began, "what kind of work do you think you'll be looking for now?"

"Work?" I looked at him absently.

I didn't know what to say so I just shrugged my shoulders and smiled.

"I haven't really decided on anything quite yet. More champagne?" My stomach twisted in a knot of angst, fearful that he might want to ask me more questions about work.

I was thankful to go upstairs and change out of the uncomfortable dress. An overwhelming sadness suddenly filled me. I had seen weddings in films and knew how I was supposed to feel, but looking at my reflection in the mirror that afternoon in my aunt's bedroom, I longed for something I couldn't even envision for myself. I felt more empty and alone than ever. Weddings are meant to be the most joyous occasion in a person's life, but for me it wasn't even a happy day. I just didn't know what my next step was supposed to be.

I was just finishing changing into my honeymoon clothes when there was a knock at the door.

"I'm so sorry to trouble you Janine darling," Uncle George apologized. "I'm going to have to collect the money for the wedding cake before you go."

He handed me a receipt through the doorway. I closed the door and looked at it. My eyes welled with tears of hurt and confusion. He had offered to buy the cake for the wedding. I had gone to the bakery with him, and we picked out a small but pretty cake covered in lilac frosting and yellow flowers. Now he expected me to pay for it.

We honeymooned for ten days in Tenerife, an island off the west coast of North Africa. It was a popular holiday spot for the English with great package deals. Clive had asked me to pay for my portion of the flight and accommodations, claiming the cost was a little steep for his salary.

Grudgingly, I emptied out my sparse bank account.

Chapter Eleven

When Clive and I returned from our honeymoon, we moved into a small one-bedroom bungalow in Saltdean about fifteen minutes east of Brighton. It was a reasonable price for a first house and he could manage the mortgage on his salary. I happily gave up my job at the hotel. I was sick of setting up tables, cleaning off tables, and serving rude middle-aged businessmen. Occasionally one of them would leave a room number on a piece of paper pushed under his plate. I'd just crumple the note into a ball and throw it out with the leftovers. I was also hoping I might lose some weight. My diet of hotel restaurant food was just adding more lard to my already voluptuous hips and thighs. I was relieved Clive didn't seem to mind.

The bungalow was my first real home since I was twelve. I felt this was the place I could finally create my own family. I wanted to cook special meals from cookbooks, grow vegetables in my own garden, and cut and arrange roses in vases for my dining room table. In my mind I would have a husband who came home from work at five, excited to see me; we would eat what I had created, and then cuddle up on the couch and talk or watch television. He would tell me he loved me and how happy he was. This was all fantasy because Clive wasn't able to give me the attention I desperately craved. He worked long hours, and when he came home, he immediately changed into his robe and sat in his favorite chair in front of the television. If I tried to cuddle up to him, he pushed me off saying I was blocking his view.

I could feel him constantly irritated by my neediness.

* * *

Clive and I were invited to my eldest stepbrother John's wedding to Lucy. My father had met Clive briefly before we got married. Now it was time to go and spend a couple of days with him and my stepmother in the countryside. The beautiful house in Plumpton was gone. The horses, my father's pride and joy, were no longer hanging their heads over the stable doors. My father's career in stockbroking had ended due to some unethical dealings of which I was never made privy. My mother told me he swindled some Japanese businessmen into buying swampland on which to build hotels, but she had no evidence to prove her suspicions. I think she enjoyed the fact that he was also now poor. Slowly, little by little, all the assets of a privileged life would disappear. In six more months, he and my stepmother would secure a living as butler and maid with accommodation included.

We drove to my father's new home, a rambling old stone house in the countryside that he was renting. Appearances were still important.

We planned to stay the night and follow them to the location of the wedding the next morning.

A few hours after we arrived, Dad went missing. Clive and I were unpacking, when my stepmother theatrically swung the bedroom door open and screeched, "Daddy is missing! You have to find him!"

Clive and I exchanged puzzled glances. We had no idea what she was talking about. We had just had dinner with them that evening in the local pub. They were arguing on the way home, but nothing more than usual.

The pitch rose in her voice. "Get your shoes on and go out and look for him. Now!" She pointed dramatically toward the door.

We drove the unfamiliar country roads, stopping at pubs. Clive stayed in the car, engine running, as I searched the crowded lounges for my dad. Exhausted, we finally returned to the house. It was late and there was no place left to search.

"Look!" I exclaimed as we approached the house. I pointed to the silhouette of a person sitting on the peak of the roof. "Is that him? What the hell is he doing on the roof?"

We pulled up the gravel driveway outside the front of the house and got out of the car.

"Dad," I yelled. "Dad, what are you doing up there?"

"I'm trying to get away from your wicked stepmother," he shouted back.

Clive turned and walked back into the house without saying a word. I followed him. My stepmother was in the kitchen nursing scotch in a coffee cup.

"We found Dad, he's on the roof," I told her as I followed Clive back up to the bedroom.

* * *

The next morning my father and Audrey were hung over and irritable. I knew Clive was uncomfortable, so I took him for a walk around the grounds while we waited for everyone to get dressed. This was the first family social event with my new husband, and I looked forward to introducing him to everyone. Clive was a good catch, acceptable in a class conscious setting, where people were judged by their parents and schooling, rather than who they were.

After the reception had come to an end, we caravanned back to my dad's house, he leading the way in his old Volvo, Clive and I following, and then some selected guests who had been invited to resume their drinking.

Suddenly, the Volvo slowed down, coming to a halt on the grassy bank adjacent to the roadside. We pulled up behind them, and the rest of the convoy came to a halt behind us. I looked around, wondering why my dad had stopped in the middle of nowhere. All I could see were fields bordered by lush green hedges; cows turned their heads to view us with suspicion.

"What the hell is going on?" Clive said under his breath.

At that moment the passenger door of the Volvo swung open. My stepmother wobbled out, holding the door handle for support. She was dressed to perfection in a black and white polka dot dress that matched the band of her wide brimmed hat. She staggered a few feet onto the grassy bank, stopped and unsteadily pulled up the many layers of tulle under her skirt. I watched in horror as she proceeded to squat and relieve herself right there on the side of the road.

"Oh... my... God!" Clive paused dramatically between each word. I slowly slid down in my seat until all I could see was the top of her wide brimmed hat. Surely if I didn't see her, this couldn't be happening.

* * *

As if my father's side of the family weren't eccentric enough, Clive was far more appalled by my mother's inappropriateness. We had only been in our new bungalow a couple of months when she elected to pay us a visit. I paced around anxiously straightening the cushions on the couch and glancing out of the living room window every few minutes waiting for the bus to pull up. Clive was watching television, unaware of my uneasiness.

I was in the bathroom when I heard the front door bell. Our white shepherd, Sabre rushed down the hallway barking excitedly. I grabbed his collar and held him back as I opened the door. She stood smiling in a knee length, blue-and-orange checkered dress with white patent leather pumps, her broad shoulders prominent in the form fitting fabric. I noticed she had made an effort to look nice.

"Hello daaahling," she slurred as she pitched forward to embrace me.

I managed to extricate myself from her ample bosom, and said with feigned cheerfulness, "Come in, Mum. Clive is in the living room."

As she traipsed past the dog and myself into the narrow hallway, I was hit by the aroma of undiluted scotch. She wobbled down the two steps into the main room, balancing herself on the arm of the couch.

"Hello Lorna," Clive greeted her, barely looking up from his horseracing schedule.

"Anything to drink here, or is this Sahara Mansions?" She looked over my shoulder at the liquor cabinet.

She was trying to keep her composure, unaware of her slurred speech. I cringed, but knew better than to refuse her a drink. Clive sighed and got up out of his chair. He poured her two fingers of scotch.

"Only one ice cube," she reminded him as she tottered to the cabinet.

She followed me around the house admiring my furniture and pausing in front of various prints I had hung on the walls. I was so desperate for her to be proud of me, yet I was always so horribly disappointed in her.

I was still meeting Abdulla for lunch and shopping excursions; Abdulla loved to shop. With his help I furnished the bungalow with a dining room set, prints for the walls, and appliances for the kitchen. Clive never asked me where the money was coming from.

My mother turned to me, lowering her voice to an almost inaudible whisper, "Dahhhling, you have done so well for yourself," she said with a malevolent smile.

Clive had retreated back to his chair. She glanced over her shoulder and then pushed her face close to mine. "Make sure you hang on to Abdullah. Just in case." She pulled back, giving me a sly wink. Assaulted by the fumes of booze, I held my breath.

"Mum you're spilling your drink!" I grabbed her glass just as the scotch was about to empty onto the new beige carpet.

When she finally left, Clive and I watched her through the living room window as she stumbled toward the bus waiting at the street corner. I lowered my gaze to avoid having to watch her as she struggled to board. She was so drunk and her dress was so tight, that she kept pitching forward as she tried to climb the steps.

Clive was riveted and kept making comments as she dropped her change on her third jaunt up the staircase, coins spilling out onto the street below. She seemed so pleased she'd finally made it to the top; she didn't even notice that the coins had dropped. The bus driver waited patiently as she rummaged around in her purse for the coins that were no longer there. I glanced sideways at Clive and could see from the look on his face that he was both fascinated and appalled.

"God, she's beyond awful. How on earth did you live with her?"

I had never taken Clive to see her at her flat, so other than the day of our wedding, this was only his second encounter with Lorna.

"I hate her," I said under my breath, "I hate her more than you'll ever know."

* * *

There was no alcoholism in Clive's family so he wasn't accustomed to it like I was. As the shameful feelings continued to eat at me, I was left feeling hollow inside, like the depleting end of an hourglass. I substituted this emptiness with food; the more I ate the better I felt, but the fix was only temporary, and then of course, I hated the way the binges made me feel afterwards. It was an endless cycle.

Clive's dwindling interest in me was confusing. I wondered what had happened to that besotted feeling he expressed to me a year ago.

He spent long days at work, leaving me alone until past dinner time. When he did get home, he changed into his favorite blue robe and turned on the television. Weekends were spent reading the newspaper, or watching horse racing on television. Inside I screamed for attention. I was twenty years old, but felt like the nine-year-old no one cared about.

One Saturday evening as he was watching television in the living room and I was in the kitchen washing the dinner dishes, I wondered what he would do if I got sick.

Would he be worried about me?

Maybe if I could make him think that I was ill, that there was something wrong with me, I could get his attention away from the television. I went into the guest bathroom, and leaving the door open I retched into the toilet bowl. I was on my knees, bent forward when one last retch caused me to gag and I managed to throw up. It wasn't very much, but it certainly made it sound as if I was terribly sick with something. I sat on the floor beside the toilet waiting for Clive to come and ask me what was wrong. After some time and no appearance from him, I realized the sound of my retching had not piqued his interest. I could hear the drone of the television coming from the living room, and now I began to feel embarrassed about my desperate behavior. I flushed the toilet and retreated to the safety of the bedroom.

Over the course of the next few days, I wondered if I would be able to make myself throw up again. Maybe if I could get rid of some of what I was eating and lose weight, he would be more interested in me. One afternoon after binging on the usual cakes and pastries, I shut myself in the toilet and vowed that if I tried hard enough, I could throw up. I knelt in front of the toilet, grabbed the sides of the porcelain bowl and stuck my index finger down my throat. My gorge rose and I emptied the puree of pastries into the toilet. When I had rid myself of everything—the food, the pain, and the self-loathing—I leaned back against the wall and suddenly felt a new and exhilarating surge course through my body. I couldn't identify this new feeling, but I somehow knew from now on everything was going to be okay.

Chapter Twelve

Over the next two years I got binging and purging down to an art.

I ate and ate until I could barely stand the weight of my stomach. I would then stagger to the bathroom and bow to my God: the toilet bowl. I didn't need my finger anymore. I hadn't for a while. I was able to relieve the feeling of being ready to burst simply by pushing my clenched fists into the center of my distended stomach. I had found a cure for my weight problem. I could stuff my feelings of loneliness and frustration with food, and then expel all the self-loathing as I purged.

Many hours of my days would be spent consuming food and then throwing up. I didn't care anymore that Clive wasn't around. His absence allowed me the time and privacy I needed to binge and purge. I lost so much weight that my thighs no longer rubbed together when I walked. The more I ate, the thinner I became. It wasn't long before I began to get the attention I had always craved.

"My goodness Janine, you're getting so thin!" Clive's mother exclaimed as we arrived at her house for the dreaded monthly Sunday lunch.

Yes, I was getting thin. I would get so thin I would disappear and then everyone would wonder what happened to me.

I now had to shop at children's stores because adult sizes were too big for me. I sorted through the clothes racks, searching for jeans that would fit twelve and thirteen year olds. My new goal was to get into a pair for a ten-year-old. I was obsessed with my shrinking form. I could pinch my collar bone between my thumb and forefinger. I could count my ribs, my fingers running along the ridges under my skin and my hipbone jutted out like a broken piece of wood.

Clive didn't mention my weight loss. I wondered why he hadn't noticed like everyone else.

* * *

In 1979 I discovered I was pregnant. I was both perplexed and excited. Because of my weight loss, my periods had become almost nonexistent and I didn't think it was possible for me to conceive. I had taken two home pregnancy tests to be sure, and waited excitedly for Clive to come home that night. I knew this was going to make all the difference; I felt I had finally achieved something.

Clive did seem happy when I told him the news, he smiled and hugged me and said how pleased his mother would be as this was going to be her first grandchild. I wondered how the pregnancy would affect my weight as I knew I was going to get fat. If I could manage to keep my focus on the baby growing inside me, I figured I'd be okay. With this concept in mind, it wouldn't be me getting fat; it would be the baby gaining the weight it needed to be healthy. I wore baggy clothes so I wouldn't freak out as the baby began to change the shape of my body.

During what was supposed to be a happy time in my life, my mother continued slipping into the bowels of insanity. I told her I was pregnant, but she seemed to have forgotten the following day. In one of our rare talks, Pete divulged some of the madness he was going through at home. He had wanted to talk to me alone, so we arranged to meet in a small coffee shop close to my mother's flat. He was now sixteen years old and the stress of looking after an alcoholic mother was showing. As he walked toward me, I noticed how painfully thin he was. His once thick, blond hair was now a dirty shade of brown and he had small scars on the sides of his neck where he told me my mother had attempted to cut it. As he smiled, I noticed his overcrowded teeth which made it difficult for him to pronounce his "r's" and "th's." I thought back to the eight-year-old boy in the hotel room who had begged me to take him with me when I ran away to Scotland.

"Hey, Sis!"

We awkwardly embraced. I felt guilty that my life was so much better than his.

As we sat sipping our coffees, my brother began telling me what had been going on at 54 Ditchling Road.

I knew my mother had had a fall recently. On one of her recent visits she was sporting a gauze patch taped over one eye. I noticed she was sober for once.

"What happened?" I had asked.

"I fell in the hallway going to the toilet in the middle of the night. You know how dark that hallway is. Well I almost lost my eye!" She said, pointing to the white bandage.

She wasn't exaggerating, but she wasn't being honest either.

Pete told me she popped her right eye out of its socket in the middle of the night while trying to get out of bed. She was drunk and lost her balance, hitting her temple on the corner of the bedside table. Alex was so drunk he slept through her cries for help. Pete told me that he woke up and found her sitting on the side of the bed screaming while Alex snored next to her. Where her eye had been, there was now an empty bloody socket, the eyeball resting on her cheek still attached by orbital muscles.

I cringed at the visual of Pete's description and wished he hadn't gone into that much detail.

He went on to tell me he realized she was drunk so he tried to calm her down, holding a towel over her face while they waited for the ambulance. Alex was so anesthetized from barley wine that he never even woke up.

The surgeon managed to save her eye, and she left the hospital sober. However, it wasn't long before she started drinking again.

Pete said he came home from school a couple of weeks later to find Alex hunched over her on the living room floor with a lamp cord twisted around her neck.

"What the hell did you do?" I asked, intrigued.

"I climbed on his back and twied to pull him off her."

I imagined the three of them piled on top of one another like a macabre circus act.

"Did you call the police?"

"No," he hung his head and then looked up sadly. "Vey would pwobably want to put me in a fostuh home and I'd wavuh stay wiv her."

It sounded to me like a foster home would have been a positive alternative.

He told me how the next day she threw Alex out, screaming curses at him out of the bedroom window as he packed up his car in the street below.

We both laughed.

I looked at him with tears in my eyes. I had asked Clive if he could come live with us, but the response was, "Absolutely not!"

* * *

It wasn't long after that talk with Pete that my godmother Patsy intervened and by all accounts saved my mother's life. Patsy had been living in New York for years, and on a rare trip to England she decided to visit her old friend. She found out where my mother was living through my grandmother. The last time Patsy had seen her was when she and her husband had come to stay with us one summer in France when we still had our house in Bormes les Mimosas. Patsy was shocked and appalled by the sordid conditions of my mother's apartment. She probably remembered my mother as a beautiful, charismatic young woman, the two of them taking London by storm. Patsy had married a wealthy American and my mother had married my stepfather.

My grandmother arranged for me to meet Patsy at the apartment. My grandmother loved my mother but had no idea how to help her eldest child. One look at my mother was enough for Patsy to diagnose her with chronic-stage alcoholism. The ravishes of her illness now bloated my mother's features. Her hair was unwashed and pulled back into a matted clump. Mascara smeared eyes devoid of emotion stared vacantly at the woman who had once been her closest friend.

"Oh darling, let me help you," Patsy pleaded, wincing as she took in my mother's appearance.

"Help me? I'm perfectly fine," Lorna responded, turning her back to Patsy and looking for something to drink.

Patsy approached her from behind, gently placing her hands on either shoulder, steering my mother towards the table and into a chair where she could make eye contact.

"I want you to come to New York with me. You can live with us for a while. Let us take care of you while you get your feet back on the ground."

"But I am managing just fine. Look! We have a roof over our heads and food to eat," my mother gestured toward our meager surroundings, knowing she wasn't fooling anyone.

Patsy smiled meekly, "A very good friend of mine is a doctor. He can treat you, and I will take you to AA meetings myself. You need a support system. Please. Let me help you."

My mother put her face in her hands and sighed deeply. It seemed as if she were silently surrendering.

"I will even help take care of Pete. I don't want you to have to worry about anything other than getting better."

Patsy slid her arm across the table and pulled my mother's hand from her face. They finally locked eyes and Patsy wrapped her hand around my mother's, squeezing it reassuringly.

"This is what friends are for, darling. Let me be there for you. You need help. It would make me so happy if you let me."

None of the family had ever even considered trying to get my mother help for her drinking. She was usually so belligerent, that even the suggestion would have prompted her to scream insults at whomever was trying to help. I had never heard of AA, so Patsy told me how it helped her sister who had a drinking problem comparable to my mother's. I promised Pete I would check on him every week. He could get the bus to and from school, and Patsy left him enough money to pay three month's rent on the apartment, pay bills, and buy food.

* * *

My mother never came back. She started a new life in United States, living with Patsy until she was financially on her feet. She asked her brother George to store her sparse belongings and notify the landlord. She sent Pete a one-way plane ticket and George took him to Heathrow

Airport where he boarded the plane to New York, with nothing but a backpack of clothes and a comic book I had bought him.

* * *

My relationship with Clive's mother had always been taxing. I felt like I wasn't good enough or smart enough for her son, and also way too young—I had been nineteen when he married me. Clive, his brother, and his sister had all attended college, experienced success in their chosen careers, and were married to their social and intellectual equals. Tongue-tied in their presence, I tried to avoid conversations around the dining table or the living room fireplace for fear of them finding out how little I knew about politics and current affairs.

I could always hear my father's voice: "You're stupid, you always have been and you always will be."

The only person I could trust with my feelings was my grandmother, but now I was no longer a child and I couldn't just go and stay with granny whenever I needed comfort.

* * *

When I was about three months pregnant, my old boarding school buddy Nina came back into my life. During my time in Denmark she was sent to an international boarding school in Saudi to complete her education. She was now living with her parents in the family's country estate about twenty miles from Brighton. My stepbrother Adam called me and told me he had seen Nina at a party.

I was anxious about reaching out to her; I was still unsure whether she blamed me for our expulsion from the convent. Nevertheless, it was six years later and I really did want to see her.

Two weeks later we sat in the living room close to the electric fireplace, drinking cups of tea and laughing about our escapades with the nuns. It felt good to have her back in my life.

My oldest friend, Nanette, had married a Syrian a year after I married Clive, and she was due to have her first baby soon after me. I knew her parents had been disappointed about the marriage, as her husband's beliefs about women were so different from the way they had raised their only daughter. Other than these two friends, there was no one else I could talk to about my pregnancy fears. I couldn't tell them the truth about how I was spending half the day in toilets voiding myself of every meal, every snack, and every calorie. They would be disgusted and horrified if they knew. Neither of them would want anything more to do with me if my secret was revealed.

Clive's mother never asked questions or offered advice about my pregnancy, and my mother was busy staying sober in Connecticut, so I bought myself a book on pregnancy and childbirth. The book contained large colored illustrations of the growing fetus and I excitedly tracked its development week by week. I looked at my little finger and imagined that was about the size of my baby. I convinced myself that my life would be different once the baby was born.

I still met up with Abdulla occasionally. He was as excited about the baby as if it were his grandchild. When he was in Brighton he would call me and we'd have lunch together and then go shopping for baby clothes and accessories.

I voiced my concerns about the bungalow being too small for the three of us. With perfect timing, Abdulla offered us the opportunity to buy one of his seafront flats for his purchase price. The high-rise flat was right behind the Metropole Hotel, five minutes from Clive's office. When I told Clive, he seemed apathetic to this amazing deal. I took his lack of interest as an agreement, and without further discussion we put our bungalow on the market. I felt we didn't talk about anything anymore. Even his initial excitement about the baby had quickly fizzled out.

We moved into the flat that winter. Sliding doors from the spacious living room led out to a large balcony. I stepped out onto it, bracing against the gusts of wind as I looked out over the frigid English Channel. At twenty-one stories I felt as if I were on top of the world. For a moment I wondered what it would feel like to topple over the rail. I looked down to the alley below and imagined my five-month pregnant body, lying broken with a crowd starting to gather around me. At that moment Clive called to me and I went back into the warmth of the living room.

I busied myself decorating the baby's room and buying all the basics, such as a carrycot and crib and tiny newborn baby clothes. Although I didn't know if it were a girl or boy, it felt safe buying unisex greens and yellows. I held up the little clothes and imagined my baby in the different outfits. My stomach was now big enough that it was obvious I was pregnant. I wondered if I would ever fit into my skinny clothes again.

My father lived about a two-hour drive from Brighton. He was now renting a small thatched cottage in the countryside. The houses were getting smaller as his income diminished, and my stepmother's health was deteriorating due to her drinking and chain smoking. I knew she had been in the hospital recently with a bout of jaundice and was sent home after detoxing, with a warning that if she continued to drink, she wouldn't live much longer. She told everyone she had pneumonia.

I decided it was probably time to visit them again. I went alone this time, as ever since my stepbrother John's wedding, Clive had made it obvious that he didn't want anything to do with my crazy family. Within minutes of my arrival, Audrey announced that we were going down to the local pub for lunch.

Arriving at the quaint country pub, I followed them through the haze of cigarette smoke around the bar and toward an empty booth next to a rain streaked window. Audrey seated herself across from me, twirling her thick gold necklace between her fingers. She drank a glass of red wine, my father had a beer, and I was nursing a small glass of orange juice. Audrey broke the uncomfortable silence by demanding that I get her another glass of wine. I eyed my father; unsure as to whether or not I should grant her request. Sometimes my father tried to control her drinking, other times he didn't seem to care.

"Shut up, Audrey, you've already had enough."

Ignoring him, she pushed her glass toward me. "Get me another glass of red wine, Chah-neen."

I hesitated, now feeling triangulated by the two of them.

She turned to shriek at me, "Get. Me. A. Fucking. Glass. Of. Wine."

Shocked into motion, I picked up her glass and took it to the bar. My eyes stung as I tried to blink back tears. The bartender eyed me sympathetically as he poured more merlot into the lipstick-stained glass.

That night as I drove home I felt hurt and angry that I let myself fall into the trap of thinking that they might treat me differently or be happy for me because I was pregnant. I didn't understand why my father would allow her to talk to me like that. He saw how upset she made me, but he never said anything to protect me from her verbal abuse.

I let myself into a dark apartment that was void of love and laughter. Clive was still at work; I turned on the lights and stood in front of our bedroom mirror, turning sideways to examine my curved belly. I placed my hand where I thought the baby might be growing. I had hoped that he or she would bring love and joy into my life. I was still binging and purging, and now began to worry that I was depriving my baby of vital nourishment. I swore tomorrow would be different and I would put all my efforts into eating healthfully for the baby.

* * *

My due date came and went. Each day crawled by and every little pain startled me into thinking contractions had started. Finally, the doctor suggested I be admitted so they could induce me. I had no idea what went along with this process and couldn't find it in my baby book.

Clive sat with me in the stark delivery room for a while, but then complained that he was hungry. Sensing his restlessness, I told him I'd be fine, and to go and get something to eat. As soon as he left, I felt the first real pain of a forceful contraction tear through my body. The intensity caught me by surprise, scaring me, and before I could catch my breath another one ripped through me, causing me to scream out loud. The nurse called the doctor and I was coached through the rest of the nightmare. I had never anticipated the primal brutality of childbirth. It felt like something was tearing through my insides, ripping at me with the force of a demon. The labor itself was only three hours, but Clive never came back. I was in a haze of pain and sedatives—and then finally it was over. I had a baby girl.

I wanted to hold her but was told she needed to be cleaned and weighed first. I also needed to be stitched up, as the force of her fast birth had torn me quite significantly. I lay in the postnatal ward for what seemed like hours, watching the other women as they cooed over their tiny babies. Then I heard a baby's wail. It didn't sound like the others, the cry was deeper, and with a sense of urgency that I instinctively identified as mine. The nurse finally brought her to me, swaddled in a soft pink blanket with a matching pink cap to keep her little head warm. As I held her and smelled her baby aroma, the pain of her arrival was instantly replaced with a feeling of intense love.

The next day I stood at the hospital window looking down at the parking lot waiting for Clive. Visiting time came and went as I watched the other husbands interacting with their wives and babies. They all looked so happy. I stole a glance at Katie wrapped in her pink blanket in her little bassinet. I had contemplated calling her Elizabeth, but then decided Katherine was a better fit. If it were a girl, Clive had wanted his mother's name to be her middle name. So here she was, Katherine Ann Darfield, wrapped up tight and sleeping soundly.

The disappointment of Clive's absence was thankfully replaced by the anticipation of lunch. I ate the tasteless meal and immediately asked for another one with two puddings. I then shuffled to the bathroom and purged all my hurt into the grimy toilet. Despite the fear of ripping my episiotomy, I couldn't stop myself. Katie was one day old, and Clive hadn't even seen her. The expected relief and numbness I always felt didn't come this time. Instead I collapsed into a weeping heap on the cold bathroom floor. I knew my binging and purging had become a problem, because I was now doing it even when I didn't want to. I wished I could ask someone for help, maybe one of the nurses? I wanted to so badly, but those three little words just wouldn't come out of my mouth.

Chapter Thirteen

Despite promising myself I would stop once I got home, I was immediately sucked back into my old habits. Now I had to schedule my binging with feeding and caring for a baby. Clive was at work all day, and when he finally came home in the evening, I tried to hand her to him. When I put Katie in his arms he looked as uncomfortable as if I'd handed him a bag of loose eggs, so I invariably took her back after five minutes. I failed at breastfeeding; it hurt too much and I was too embarrassed to ask anyone what to do. After enduring three weeks of torture, I turned to the relief of bottled formula. The pain of engorged breasts is to make sure women don't forget to feed their babies. I didn't know what was worse, the pain of breastfeeding or my breasts feeling like they were on fire and about to explode.

I was disappointed that Clive's family weren't more excited about the baby. We drove to Kingston once a month to visit his mother, Katie sleeping in her wicker carrycot on the backseat of the car with Sabre curled up beside her. Sabre loved to barrel past his mother as soon as she opened the front door of the imposing Tudor house, sliding the Persian rug into an accordion at the end of the long hallway.

Clive's siblings and their spouses paused what they were doing to say hello to me, briefly acknowledging Katie, before Clive joined them to talk about their jobs, politics, and local gossip. I felt I became invisible again.

Clive's father had died of a fast-spreading cancer during my pregnancy, yet no one mentioned him or seemed to miss him.

I felt like the nanny, the waitress, the nothing girl. I was afraid to join in their conversations in case my lack of intellect or education became too apparent. None of them knew I had been expelled from school when I was sixteen.

What would they say if they found out I'd never finished school? I would be the priority on their gossip list, that's for sure.

I was expected to take Katie upstairs and place her in her carrycot in one of the spare bedrooms and then come back down and eat dinner with everyone. I could only relax when she was sleeping, and there was no way I could leave her alone. The dining room was at the other end of the large rambling house and I would never know if she woke up and started crying until her demanding screams resonated through the house. I knew if she got that upset it would take forever to calm her down again. I was also afraid her crying would disrupt their family dinner. In the end I simply decided it was easiest if I stayed up in the room with her.

Katie was christened when she was five months old. Clive's mother decided the service should take place at her Catholic church in Kingston. Although I had been raised Catholic, I had never taken first communion, therefore it wasn't appropriate for me to receive the holy communion. I sat in the pew with Clive's family and when they lined up to receive the Eucharist, I slipped out and hid in the bathroom.

After the service my father and Audrey followed us to Clive's mother's house for the reception. This was their first introduction to his family, and I was glad this time I didn't have to choose between my parents as I had for my wedding. I was anxious Audrey might get drunk, but it would turn out that my father was the embarrassment this time.

As the guests were leaving the reception, I nervously watched him approach my mother-in-law. He was wearing a long camel hair coat with deep pockets. As he extended his hand to say good-bye, a loud clatter drew everyone's attention. The room fell silent as silver trinkets he had gathered from around her house dropped from under his coat and landed noisily at his feet. As he bent over to collect them, an empty silver sugar bowl dropped from one of his pockets.

"Oh dear, oh dear!" he exclaimed, as he looked around in amazement. "My goodness, how did all this get into my coat?"

Clive's mother was not amused by his prank; she curtly told him that he had better leave and escorted him to the front door. As he handed over her valuables, he turned to me and winked.

"Can't really take a joke that one, can she?" he muttered under his breath.

* * *

When Katie was eighteen months old, I took her to the States to meet my mother and her uncle Pete. My mother had acquired a little apartment, a job, and a car in Millerton, Connecticut. It seemed from her letters that she was trying to build a new sober life for herself and Pete.

Odds and ends and items from garage sales furnished my mother's sparse apartment. I noticed she had tried to make it as homey as possible. The picturesque little town boasted one junction and a single traffic light. She had secured a job as the pastry chef in a beautiful old mock-Elizabethan hotel restaurant a couple of miles outside the town and Uncle Pete worked with her as a waiter. The enormous house had been converted into a high-class inn for those who wanted to experience the luxury of stone walls, huge fireplaces, four poster beds, high beamed ceilings, and gourmet cooking. The grounds were surrounded by expansive woods, and during hunting season some guests checked out with a deer carcass strapped to the roof of their car. This was a far cry from the cheap hotels we had lived in during my childhood.

My mother was now a proud member of AA. Her entire vocabulary was interspersed with AA clichés and references to God. It was as if she had taken on a new identity that bore little if any, resemblance to her former self. Gone was the slurring, stumbling, disheveled woman who lived in the sordid flat with Alex. In that woman's place now existed a self-assured, neatly dressed woman in her fifties. I enjoyed hanging out in the richly decorated hotel lobby watching the privileged guests come and go or taking Katie for walks in the grounds.

Red maples adorned the streets of the town, their silvery bark glinting in the afternoon sunlight. Brick store fronts and pale awnings lined each charming little block. When not at the hotel, Katie and I spent our days exploring the town.

Unbeknownst to me, my mother had arranged for me to go to a party one evening. She seemed very excited, and I wondered what her motivation could be. I had a feeling she was plotting something.

"But I don't want to go," I complained.

"Come on, Janine," she reasoned. "He's the owner's son, a wonderful young man, and a college graduate."

My mother was impressed by college graduates, both intimidated and awed by those with college degrees. She had been pulled out of school when she was only fourteen to look after her siblings and she had chosen not to resume her education after the war. Instead she was a graduate of the "school of hard knocks," as she liked to call it.

"Come on," she pleaded. "I'll look after Katie and you go out and have a nice time.

"But I don't have anything to wear," I said, hoping that this would solve the problem.

"Well, actually…" she responded slyly, pulling a dress out of her closet. "One of the girls at work lent me her graduation dress for you to wear."

At that moment I realized that she had planned the whole thing, right down to the dress. I knew she didn't like Clive and felt his parents had shunned her at our wedding. She wouldn't even consider that her being drunk might have anything to do with their scorn. Grudgingly I retreated to the little bedroom to change; Cinderella was going to the ball.

I looked at myself in the mirror. The white sequined dress hung loosely over my right shoulder, and came with a matching headband. My collarbones jutted out, I had become very thin again. I curled my hair with a curling iron and borrowed a pair of my mother's gold hoop earrings. As I applied the finishing touches of make-up, she came into the room.

"Oh darling, you look lovely. You'll fit right in!" She clasped her hands.

She turned to Katie who was playing with one of her necklaces. "Look Katie, doesn't Mummy look beautiful?"

"Mummy booful," Katie mimicked.

She picked up Katie and carried her to the front of the hotel to see me off. My date was tall and thin in his tuxedo; he slicked back his thick blond hair and smiled nervously. I assumed that he must have been set up too.

A horse and carriage waited at the curb.

This was our ride?

Katie appeared more excited than I did, bouncing up and down in my mother's arms crying, "Horsey, horsey!" as she pointed to the well-groomed horse.

Shortly thereafter we arrived at an impressive mansion and I realized immediately that I was completely out of my element and regretted that I had agreed to come. I felt uncomfortable around preppie intellectuals and had no idea how on earth I was going to manage to get through the evening. We entered the main room and I felt everyone's eyes on me. I wondered if they knew that I was an imposter in a borrowed dress. I felt stupid and ugly and wanted to disappear into the woodwork.

My date led me upstairs to a large den where most of the twenty-something crowd were hanging out. I noticed a group gathered around a mahogany table in the middle of the room. I could see that the table displayed lines of white powder, like little tally marks on a chalkboard. Every so often, a guy or girl would hunch over the table and sniff whatever was on the table through a rolled up dollar bill.

One of them glanced up at me and smiled as he caught me eying the table. "Want a line?"

I panicked as I hadn't meant to be caught watching. Now they might expect me to join in, and I was completely clueless. I just wanted to go home. I found a bathroom in the hallway and locked the door behind me feeling like a trapped animal. My heart was pounding and all I wanted to do was take off the stupid dress and put on my pajamas. It took me a while to calm myself down until finally I mustered up enough courage to leave the safety of the bathroom. Somehow I managed to avoid the drug activity for the rest of the evening. I'm sure my date was thrilled that he had brought someone like me along; a boring girl in a borrowed dress who was anything but cool. I was relieved when we finally left the mansion to return to my mother's modest little apartment.

Two days later Katie and I flew back home.

Chapter Fourteen

The week after I returned home from the States, Clive surprised me by informing me he had accepted a job at the Barbican Center in London as the head banqueting manager. We had a month to sell our flat in Brighton and make the move. It took us only a couple of weeks to find a house we liked and could afford. It was out in the suburbs, but the train station was within walking distance and Clive could just hop on the underground to the Barbican. The next two weeks were spent packing up our lives from the twenty-first floor of Sussex Heights. I was excited we were moving into a real house. Our new home was a three-story Victorian semi-detached house in Dulwich, South East London. The very top floor was a huge attic that I excitedly transformed into a playroom for Katie. I painted the walls bright yellow and filled the room with a plethora of toys; a dollhouse and a big wooden rocking horse were among her favorites. I covered her bedroom with Paddington Bear wallpaper and fitted her bed in a matching bedspread. We even had a spare room in case anyone should want to come and stay.

The house was new and different and this was the closest I had lived to London since I was five. Clive was still gone most of the time and I was left by myself with Katie. Carbohydrates and sugar seductively beckoned me, promising me the comforting, sweet numbness I craved. Taking Katie in her stroller for her afternoon walk through the neighborhood, I found a fish and chip shop and bought sausages deep fried in batter with two servings of chips. As I pushed

Katie home, I could feel the warm grease seeping through the paper. The anticipation of what was to come hurried me along.

Once home, I placed Katie in her crib with some toys. First, I ate the sausages and salty chips smothered in ketchup. Then I had two bowls of cereal, a bar of chocolate, a jam sandwich, and whatever else I could find in the kitchen. I ate and ate until I could hardly stand the weight of my straining stomach. At what felt like the last minute before my stomach burst, I staggered into the bathroom, purging all that had been consumed. Following this ritual, I felt in control once again,. energized and motivated to clean the house or take on a project. Despite the euphoric feeling, I experienced times when I was afraid that I might die of a heart attack surrounded by the evidence of my awful secret.

I had read an article in the local paper about a young woman who had been found dead in her bedroom, surrounded by cakes, opened packets of biscuits, boxes of cereal and sodas. The article said she had died of a ruptured stomach due to binging. There she was, exposed for all to see, hemmed in by mountains of half-eaten food. Bearing this in mind, I was very careful to clean up after myself as I ate, throwing out remnants of my binging into the outside garbage bins, much like an alcoholic gets rid of their bottles. I vigorously scrubbed the toilet, leaving it sparkling clean and looking as if it had never been used. Then I would obsessively brush my teeth; I had read that purging stripped teeth of their protective enamel causing decay. I lived in fear that they would eventually rot and fall out. Sometimes I had lucid dreams that my teeth were crumbling in my mouth. I would wake feverishly running my tongue over them, feeling relief they were still intact.

My abnormal eating coupled with the constant fear of being caught kept me feeling anxious and on edge. I could never relax, always preoccupied about how I would get through the next meal without anyone finding out. I couldn't be emotionally or mentally present for Katie or anyone else. The only respite I had was when I slept. As soon as I woke, the nightmarish cycle started all over again.

Clive yelled out the names of horses racing neck to neck from his recliner in the downstairs living room while I sat on our bed binging on éclairs and fruit tarts. I numbly savored every morsel, slowly licking the chocolate icing from my fingertips, and using my tongue to rid the pastry papers of their last remaining crumbs. My ritual after purging was to weigh myself. If the numbers crept up above ninety-eight pounds, I immediately jumped off the scale. I could never weigh more than ninety-eight pounds.

* * *

When Katie was three years old my mother moved from Connecticut to Palm Springs, California. Having complained to her doctor about her various ailments over the years, he told her it might benefit her to live somewhere that had a warmer, drier climate. I wondered if her doctor suggested this so he would no longer have to have her as his patient. Her health was always precarious; I seldom paid attention as she ran through the list of all her medical issues anytime she called me. Her fibromyalgia, hip problems, bowel issues, arthritis, neuropathy, and constant bladder infections were just some of the conditions she would want to discuss for as long as I was willing to listen.

This time she was excited about her latest move and told me about the little house she had found to rent just outside Palm Springs. She claimed she was five years sober now and had found a job as a pastry chef at a Sheraton Hotel. She managed to get Pete a job in the same hotel as a busboy.

"Why don't you bring Katie and come and visit me again? You'll love it here Nini!"

This was all I needed to hear. Any excuse to get away from Clive sounded perfect. I told Katie we were going to the States to see Granny again. Katie was old enough to understand what I was saying and she was used to talking to my mother on the phone. She jumped up and down excitedly on her bed.

"We gowin to see Gama, we gowin to see Gama!"

Clive had no comment to make about us going. He didn't seem to miss us when we went last time and I wondered if he preferred life without us.

I loved Palm Springs. It was so different from the cold and lifeless landscape of Dulwich. Palm Springs was warm and busy with trees trimmed to perfection. The flowers and grass looked artificial, symmetric and arranged. The stores sold colorful clothes, souvenirs and knickknacks. It was an oasis of life and color in the middle of a desert.

I was used to the corner off-license and the fish and chip stand, wearing layers of clothing and a parka to endure the brisk ten-minute walk to get my fix. Here, there was bustling activity on the sidewalks. Men and women passed me wearing the briefest of shorts and the tiniest tank tops I had ever seen, their skin proudly bronzed from the California sun or from tanning salons which I had never previously heard of. I looked down at my thin arms, completely devoid of color. I was not used to the blue, cloud free sky. I kept looking up and marveling, announcing to strangers and storeowners what a beautiful day it was. They seemed unaffected by the climate, and after a few days I realized that every day was a beautiful day during springtime in Palm Springs.

My mother introduced me to her friends in AA and some of the young men and women who worked with her at the hotel. She proudly announced, "This is my daughter Janine who lives in England and this is my beautiful granddaughter, Katie."

My mother let me borrow her car and I navigated the streets, trying to remember to stay on the right side of the road. I met people at cafés or bars in town. I wasn't used to any kind of "nightlife" and now, for the first time, I was having fun.

One afternoon I was at a Mexican restaurant in town, when a man in his late thirties approached my table. I was watching Katie twirl in the middle of the lounge, entertaining couples at adjoining tables.

"Hey there! Haven't seen you here before?" the stranger asked.

I didn't know how to respond, so I just smiled shyly at him and turned my attention back to Katie.

"You got a name?"

"Yes, it's Janine," I replied uneasily.

"Janine," he said my name as if it were a dish on the menu he was considering ordering. "So…are you here on vacation Janine? I'm guessing by your accent that you're not a local."

I was amused at his pick-up lines.

"Yes, my mother lives here. I'll be staying with her for the next month."

"Oh, right on! That's great," he said flashing me a dazzling smile. "How do you like Palm Springs so far?"

I started to relax. "I like it. It's so different compared to where I'm from in England."

"Are you from London?"

I had noticed that whenever someone found out I was from England, they assumed that I was from London.

"Sort of," I replied elusively.

He told me his name was Richard and he had a furniture business in town. I had immediately labeled Richard as the Palm Springs lounge lizard. He had a slim build and proudly wore a pair of the shortest bright orange corduroy shorts I had ever seen on a man, coupled with a bright blue Hawaiian shirt, unbuttoned and splattered with palm leaves and colorful toucans. He had deeply tanned, leathery skin and light brown feathered hair. A gold medallion rested in the soft hairs of his chest. I was sure he cruised the bars and restaurants of the town looking for easy targets.

He smiled at me again and I wondered if his teeth were false, they seemed so white and perfectly straight against his bronzed skin.

Katie, bored with her twirling was now crawling underneath the table. I got up to say good-bye when he made his move.

"Come with me and my friends tonight, we are going to have sushi at this really cool Japanese restaurant. It's not far from here."

I hesitated a moment. I knew my mother could give Katie dinner and put her to bed. Going out with Lounge Lizard might be fun if other people were going too. I could take my mother's car, so if I wanted to leave I'd have an exit plan. I had never tried sushi and was ready for a new experience.

A few hours later I anxiously drove my mother's car to the Japanese restaurant. Richard had written the directions on a paper napkin, and he now waved to me from the bar. Feeling self-conscious, I quickly walked over to him. As he pulled out a chair from the bar, my nostrils were assaulted by the vapor of his cheap cologne. We sat at the bar sipping mai tais, waiting for his friends.

After a few minutes of uncomfortable chit chat, I noticed a couple walking toward us. She was wearing a short leather skirt and one of her stockings had a long tear down the front. As she got closer I saw that she had a ring in one nostril and what appeared to be a large cold sore on her lip. Her date looked like he was in his late thirties, dark haired, about five-foot-ten and stocky. He carried a men's soft brown leather purse under one arm. He was wearing a brightly colored short sleeve shirt tucked into a pair of tightly cinched jeans. As he approached I noticed his dark body hair, exposed at areas not covered by his clothing. I noticed he too had a cold sore on his lip. My spirits diminished as I realized this was the couple we had been waiting for.

We introduced ourselves and sat down at one of the tables. Several drinks later I found myself eating creatures with unseeing eyes, perched atop small mounds of rice. Richard's friend Paul was very charismatic. He told me he was Jewish and that his parents left Austria at the beginning of World War II. He and his sister grew up in California with two Austrian grandmothers who couldn't speak a word of English, other than yelling, "Shurrup" at the kids all day long.

Paul told me how his parents had both worked full time, establishing a life for themselves in the United States, while his grandmothers raised him and his sister. Paul's father had recently employed him at his new car dealership in Palm Springs. I pictured Paul writing prices on the windshields of newly delivered cars and spraying them down with soap and water every morning so they were nice and shiny before the customers arrived. I also discovered he was fourteen years older than me.

As the evening wore on, I realized we had split into two couples, Paul was talking to me, and I noticed cold-sore girl was in deep conversation with Richard. I wasn't used to drinking, and never really liked the taste of alcohol, however, this night I drank wonderful, fruity tasting beverages with names I had never heard of. I felt light-headed and wanted to go back to my mother's mobile home and lie down. As I said my good-byes, Paul asked for my mother's phone number and address. I told him where she lived, feeling embarrassed that he might know it was in a run-down trailer park.

On the way home I was nervously trying to keep the over-sized L.T.D Ford on the right side of the road, when I noticed flashing lights in my rear view mirror. The car was like trying to maneuver a boat as I pulled over. I held my breath and watched the policeman walk toward me in the mirror.

"Do you know how fast you were going miss?" he asked as he walked up to my open window.

"No, I'm so sorry, I'm not used to driving here, I'm from England and this is my mother's car and…"

He silenced me with his hand. I looked at his palm, frozen in mid-sentence.

"Let me see your driver's license please," was all he said.

I nervously pulled out my British license, which was valid for the next fifty years. The officer started walking back to his car, unraveling the document that was encrypted with codes and numbers. He stopped mid-stride and turned back.

"I'm going to let you go this time because you're on vacation, but I suggest you go right back to where you're staying."

I took my unraveled license from him and with shaking hands stuffed it back in my bag. "Thank you," I mumbled, not moving until I saw him get back in his car.

* * *

The next day, I dragged myself out of bed, head pounding and mouth as dry as cotton. I poured myself a tall glass of orange juice.

"Janine," my mother's voice came from the front room.

I walked in to find her holding two large envelopes. "These were hanging out of the mailbox, someone must have put them there late last night, because the mail doesn't come until the afternoon."

We sat down on her second-hand tattered corduroy couch as I

read the cards from Paul out loud. They were filled front and back with endless expressions of desire and intention.

I had only spent a couple of hours with this guy.

I turned to look at my mother's reaction.

"What the eye doesn't see, the heart doesn't know," she raised her eyebrows and smiled wickedly at me.

Was she actually encouraging me to cheat on Clive?

The last time she had tried to fix me up on a date it had failed.

At that moment Pete came through the swinging aluminum door after his night shift at the hotel. "What's going on?"

"Your sister has a date this weekend," my mother answered for me.

In one of the cards, Paul described his ranch house in a place called Malibu. He wanted me to go there with him for the weekend.

"You will love it!" Pete said. "It's where all the stars live."

To me it sounded like I would be out of my element once again.

* * *

My mother suggested I leave Katie, and even if she had to go to work, she would take her. All the staff at the hotel loved Katie.

I nervously dialed the number at the bottom of one of the cards and asked to speak to Paul. A moment later I was telling him that he could pick me up the next day.

I was going to Malibu.

* * *

The following afternoon I was sitting on the steps of the trailer with a small overnight bag between my legs. I didn't want him to come inside and see the sparse, mismatched furniture which had been donated by hotel employees. Just as I was beginning to think he had changed his mind, I heard the low roar of an engine coming around the corner. There was Paul, sitting behind the windshield of a black Porsche convertible. I took in the flared fenders, extra-wide tires, and large spoiler. The rear windows and rear windshield were tinted. I had never seen such a display of extravagance and suddenly regretted my decision of going off with someone so obviously flashy.

How could a guy who worked at a car dealership afford to drive such an expensive car? Did he borrow it from the lot?

My date hopped out and ran around to the other side of the car, opening up the passenger door for me. No one had ever treated me with such courtesy. I slipped into the hot leather bucket seat. The heat of the day was now beginning to intensify. Mornings in Palm Springs were beautiful, but by lunchtime I felt as if I were trying to breathe in an oven.

Driving the freeway, I caught a glimpse of myself in the passenger mirror. Sitting against the black, leather interior with my sunglasses on, I didn't recognize myself.

"What are you thinking about?" Paul asked.

"Nothing really. Just wondering what Malibu is going to be like."

"Well, the ranch is nestled in the Santa Monica Mountains. I have fourteen acres up there. It's quiet and beautiful, and only a few minutes from the beach. It will be much cooler than Palm Springs."

I pictured myself lying on a beach towel near the shore, sifting warm, golden sand through my fingers as the waves crashed near my feet. "Sounds amazing," I said, pulling myself out of my daydream.

"It really is. Just a couple of hours away."

I studied his profile for a few seconds. He wasn't bad looking; his hair was thick, wavy and dark. His T-shirt exposed biceps which were tanned and muscular, extending into hairy forearms, and strong calloused hands which gripped the steering wheel of the powerful car. I thought of Clive's flabby, hairless white arms and soft hands never used for any kind of manual labor.

I leaned back against the headrest and closed my eyes, pushing any guilt out of my mind.

"So, what exactly do you do at the car lot?" I asked him, trying to fill the uncomfortable silence. "Do you have to wash the cars every day? That must get so boring…and so hot outside!"

Paul threw his head back and laughed. "I don't wash the cars. We have employees who do that for us. I thought I told you that my father and I *own* the dealership."

"Oh," I was embarrassed that I had misunderstood.

I was quiet the rest of the drive.

Eventually we exited the freeway, winding our way up a canyon road. After about twenty minutes of sharp bends and curves we turned onto a long driveway lined with pine trees, which ended at a grassy island surrounding a beautiful old oak tree. Past the tree I could see a small wood-paneled rust colored ranch house set back from a white painted porch. I stepped out of the car onto the gravel and looked around. On either side of the driveway were large pastures. Each pasture contained a couple of dilapidated barns and I noticed a pig and a donkey grazing side by side. He was right; the weather was much cooler here.

I followed Paul to the porch which was covered in an abundance of pink, red, and white blooming bougainvillea. My mother had identified the native plant to me. I loved it and remembered seeing it cascading colorfully over trellises adorning houses in Tenerife on my honeymoon.

"I have to go and do some work on the plumbing system," Paul said. "Just make yourself at home. We'll be leaving at seven to meet some friends for dinner."

I sauntered through the house, stopping to admire the countless antiques. They were nothing like the ones I was used to at Woodlands. These were trophies of the Wild West.

From the time I was a young child, I was obsessed with cowboys and Indians. I loved watching Westerns on our small black-and-white television. When I was home from boarding school, I couldn't wait to play with my small-scale Dodge City replica and container of plastic cowboys and Indians perched on horses. For hours I recreated scenes from the Westerns with my miniature characters. My Dodge City even had a saloon with swinging doors, a general store, and a jail. There, I was in charge of the show; I would decide who was going to live and who was going to die.

Now I was walking onto a real-life set of my childhood fantasy. There was an old phonograph sitting on an antique table by the window. I ran my finger across the smooth vinyl record, as it wobbled unsteadily beneath the needle. In a corner of the room was a vintage wheelchair carved out of polished mahogany and upholstered in a faded floral printed tapestry. Against the wall in another room was an antique, freestanding shower, its long, cylindrical base made out of copper and a huge metal showerhead affixed to the top. I stood underneath it, imagining what it would have been like to bathe in those days. Paul had old cash registers, tea sets, and knickknacks throughout the entire house, enough to fill an entire Western memorabilia store.

Smiling, I took my small overnight bag into the bedroom and placed it on a cherry wood rocking chair by the bed. The bed was an antique four-poster with polished brass rails; two thick mattresses stacked atop each other made it high off the ground. I pulled out the one dress I had brought with me from England and quickly changed, glancing at myself in the mirror. The dress was not flattering, and I looked much better in jeans or shorts and T-shirts. My eating seemed to be more controlled when I was away from home and distracted by people and activities. I wondered where we were going tonight. I was nervous about meeting new people and felt self-conscious in my dress.

At that moment Paul came into the house. "Wow, you look great. Is that what you're wearing tonight?"

"Yes," I said, looking down at my dress. It was beige, fine knit, with delicate embroidery on the sleeves and around the hem.

"Looks fantastic," he said eyeing my legs.

I pulled the dress down, trying unsuccessfully to cover them. I wished he would stop looking.

"Is that what *you're* wearing?" I joked, a desperate attempt to turn the attention back onto him and away from myself.

He had on yellow shorts and a T-shirt that were covered in grass stains and mud.

"Ya," he laughed. "Wouldn't we make quite the pair? Listen, I'm gonna go get cleaned up. Why don't you hang out in the living room and watch some television while I shower and get changed?"

I walked back into the living room and sat down on the rich burgundy velvet couch. The fabric felt scratchy against my legs. Picking up the remote from the coffee table, I switched on the television and began thumbing through the channels. I was fascinated by the amount of choices available, there were what looked like hundreds of shows and programs. I was used to three channels at home. I wondered how people could decide what to watch.

When Paul was finally ready, we got back in the sports car and drove down to the coast. Twenty minutes later we pulled into an ivy-covered restaurant overlooking the ocean. A sign painted in red on a white background read "L'Hermitage."

Paul explained that the nearest gas station or store was twenty minutes from the ranch no matter which road one took. "If you forget the milk, you're not going to drive forty minutes to go back and get it," he stated matter-of-factly.

A valet in a tan and red uniform with a matching cap opened my door and helped me out of the car. Paul quickly snatched my hand from his and led me into the restaurant.

There were only a few tables inside, lit by small votive candles. Couples sat close to one another, smiling and enjoying their overpriced entrees over a glass of wine. The maître d' appeared and led us to a table in the back of the room where I met Paul's old school friend, Larry, and his lady friend who's name I forgot soon after I was introduced. I timidly said hello, sat down, and picked up the leather bound menu.

Luckily, it seemed the three of them had plenty to talk about without much of a contribution from me. We finally ordered, and I sat absorbed in my meal, feeling relieved as my date and his friends continued to talk amongst themselves. I wished I had not made the decision to come, and found myself yearning to be back in my mother's trailer with Katie.

The food kept coming; we had seafood appetizers, the finest filet steaks topped with gorgonzola and roasted vegetables, followed by an array of desserts. I could not eat like this without purging, no matter how hard I tried to control myself. I politely left the table at the end of the meal and looked for the ladies' room.

In the bathroom I stood and looked at myself in the mirror. *What makes you think you belong here?* I silently asked my reflection.

I felt a surge of guilt as I thought of Clive back home in England. I quickly shrugged off the bad feelings again, reminding myself that he didn't love me, and he certainly didn't care about what I was doing. He was probably glad to be alone. Now he could spend all day in his threadbare bathrobe, watching horseracing on television, pausing every now and again to pick up the phone and place a bet. I knew his little secret, as I had heard him placing bets when he didn't know I was listening.

As I walked back through the restaurant, I could see that there was some kind of commotion going on at our table. Paul had taken off his watch and was holding it out to the waiter who was shaking his head. As I approached, I realized that the waiter was telling Paul that his credit card had been declined. Apparently Paul had tried giving the waiter two other cards, but they were maxed out as well. He had not brought any cash, so now he was trying to barter our expensive meal with his Rolex.

I found out later that Larry had not brought any money because Paul owed him money and he assumed that Paul was paying.

I nervously cleared my throat. "How much is the bill?"

Everybody turned to look at me.

"How much do we owe?" I asked again.

The waiter seemed frustrated, "Two hundred ninety-eight dollars and fifty-three cents, mademoiselle."

Had we spent that much money on food?

I took note of the two empty champagne bottles nestled upside-down in a bucket of ice by the table. For a moment I was annoyed with myself for just having flushed eighty dollars' worth of food down the toilet.

"Do you take American Express travelers checks?" I asked the waiter.

"Yes we do, mademoiselle."

It was making me nervous that the people at other tables were watching us. Both my father and my stepfather had always been very low key about money; you don't let anyone know when you have it, and you certainly don't let anyone know when you don't. I had exactly three hundred dollars in traveler checks for my holiday spending. I signed each check and handed them over.

How foolish I was to believe that for a moment I was special.

* * *

Later, at the ranch, I wasn't sure where I was supposed to sleep.

Was he expecting me to sleep with him?

Paul hadn't discussed any type of sleeping arrangement. When I came out of the bathroom, he was already in the bed waiting for me, proudly displaying his hairy torso. There was only one bedroom and one bed, as he had converted the other bedroom into an office. I nervously climbed in beside him, keeping on a T-shirt and panties and started telling him stories about my family in England. I knew I was talking too much, but I just didn't know how else to handle the situation. I finally turned to look at him and noticed he had fallen asleep. I let out a sigh of relief. The evening had cost me just about all my money, but at least the champagne had dulled his senses.

* * *

I was awakened early the next morning by a grunting noise outside the bedroom window. I sat up in bed taking in the unfamiliar surroundings. Paul was snoring next to me.

No, that's not what I heard. It was something else.

I heard the grunting again, and it was followed by a loud, rustling sound outside the window. I got up and looked out at the front porch, and there it was, an enormous pink pig. I turned back to the bed and shook Paul awake.

"There's a huge pig on the porch!" I shouted.

"What?" he mumbled, rubbing his eyes awake.

"On the porch," I repeated. "A giant pig."

"Oh shit," he responded, and threw back the covers. I quickly turned my head away, realizing he had been sleeping in the nude. He pulled on his jeans and bolted out of the room. I looked back out of the window in time to see him running up to the pig, arms flailing and yelling, "Hey! Hey!"

The pig totally ignored the human display of authority and carried on with its task of examining the porch. Paul picked up a stick from the ground and started to whack the pig on its thick, leathery hide. With an indignant snort, both pig and Paul slowly made their way back to the pasture. I realized it was the pig I had seen the day before with the donkey.

* * *

Later that afternoon and back in Palm Springs, I recounted the weekend to my mother.

"The ranch was amazing! It's only a little house, but there are two huge pastures with pigs, chickens, a donkey and a horse," I said excitedly. The horse belonged to a neighbor and Paul let her keep him on the property in return for her taking care of the other livestock.

I went on to tell my mother that Paul had surprised me the next morning with a tray of breakfast, accompanied by two tall glasses of mimosa. It was the first time I had ever tried champagne mixed with orange juice, and I liked how the sweet juice covered up the sharp taste of the alcohol. He had even cut two slices of fresh orange and wedged them on the rim of each glass. We had our breakfast at a little wooden table on the porch under the bougainvillea.

I left out the altercation with the pig, and thankfully she didn't ask me where I slept.

"We sat on the porch and talked for hours. He told me how he had bought the house in the late 1970s and was married under a maple tree in the front yard. His wife had a son from a previous marriage, but apparently the boy never took to Paul. They were divorced about five years ago. In the divorce, she had tried to get the ranch, but he took her to court, and with the help of his friends, made her out to look like an alcoholic gold digger."

I felt sorry for her when Paul had first recounted this story to me. Even though I had never met her, the idea of people purposely ganging up and showing what a piece of shit she was made me sad. I had always sided with the underdog.

"He told me she had a drinking problem when he first met her," I continued.

"Ah," my mother said, perking up at the mention of someone with an alcohol problem.

I could tell she was feasting on all the gossip. Her world lacked

140

the drama it used to have when she was drinking. Now she went to AA meetings for excitement. Stories of other people's struggles and personal anguish became her solace.

I finally told her about the nearly three-hundred-dollar meal I paid for.

"You make sure you stay with him until you get your money back," was her motherly advice.

Chapter Fifteen

Over the next few days Paul wanted to see me every free minute. Now I was starting to feel myself in a dilemma. Clive was scheduled to come out and join me in less than a week.

What the hell was I going to do?

I had told Paul about Clive, but he responded as if I'd told him I had left a little dog at home in England. By now we had started an intense love affair, although I wasn't sure if I was in love or flight from reality with him. I felt carried away on the high of passion and excitement. It was so different from the feelings I had for Clive and the nihility between us. I was unaccustomed to the unwavering attention I was getting from Paul. I remembered when Clive told me that he was besotted with me and how good that made me feel. Paul's fixation with me was intense and incessant.

Every morning I jogged around the perimeter of the trailer park. I was trying to switch to some healthier methods to keep my weight down, as my mother's mobile home wasn't equipped with the best of plumbing. Once I had to go outside and vomit into the shrubbery after a meal, hoping that no one would observe me in what I felt to be the most degrading and disgusting behavior ever. I felt that was as bad, if not worse, as my stepmother peeing on the side of the road.

The day Clive's flight was due to land, I arranged to meet Paul for breakfast after my morning jog. Once sitting in the cafe, Paul presented his plan for me to leave Clive and live with him in Palm Springs. When I asked him about Katie, he assured me that he would take care of the two of us; all I needed to do was tell Clive that I wanted a divorce as soon as possible.

* * *

I took Katie and picked Clive up from Palm Springs airport where he had made a connecting flight from Los Angeles. He greeted us with the same enthusiasm as one would give to a couple of luggage handlers. On the drive back I attempted small talk, nervously telling him about the town, the glorious weather, and how strange it was to see my mother sober.

"Is she still just as nuts?" was his only response.

He didn't say anything to Katie.

Once back at the trailer, Clive briefly acknowledged my mother and then informed us he needed to take a nap. As he slept unknowingly on the spare fold-out bed, my mother whispered to me that Paul had already called several times to see if I was back. I called him and said I could meet him for a few minutes at the park while Clive was sleeping.

I hung up the phone and checked on Clive, his back was to me but I knew from his deep breathing that he was asleep. I whispered to my mother to watch Katie and try to keep her quiet, and if Clive woke, she was to tell him I had gone for a walk.

It was a typical Palm Springs afternoon, quiet and balmy. An old woman drove by in an enormous Cadillac, her head barely visible above a sheep skin covered steering wheel, tires weaving back and forth across both lanes. A couple of aging men loaded a golf cart in slow motion, probably bickering about which tennis pro was likely to take this year's title. The geriatrics reminded me of reptiles, attracted to Palm Springs by the sun, the sand, and the dry heat.

As I approached the park, I immediately saw Paul standing against a tree excitedly waving to me.

Wasn't this what I'd always wanted?

He grinned like a boy who had just won a trophy. I slowed my pace and approached him apprehensively, everything I was doing felt so wrong, yet I couldn't stop myself. He took me in his arms and told me he couldn't stand being apart.

It hadn't even been a few hours since I'd last seen him.

I told him I needed some time to be alone with Clive and pretend everything was all right. I felt there was no way I could let him suspect anything right now. Paul told me that all he wanted was to be with me, and that he could wait if he had to. We kissed passionately under the tree and as I pulled away, anxious to get back, he grabbed me and looked intensely into my eyes.

"Janine, it's going to be okay. You and I are meant to be together. You can do this."

I reluctantly freed myself from his grip and jogged back to the trailer.

When I got back my mother told me Clive had taken Katie to the pool. I put on my swimsuit and went to join them. My stomach was doing summersaults. I found him sunning himself by the trailer park's above-ground pool, while Katie played with her toys nearby shaded by a dirty yellow umbrella. He didn't acknowledge my presence, or ask where I had been, as I settled down on a lounge chair next to him.

I pushed my sunglasses on top of my head and looked at him, lying on the cheap plastic lounger next to me. His face was turned up to the sun and his neatly parted hair was a bit messy. He was wearing his favorite union jack swimming shorts. His body, soft and white, would soon turn pink in the sun. If I reached out my hand I could touch his bare thigh, but at the same time he was a million miles away. He hadn't seen me in over two weeks, and he had yet to embrace me. He was just lying there, completely unaware of my existence. I watched as beads of sweat formed at his temple, glistened in the sun, and then trickled down the sides of his face, collecting in a small pool above his collarbone. I studied this stranger next to me and realized in that moment that I hated him.

"Clive?" I realized I was speaking before I really knew what I was going to say.

"Yes?" He answered, not moving.

"I want a divorce."

My heart pounded as I watched him intently, waiting for some kind of reaction.

He swatted away a fly absentmindedly. "Fine," he said, talking to the sun. "I'll fly home in the morning."

That was it? Fine?

I knew he was hurt, if not emotionally, certainly it had affected his pride, and I felt guilty that I hadn't waited until our holiday was over to tell him. I wasn't surprised, though, that he didn't even want to know why.

We avoided each other the rest of the day. I took Katie for a walk in her stroller and met Paul a short distance from the complex. I told him what had happened. He hugged me happily, and told me I needed to let Clive go home and process what I had told him. I could get an attorney when I got back to England and then return to Palm Springs as soon as possible.

When I got back to my mother's, Clive continued to ignore me; I knew he had told her, probably trying to elicit pity from her. Out of sympathy she offered to drive him back to the airport. I shut myself in her bedroom with Katie and listened as he packed up his belongings and left.

I knew my mother would offer him solace on the drive. I also knew she would encourage him to let me go and move on with his life.

He would be unaware that this was also in her best interest.

* * *

Katie and I returned home a week later. There was no one to pick us up from the airport, so we took the train and the bus back to Dulwich. Gone was the blue sky and baking sun. It was muggy and drizzling with rain. I enrolled her in preschool and tried to adjust to living in the house while avoiding Clive. He made no attempt to tell me how he was feeling and I was afraid to ask. Tension filled our home. While Katie was at pre-school during the day, I set about finding myself an attorney. My main objective was to find a way to take her back to the States with me. There was no way I was going without her.

I visited my grandmother in Brighton. She didn't know what was going on, but she was always pleased to see me. She made me a cup of tea and offered me dipping biscuits from the same silver container

I remembered as a child. She adored Katie, and was the only person who seemed to have genuine interest and unconditional love for both of us.

On one visit I discovered that my grandmother's new neighbor was friends with my dad and Audrey. Sheila was recently divorced and her daughter Lindsey had moved back in with her. When Lindsey and I were teenagers, she would join myself and my dad or an occasional Sunday hunt. We used to giggle at the overweight riders in their tight red jackets, jodhpurs and shiny black boots as they toasted each other with glasses of port at seven in the morning. I would inevitably fall off my pony and Lindsey would always abandon the hunt to accompany me home.

I had really liked Lindsey and was excited to have found her again.

* * *

One day as I was sitting in Sheila's kitchen, reminiscing about our crazy families, I impulsively asked Lindsey if she wanted to move in with me for a month as I went through my divorce. She thought this was a great idea, and we formed a plan to temporarily convert the guest bedroom on the second floor into a bedsit that we could share. I didn't ask Clive if he minded. I needed a friend.

I helped Lindsey move her things into the spare bedroom. We brought a television, a table and two chairs, and we shared the queen-sized bed. We split the three-story house in half; Katie's bedroom was next to ours, and Clive lived on the floor below us. He kept our old bedroom and bathroom, allowing us to use the kitchen and dining area while he was at work.

We continued to ignore each other, but at least now I had an ally.

On one occasion I showed Lindsey the cellar and discovered a rack of bottles of Dom Perignon champagne and vintage port. These collectables were from Clive's years of working in banqueting. I had no idea they were there, as the cellar was always Clive's domain. Little by little, over the next few weeks, Lindsey and I drank champagne for breakfast, lunch, and dinner.

Over the next month I became accustomed to champagne as a daily beverage, and enjoyed the happy carefree feeling it gave me.

Each bottle emptied was refilled with water, sealed, and placed back on the rack. I went out with Lindsey's friends in the evening and come home at all hours. I had an understanding next-door neighbor who did not mind Katie spending the night at her house with her three young children. One evening Lindsey and I tried to quietly re-enter the house after a night on the town. We were giggling as we stumbled blindly up the staircase.

"Where the hell have you two been?" Clive barked at us as he came down the stairs, switching on a light.

Lindsey was not intimidated by Clive. I had always admired her self-confidence and bravado. She paused and swayed as she turned to face him, "Oh do shut up and mind your own business, Clive," she slurred.

Clive's face turned red with anger and his jowls vibrated in disbelief. I giggled at her bravery, for saying the words I had never dared. We then staggered into the bedroom holding each other for support.

* * *

It was during this period of drinking that I experienced my first alcohol blackout. Clive had taken Katie to his mother's for an overnight visit. I decided it would be fun to join Lindsey and her friends who were going out for a night of pubbing and clubbing in London. Several hours later the evening faded into a blur.

My next conscious experience was waking with a blinding headache to the shrill ring of a telephone. I was in a bed that was not mine, next to Robbie Simpson who was now reaching for the phone. He passed it to me, "It's Lindsey, and she sounds pretty upset."

What was I doing here in his bed, and where were my clothes?

I had no idea if we had sex, but I assumed since we were both naked, something must have happened. I had had a crush on Robbie for a while, but he had never given me the time of day before this.

Lindsey was calling to tell me that Clive had come back early with Katie and I had better get home.

I navigated my way to Robbie's bathroom and found my clothes strewn all over the floor. I hurriedly dressed and told him I had to go.

I was surprised to find my car parked outside his London flat. I could have sworn I had taken a cab.

Did someone spike my drink? Where was I last night...and what did I do?

Anxiety gripped me as I approached the car and walked around it looking for dents.

Nothing.

It was even impeccably parallel parked. I was baffled.

Back home and later that day I tried to figure out what had taken place. Katie was at school and Clive and Lindsey were at work. I wandered around the house attempting through sheer determination to recollect the events from the night before. I remembered being at the pub for a couple hours, laughing and drinking with Lindsey, Robbie and a couple other people... but nothing after that.

Lindsey didn't get back until after six, and she couldn't fill in the gaps.

"Where did I go after the pub?" I asked her again.

"I don't know," she said handing me a couple of aspirin and a glass of water. "You left with Robbie instead of coming with us."

I felt my face burn. I turned away from her and went into the bathroom where I stood looking at myself in the mirror.

How could I walk around all night without knowing whom I was with or what I was doing?

Overcome with shame, I drank down the aspirin and decided the best way to deal with this event would be to put it out of my mind and never think about it again.

* * *

Meanwhile Paul was calling me every day.

"What's happening? Do you have a court date? Where were you yesterday when I tried to call you?"

I felt pressured from six thousand miles away. He told me that if I wasn't back in Palm Springs the following month, he would come to England himself and get me.

I still met Abdulla occasionally for lunch in London. This time I

148

took Katie with me. He was upset when I told him I was going to live in the States. Katie was sitting on his lap giggling as she tried to pull his headdress off.

"Those Americans are bad people, you will only have trouble if you go there," he warned me. "You cannot even understand what they are saying because they speak so funny, twang, twang, twang," he mimicked an American accent, which made Katie giggle even more.

I told him I would stay in touch and write him letters and I thanked him for all he had done for me, such as paying for my fares to the US. I saw tears in his eyes as we hugged good-bye.

* * *

The divorce was simple and quick. I agreed to let Clive keep the house, the furniture and the car. In exchange, I would take Katie with me. I received sixteen thousand pounds of equity money from the house, which I decided to keep in my bank account in England—just in case I needed to come back. I told Lindsey I would be leaving in a week, so she and I threw our final farewell party while Clive was at work.

We finished off his last three magnums of champagne.

* * *

A week later I arrived in Los Angeles with two suitcases and Katie—all I possessed in the world. I scanned the sea of strangers for Paul.

What if I see him and regret my decision?

Then I spotted him waving to me through the crowd, a huge bouquet of flowers in his hand as if he were directing a plane on the runway. My mother was by his side holding his other arm for support.

He eagerly approached us, smiling from ear to ear and hugged me tightly for a little too long. I felt embarrassed by his public show of affection. He took my trolley and led the way to his car.

He opened the car door, and I stood mesmerized by a plethora of flowers on the backseat.

Were all these for me? What was I going to do with so many bouquets?

Paul beamed at me, "Do you like 'em?" He asked. "They're all for you!"

I looked back at the dozens of red, long stem roses, pink chrysanthemums and yellow lilies. The fragrance was overwhelming as Paul gathered them by the armful and shoved them into the trunk so my mother and Katie could have the back seat.

He turned to us and smiled, "Come on girls, it's time to go home!"

As Paul drove to Palm Springs I stared absentmindedly out of the window. I felt like a ship at sea without a compass. Katie was chatting excitedly about going to the pool.

A vague feeling of impending doom settled in my stomach.

Had I made the decision to leave England too quickly?

Chapter Sixteen

Paul had moved in with his parents a few months before we met. His father opened a new Chrysler dealership in Palm Springs, so Paul left the ranch and his used car business in Los Angeles to help his dad get the recently purchased dealership off the ground. Paul told me he owed it to his dad, who had given him his first opportunity to run a business when he was seventeen. Paul shared with me how his dad gave him a shop from which to run a car parts business. While Paul's friends were all out partying, he had to be a responsible business owner. Now his father needed his help and Paul felt he couldn't say no.

My first meeting with his family was lunch at a Jewish deli in Palm Springs. His older sister Sandra wore a sequined blouse fitted with shoulder pads and big, gaudy jewelry. Her teased hair was dyed red and I noticed that she had escaped the family nose. She was extremely critical, and I squirmed in my seat while she complained about everything that came out of the kitchen; the food took too long, the sauce wasn't creamy enough, how long did she need to wait for a refill on her drink? I grimaced apologetically at the waiter every time he approached our table.

Her husband Steve had made a name for himself racing dirt bikes; he was never without a toothpick in his mouth, even now at the lunch table. I had noticed his white snakeskin cowboy boots when he first walked over to our table. His face had a strange bright pink coloration, and was pulled so tightly over his features, that it resembled the skin grafting of a burn victim. I watched in amazement as he ate a salad with the toothpick choreographed skillfully around tomato wedges and slices of cucumber. Never once did it fall from the grip between his teeth. Paul's mother Harriet appeared uptight and never smiled once throughout the meal, she looked disapprovingly at everyone, and I got nervous whenever her critical eyes scanned in my direction. Paul's father Ernie was quite the opposite, charismatic and funny, oblivious of his unhappy wife by his side.

His family left much to be desired with their table manners. I watched in horror as Steve tossed his napkin he had used to blow his nose onto the table by his plate and Sandra noisily slurped down her soup next to him.

Before booze-impaired mealtimes, our family observed strict table manners. As a child I recalled my stepfather sitting at the head of the mahogany table disparagingly overseeing his small kingdom. Pete and I usually ate with the nanny in the kitchen, but on weekends we joined our parents, along with the nanny, at the formal dining table. No one was allowed to take a bite until my stepfather had picked up his knife and fork. There was always so much to remember, especially when you were hungry and only nine years old. Chew with your mouth closed and your hands folded neatly in your lap. Count silently to twenty before taking your next bite. No elbows on the table. Meat should always be closest to you, vegetables furthest away. Always cut the meat, never tear it. When pausing to chew, knife and fork should be placed at ten and two on the plate, serrated side of the knife facing inward and prongs of the fork downward. The soup bowl was the most challenging to master. It should be held tipped backwards and away from you, with the soup spoon poised delicately between index finger and thumb, as if holding a pen. Gently dip the spoon into the soup, always away from you and in a clockwise manner. Bring slowly to your lips and gently sip from the side of the spoon, *never* the front. Do not *ever* put the spoon into your mouth, and under no circumstances should you ever make slurping noises.

I was now horrified watching Paul's family consume their meals like a group of farm animals eating out of a trough. I thought I'd finally seen it all, when his mother picked up the dessert menu and, using one of the corners, proceeded to pick a piece of shredded meat from between her molars.

* * *

Ernie and Harriet had a large condo on a golf course in Palm Desert with wall to wall white shag carpeting and avocado green and orange painted walls. The plastic furniture and gaudy porcelain fox statues that adorned every corner attested to the fact that the condo had probably been styled in the late 1960s, and although we were now past the mid-1980s, not a thing had changed.

It hurt me that his mother continued to be rude and unfriendly when I tried so hard to be nice to her. It brought me no solace that she was like that with others too; constantly critical and judgmental. I could feel her watching me even when I couldn't see her.

"Vhat are you doing?" I was startled by the thick Austrian accent behind me while I was standing at the kitchen fridge one morning.

"I'm just getting Katie a glass of juice," I said nervously, keeping my back to her.

"Vhat glass are you using?"

Katie held tightly onto my leg when Harriet was around; perhaps because she was afraid she would get snatched up if she let go of me.

Every weekend Paul drove us down to the ranch in Malibu to labor over his plethora of never-ending projects. As Fridays came around I felt excited that I would get a couple of days' freedom from under Harriet's watchful eye.

Thankfully, it wasn't long before we found our own condo in Rancho Mirage, and with relief, I was finally able to get out from being under constant scrutiny. Paul went to work during the day as I attempted to shift into my new role of housewife, even though we weren't married. There was a large swimming pool in the condo complex surrounded by palm trees and chaise lounges shaded by sizeable green umbrellas. I liked to take Katie there in the mornings before it got unbearably hot. Then we would visit my mother in the impressive kitchen of the Sheraton Hotel. She loved introducing us to her friends and coworkers, most of whom I had already met, but

I didn't mind meeting them again. I knew she was happy to finally have her daughter and granddaughter close by.

My mother was the pastry chef, so Katie and I would always get to sample the dessert of the day. Returning home a few hours later, I put her down for a nap as I did housework, puttered in the garden, and then together we'd go to the market and shop for dinner that night.

I gradually became familiar with the town and in the process of grocery shopping, I learned the names of American cuts of meat and vegetables that were not to be found in British supermarkets. I then returned to the condo after getting new recipes from my mother and practiced cooking dishes that I was unaccustomed to. I was eager to be the perfect girlfriend for Paul. I was sure to ask him about his day when he got home and feigned interest as he told me about cars and making great deals.

My mother offered to watch Katie when she wasn't at work so I could keep up with my exercise regimen and jog around her complex. She would also watch her some nights so Paul and I could go out on the town. It seemed my binging and purging had become more sporadic and no longer as severe as when I was living with Clive. It didn't consume my life anymore as it had for so many years. Every now and again I would eat too much and need to throw up to relieve the abdominal discomfort, but gone was the routine binging and purging.

I wondered if it was because I was happier. I had a house in a place where the sun shone all day, my little girl, a man who loved me, and a sober mother. I had found joy in my life at last. I was happy laying by the pool watching Katie as she ran around the perimeter shrieking, "Watch me Mummy, watch me jump in!"

I even had a new car to drive that Paul had given me from the dealership lot.

He liked us to go out at night to a restaurant, or frequent one of the many clubs in Palm Springs or Palm Desert. He was constantly buying me things, like clothes, jewelry, or bouquets of flowers, and expressing his undying love for me in cards.

This was what I had yearned for, to be loved, needed, and cared for. All the things I missed in my childhood. I misread his subtle forms of control as a genuine interest in me and everything I did. He always wanted to know whom I was talking to when I was on the phone, where I was going, and when would I be back.

On weekends Paul and I drove to Malibu while Katie sometimes stayed in Palm Springs with my mother. Once at the ranch, Paul worked non-stop making changes or repairs to the property, while I cleaned and reorganized the inside of the house or planted flowers in the front and rear gardens. Beautiful new white three-rail fencing was installed around the perimeter of both pastures; this was quite an undertaking, but something Paul told me he always dreamed of doing. Sapling trees were planted in the long driveway to replace the ones that had been lost to bark beetle years before. After a long day of work, we showered and then headed into Los Angeles for the nightlife.

* * *

One such night, we had driven to the ranch in a brand new Chrysler New Yorker that Paul had "borrowed" off his father's lot. The car had no miles and the stickers were still pasted to the windows. He told me he disconnected the odometer, keeping the vehicle seemingly unused. I wondered if his father knew.

On the drive home from the nightclub we got into an alcohol-fueled argument. We had been drinking champagne and Paul felt that I had been flirting with a guy on the dance floor. I was angry and hurt by his accusations and the unfairness of his mistrust.

We finally pulled up the gravel driveway outside the front of the ranch. Paul threw the car into park and, leaving the key in the ignition, strode into the house, slamming the front door behind him.

"Fuck you!" I yelled at him from the safety of the vehicle. I pulled myself across to the driver seat, put the car in drive and accelerated. I had no idea where I was going but I was going somewhere. The wheels locked on the gravel, and the car careened sideways out of control, crashing through the brand new fence. Shocked sober, I hung onto the steering wheel like I was riding a bucking bronco, my foot somehow glued to the accelerator.

The car bounced roughly across the pasture, as I drove a sweeping arch, back through another section of the fence, impaling one of the newly planted saplings through the windshield.

I managed to steer the battered car back onto the driveway, navigating through an area of the windshield the tree had missed, until it ultimately sputtered and died at the side of the road. I sat in the demolished vehicle for a few minutes in shock, trying to register what had just taken place. I watched the smoke rise out from the hood, the trunk of the sapling just inches from my right cheek. Feeling even more sober now, I pushed the door open and stepped out to survey the damage. I looked up the driveway and saw that two large portions of the fence were missing; white painted wood debris was strewn across the driveway. I took off my heels, and walked dejectedly back up the driveway and into the house.

In the bedroom Paul was already snoring loudly, several hours away from a hangover. I reached out and shook his shoulder.

"Paul," I whispered my face close to his, my heart thumping in my chest.

His eyelids fluttered.

"Paul?" I repeated, still fearful of bringing my voice to full volume.

"What?" he grunted.

"You have to come outside, something has happened to the car."

Still somewhat under the influence, we both walked unsteadily down the dark driveway and past the destroyed portions of the fence. The New Yorker was where I left it, wrecked at the side of the road, looking as if it had been used as a stunt car. I braced myself for his reaction.

"Jesus Christ, what the hell am I going to tell my dad? What the hell did you do Janine? I just had all the new fencing installed last week!" Paul ran his hands through his hair. "Janine!" he turned and barked at me, but I was already walking back up the driveway toward the house.

* * *

156

The following morning, sun shone brightly on the wreckage from the night before. Paul arranged for a rental car to take us back to Palm Springs. He rehearsed the story for his father. A truck had come around the corner on the wrong side of the canyon road. Paul had to swerve onto the embankment to avoid hitting the truck, and crashed the New Yorker into a tree.

We drove back in silence. As bad as I felt, I was relieved not to have to take any responsibility.

I had found myself the perfect enabler.

* * *

We had been living in Rancho Mirage for about six months, when one morning while I was busy cleaning the condo Paul called out to me.

"Hey Janine, come out here!"

I was scrubbing the tub and emerged from the bathroom, Comet in one hand and scouring brush in the other. He had told me he had to go in late to work that day because he was waiting for a phone call at home. The bedroom was on the second level of the condo and Paul was standing out on the large balcony.

"Quick, come here," he beckoned impatiently.

I went onto the balcony and looked up, following his finger. A single engine plane was flying over us.

A brightly colored banner streamed behind the plane, "Petite Nini Will You Marry Me?" *Petite Nini*—my nickname from my childhood in France, given to me by Mimi and Fanny and then picked up by my mother. Paul had remembered me telling him this and used it in his marriage proposal.

What do I say? Do I tell him that I need some time to think?

I was really happy with our life, but I felt I hardly knew him; we'd only been living together a few months. I was afraid if I said I needed more time I might lose him. So instead of saying anything, I threw my arms around his neck and buried my head in his shoulder so he couldn't see the agony of indecision on my face.

He interpreted my silence as consent.

* * *

157

The next morning, Paul told me to look under my pillow and waited eagerly as I pulled the pillow back to reveal a large, vulgar ring nestled on the mattress below. I picked it up and examined it.

"That's your engagement ring," he said looking at me expectantly.

I had never seen anything so gaudy. The band was thick gold, and the centerpiece was a large, smooth ruby surrounded by diamonds. I didn't like gold, and I hated rubies. I noticed the ruby had a hairline crack running across the surface.

"See if it fits." He took the ring and slipped it on my finger. I stared at it in dismay.

"I've decided we'll get married in April," he stated.

That was the month of my twenty-sixth birthday.

"You don't seem happy?" He looked at me concerned.

"It's not that. I'm just overwhelmed."

"Come on," he said excitedly. "Let's go and tell my parents!"

Chapter Seventeen

We traveled to England a couple of months prior to our marriage. Nina arranged a party for us in a nice pub inviting my family and friends. My father and Audrey made jokes about Paul being Jewish.

"I see you found a nice Jewish boy this time," my father laughed.

We then flew to France where Paul had arranged to purchase a Mercedes 500 SEC in Paris. We spent a couple of weeks of a pre-nuptial honeymoon, driving from Paris to the south of France on the auto route, carelessly exceeding speeds of a hundred miles an hour, listening to Lionel Richie sing "All Night Long" on cassette.

Once in Le Lavandou we surprised Mimi at his shop, and then followed him back to a new house they had purchased a few miles outside town. Fanny couldn't believe her eyes when she saw me.

"Petite Nini!" She gave me a big hug and kissed me on both cheeks. I introduced Paul to them, who appeared a little uncomfortable with their hugs and kisses. Paul spoke no French, so he watched in amusement as we talked and laughed late into the night. Fanny had called Martine and Danielle, and we all feasted on delicious foods: fish and game caught by Mimi and vegetables from their garden, and wine from their vineyard.

At the end of our vacation, the Mercedes was shipped back to Long Beach, still bearing French license plates and amber headlights.

* * *

Our wedding was planned to take place in Idyllwild, a small community in the mountain range north of Palm Springs. Paul wanted to get married in the beauty of nature and I liked that idea. I didn't want to go through another spectacle as I had with Clive. It was agreed that Paul's friend Richard take a limo from the dealership for Katie, my mother, and myself; and Paul drive separately with his parents in his Mercedes.

Richard was dressed in his Lounge Lizard signature style, only now he had traded his little shorts for a pair of tight white leather pants. His Hawaiian shirt was a shocking orange, and I grimaced as he got into the driver seat.

"Come on ladies, let's roll!"

A half hour into the trip, the heat became unbearable.

"Sorry, no air," Richard said after turning some knobs and flipping switches on the dash. No longer being able to tolerate the temperature, I took off my brown suede skirt and boots I had purchased for our "casual" wedding and placed them on the seat next to me. Katie raised her hands over her head, signaling for me to take off her cream bridesmaid's dress.

"Me too, me too!"

Her little bouquet of freesias were already starting to droop in her hands.

The limo sputtered and came to an abrupt stop on the side of the road.

"What's wrong?" I asked Richard.

"I think we just ran out of gas," he replied tapping on the plastic, "looks like this gauge here's defective."

"Fantastic," I muttered under my breath.

"No problemo fair maidens." Richard hopped out of the car and ran to the back to open our door. Katie and I struggled hurriedly back into our uncomfortable clothes, and we all piled out, abandoning the sweltering vehicle on the side of the road in the hope that Paul wouldn't miss us as he drove by.

Several minutes later, Paul's car crested the hill, and we waved at him like survivors of a shipwreck. He flashed his lights in acknowledgement and pulled over. His parents were sitting in the back, and I watched in disbelief as he motioned for them to get out of the car to make room for all of us. Now, however, there was no longer room for his parents. Paul told them not to worry, he would be back to get them. As we drove off I turned and looked through the rear window. Ernie and Harriet were holding hands, looking confused and cast off at the side of the road next to the disabled limo.

We dropped Richard at a gas station in the town of Idyllwild, and the rest of us proceeded to the nuptial site. Just as we were approaching our destination, I thought I saw the rabbi pass us in his red Chevrolet.

"Wasn't that the rabbi?" I asked, craning my neck over the passenger seat as his car disappeared behind us. I had met him several times and thought it was funny that an old rabbi drove a red Chevy.

"Hang on everyone," Paul yelled, executing a fast u-turn with race like precision.

My mother gripped the handle on the door, and Katie squealed excitedly sliding across the leather seat as the car did a one-eighty. Tires screaming and burning rubber, Paul sped up to the rear of the rabbi's car. Flashing his amber headlights and honking his horn, the rabbi finally noticed us and pulled into a turnout. The Mercedes came to a stop behind him and Paul got out of the car. I watched the two of them exchange words, and then Paul jogged back smiling.

"All right, we're back in business. The three of you are going to the wedding site with the rabbi while I go back for Richard and the can of gas, and we'll go get my parents. I'll meet you at the site as soon as I can."

"Is this is okay with the rabbi?" I asked, feeling anxious about all the chaos and drama.

"Ya, Janine. Would you get out of the car? Time's a wastin'."

The three of us got out, and managed to squish into the Rabbi's car.

"Sorry about this," I said sheepishly.

We then drove to the nuptial site in silence. My mother, Katie, the rabbi, and I, waited without exchanging words, each churning on our own resentments, until finally Paul returned with his parents and Richard following closely behind in the limo. I breathed a sigh of relief as all of us finally seemed to be arriving in the right place. At one point

I was so anxious from all the stress I felt I might throw up. Paul and his father exited the car quickly and began walking toward us, when we heard a shrill scream. In his haste Paul had forgotten to put the car in park and Harriet had been overlooked in the back. We watched in horror as the Mercedes began rolling down the hill, his mother's arms flailing out of the open rear window.

"The car eez rrolling, Villiam, the car eez rrrolling!" she shrieked.

Paul leapt into action and managed to make it to the vehicle, open the driver's door, fling himself inside, and slam his foot on the brake before it collided into a tree. He then helped his traumatized mother out of the car. She was looking shaken and haggard in her now crumpled dress. Paul led her over to the clearing where the rest of us were waiting and we walked to the site we had chosen for the ceremony. The terrain was steep and rocky and Harriet complained that she couldn't walk in her heels. In the end we all had to stop and wait as Paul scooped her up in his arms and carried her as if she were his bride. We made it to the grove of trees and babbling brook by dusk, where we were greeted by hordes of mosquitoes.

As we waited, the rabbi searched for his notes. I observed everyone slapping themselves trying to evade the persistent bites from hungry mosquitos. I was hungry myself, as well as resentful toward Paul, frustrated, embarrassed, and tired. Paul approached me and rested his hand on my shoulder; I turned to him and snapped under my breath.

"Don't touch me. I'm never going through anything like this again."

He looked confused as he backed away from me. I wondered how anyone could be so unaware of the negative effects caused by their behavior. I glanced over at Katie, who was standing under a tree, holding her bouquet of now completely limp flowers. In a perfect conclusion to our vows she gave me a defiant grimace, threw her bouquet to the floor, and ground the flowers into the dirt with the heel of her new patent leather pump.

Paul, still oblivious to all the drama he had created, turned to me beaming with joy.

* * *

Marriage to Paul was nothing short of excess: expensive clothes, restaurants, fast cars, and I was soon to find out, drugs. He would be gone long hours at the dealership; and Katie was in pre-school. Alone during the day, I found myself doing exactly the same at the condo in Palm Springs as I had been doing in the house in Dulwich. It didn't take me long to fall back into my eating disorder of binging and purging whenever I could. My two basic needs were simply a good supply of food and a working toilet.

On weekends Paul would take me to his friend's houses, encouraging me to make friends with their girlfriend's or wives. I felt we had nothing in common, they all liked to drink, talk excessively, shop, and snort cocaine. Before I met Paul, I had witnessed people doing drugs a couple of times; I was simultaneously curious and afraid. I couldn't imagine that was something I would ever do.

* * *

We frequented his single friend Al's house in Encino. Al had an impressive house with marble floors and white leather furniture. Beautiful skinny young girls lounged by the pool and adorned the living room couches, outstretched like expensive blankets. They never gave me the time of day and I felt like an outsider.

I was the square girl.

One evening, I was sitting at a glass table where the drug use was taking place. I usually declined politely whenever offered the white powder. This time I accidentally disturbed a line of cocaine with my elbow, brushing it onto the sheepskin rug below, completely oblivious of the cost and meaning that seemingly innocuous white powder represented to those around the table.

"Oh my God! How could you be so stupid!" one of the women snapped at me.

I quickly got up and pretended I had to use the bathroom.

I spent the rest of the evening avoiding everyone and hanging out with Al's tabby cat Bootsie.

* * *

I finally succumbed in Las Vegas, of all places. Paul and I had gone there for a weekend get-a-way, when an old friend of his came by our hotel room with drugs. I found out later that Paul had made the deal before we left Palm Springs.

I was standing at the window, sipping a glass of Dom Perignon, looking down at the glittering strip below, when the stranger arrived. The "friend" was gone in less than five minutes.

"So, what do you think?" Paul said, wagging the vial back and forth in front of my face.

"Think about what?" I said, playing dumb.

"Trying some of this with me? I think it's time and I think you'll really like it. It'll help you keep it together while we're out drinking tonight."

I turned my head away from him and looked back down at the excitement on the streets.

"Look, if you don't like it, you never have to do it again. But if you don't try it, you might be missing out on something fantastic. At least this way you'll know."

He does have a point. I'll just try it, and if I don't like it then that will be that. No big deal.

"Let me see that," I said, reaching out my hand.

Paul beamed in anticipation and handed me the little glass vial. I rolled it slowly between my thumb and forefinger.

"Okay," I said. "Let's do it!"

"That's my girl."

Paul took the vial from me and tapped a little of the white powder into the cap. He showed me how to put it up to one nostril, close my other nostril with my index finger and inhale. I nervously followed his direction, coughing as the unfamiliar chemical taste hit the back of my throat, I felt my throat go numb and my nose started to run. I contorted my face.

How can people enjoy doing this?

"Good, now do the other side," he instructed.

Within a few hours I found myself laughing and talking excitedly —suddenly there was so much I had to say. I felt energized and focused. We spent the rest of the night dancing at a club; my awkwardness was replaced by confidence and a new sense of rhythm on the dance floor. The drug took away all my insecurities and we had a fantastic night out. I felt like Cinderella, only midnight never came. As I danced, I finally felt carefree and in tune with everything that was going on.

After that night, I wanted to use cocaine whenever I could. I no longer had the desire to binge and purge, I was now full of energy and no longer hungry. A small amount of white chemical powder had replaced all the pounds of food my broken brain had forced me to eat for the past twelve years.

I had been extremely naïve to the opulent lifestyle that I had landed in so quickly. My days of pushing Katie in her stroller to the corner fish and chip shop were exchanged for expensive jackets, leather outfits, miniskirts, and stilettos. Aside from the gifts, Paul would give me cash and suggest that I make myself look more seductive. My light brown hair already bleached blonde by the sun, was now highlighted at an expensive salon. I sat for hours in a chair as a woman bent over my hands laboriously applying acrylic nails over my bitten ones. I cooked my fair English skin in a tanning salon, and began making friends with the wives of his friends.

Now we had something in common.

As far as finances went, I was totally dependent on Paul. The bank accounts were all in his name. I didn't have any money of my own. I didn't have a car or even a credit card. I had come from England with Katie in one hand and my suitcase in another. I did have the settlement from the sale of the house in Dulwich still safely tucked away in a savings account in England.

Al the dealer, Richard the Lizard, and Paul would hang out in clubs, bars and restaurants. The three of them epitomized Palm Springs living. Champagne was flowing and cocaine passed openly, palm to palm in little glass vials. Richard latched onto the older, wealthy single women and Al usually had a couple of young, anorexic looking girls with him. I never knew their names. I was always curious about Al, and how he came to be a drug dealer. I discovered that he had given

Paul a trade of an uncut ruby stone for a cash loan. This was a good deal for Paul who liked to barter whenever he could. He had taken the stone to a jeweler and instructed them to set it in a ring — the engagement ring that had been hidden underneath my pillow.

Al had the style of someone who was once affluent. I imagined him sitting casually in a rich leather armchair holding a cigar in one hand and a glass of scotch in the other. I never saw him snorting cocaine with everyone else, but there was one night I caught him alone in his kitchen, sucking on a glass pipe under the hood of the range. I quickly turned and left the room, but not before he saw me. I knew I had seen something he meant no one to see. I didn't understand what he was doing, but the urgency and the madness in his eyes scared me.

Paul had told me Al once managed some well-known bands. I had seen gold plated albums hanging in his den, but I was afraid to ask him who they were. Someone else said he had been married with two children; the kids were adults now and didn't talk to him. He drove a Chrysler convertible from the Palm Springs car lot, probably the result of a barter with Paul. I had been in his car a few times and knew he kept a handgun in his glove compartment. There was always a box of Kleenex casually tossed on the passenger floor, perhaps because his nose was constantly running from cocaine or because sometimes he would pull over and cry for the family he had lost.

* * *

Paul's plan was to remodel the small ranch house and replace it with a bigger customized house. He viewed his domain and saw, in his mind's eye, the large house sitting on fourteen acres surrounded by white picket fences. He wanted a pond with a bridge, encircled by weeping willow trees. Behind the house he planned to transform the standard swimming pool, putting in boulders, a cascading waterfall, and walkways bordered by flowers and lit by expensive outdoor lighting. I followed him around, an extension of himself, and stood with him in lumberyards, kitchen stores, and hardware stores. I feigned interest, but really had none.

I usually ended up waiting in the car for hours while he ran his errands; Paul lost track of time when he was immersed in a project.

* * *

Paul told me that before I came along, his mother had given up trying to coax him into marrying a nice Jewish girl. At the end of our first year of marriage, we took a two-week vacation to Israel. I immersed myself in his family's heritage as we followed our personal guide from cities to towns and villages. I missed the drugs, but was not so dependent that I couldn't go without for a couple of weeks. The trip was paid for by his parents, probably in the hopes that I might convert to Judaism.

Upon our return, Paul quickly became engrossed with his business and rebuilding the ranch house, as I became preoccupied with my newfound chemical friend. I discovered a select group in Palm Springs who did drugs, and then when Paul and I were in Malibu we usually hung out with his old school friends who were also users.

Around this time Al introduced us to his friend Nikki. She was unlike the other young girls who tagged along, girls I felt should be doing their homework or hanging out at the movies with their teenage boyfriends, not passing the time with a middle-aged drug dealer.

Nikki was about my age, self-assured and intelligent. I discovered she was a freelance artist and she loved doing coke. It didn't take me long to find out she sold for Al. He liked to go to bed early, so Nikki would take the calls after nine at night.

I made one of those calls for Paul and myself one night, and that was it—I was in. After the initial awkwardness of asking her if I could purchase coke from her without Paul's knowledge, I was now able to access my own secret supply.

Chapter Eighteen

It didn't take long after our marriage for me to start feeling trapped and controlled by my new husband. All I had wanted was to have a family and be happy. I chastised myself for my inability to make it last. Here I had a man who loved me, I lived in a beautiful house in Malibu, I was given a car to drive, a little cash to spend every week, and I didn't have to work. *Wasn't that enough to make me happy?* Yet I had no life of my own. His life was my life. I also realized I had no other options; having no job skills or experience, I was afraid to even try to get work. I had no credit or debit cards and nothing material in my name; I was completely dependent on him. My life lacked significance or meaning. Paul would either be working on different projects on the ranch, wrapped up in his work at the car dealership in Palm Springs, or in his father's tow yard in the Valley. His father owned a large established tow yard in Van Nuys that was used by the Los Angeles Police Department for everything from impounds to homicide investigations involving cars. This was the main source of income and security for the family. Cars that weren't immediately claimed, Paul sold.

I wasn't used to the dynamics of a family business, unprepared for the hours of what I considered torture spent at Paul's parents' home in Palm Desert. Paul, his father, and sister conversed endlessly about the tow yard and their respective car businesses. His sister Sandra had a car rental lot in Palm Springs and Paul still had the used car lot in Van Nuys that his father had given him when he was seventeen. I had no interest in their discussions which would drone on for hours.

Harriet was as disinterested as I was. I could either hang out with them or with her.

I chose to jog around the complex.

My only friends were his friends—and Nikki. I arranged to meet her at least twice a week in a commercial parking lot in Woodland Hills close to her apartment. There I waited anxiously, hungrily scanning vehicles coming and going for her little gray convertible VW Rabbit. She always had the roof down, rain or shine, her hair pulled up on the top of her head in a Scrunchie, making it easier for me to spot her.

I had peeled a hundred-dollar bill off the stack that Paul kept in his sock drawer. I needed something to help me not care.

* * *

It was around this time I set about applying for U.S citizenship. I didn't want to run the risk of deportation as did my mother. When I asked her if she was worried, she assured me she wasn't.

"It's the Mexicans they're looking for, not us Brits."

As I filled out the stack of paper work, one of the questions caught my eye: Are you, or have you ever been a habitual drunkard?

I marked an X in in the "no" box and wondered who would ever answer "yes" to such an incriminating and degrading question. I speculated this was a reason why my mother had avoided the process of citizenship. I vaguely remembered a time when a policeman brought her home for being drunk in public.

The process of my citizenship culminated at the Los Angeles Convention Center. I stood waving a miniature United States flag above my head, a flag tagged with a "Made in China" label sewn to its edge. I looked around and noticed I was flanked by elderly Korean war veterans proudly waving theirs. There was a feeling of camaraderie amongst us while a recording of John Denver singing "Country Roads" filled the room from the large overhead speaker.

* * *

Back at the ranch I tried to please Paul by cooking, cleaning, and keeping the gardens beautiful; but I felt as hard as I tried, I could never live up to his expectations. As my obsession with cocaine increased, we started to have more episodes of conflict. The drug fueled my ability to speak up about my frustrations. Once I had been too afraid to talk back; now fortified by a stimulant, my inhibitions disappeared. While we were having dinner one evening, arguing over some seemingly innocuous impulse purchase I had made, he looked up at me exasperated and said, "You know Janine, most of the time you're 98 percent perfect, but unfortunately the other 2 percent of the time you screw everything up." He validated my father's opinion of me, although I hardly doubted my father would have ever considered me 98 percent perfect. More like 2 percent of the time I might have had the ability to do something right.

* * *

We had been married two years, when Paul decided we would go to Hawaii for a week's vacation. I was excited to be staying in a high-end hotel right on the beach. I felt a vacation and quality time together was just what we needed to improve our relationship. Five days into our blissful stay, Paul offered to buy me a massage. I called down to the lobby and was told that the only available massage therapist that afternoon was a man. I was a little hesitant to use a masseur, but Paul told me it was okay and to go ahead. I excitedly gave him a peck on the cheek and skipped out of the room. This was going to be my very first massage.

I left the spa feeling wonderfully relaxed by my new experience, my skin soft and smelling of oils. As I walked into our hotel suite, I noticed Paul was sitting on the couch, a newspaper blocking his face.

"What were you doing?" he asked from behind the paper.

"What do you mean, what was I doing? I was getting a massage, remember?"

I was confused by his demeanor, and his question.

"I meant what were you doing *after* the massage?"

His words were clipped and precise.

"How do you explain the massage being an hour and ten minutes?"

he sneered, finally putting the paper down on his lap and looking at me in a way that scared me.

"What did you do in those ten extra minutes?"

"I didn't do anything!" I said, my voice shaking, close to tears. "He just went on longer than he should have, I don't know why."

"Did you give him a blow job?"

I burst into tears and ran out of the room into the hallway, slamming the door behind me as hard as I could. Injustice and hurt coursed through me as I strode down to the lobby and out onto the beach. My heart was beating hard in my chest as I kept walking until I was down to the water's edge. It was the end of the day and everyone had left to go back to their rooms and get ready for dinner. I sat down on the cool sand and pulled my knees up to my chest. I cried, hugging them tightly to my body. I couldn't understand what I had done wrong.

After a while I felt a presence behind me, and thought Paul must have followed me because he felt badly and wanted to tell me that he was sorry. I turned, and staring at me with its soulful eyes was a shaggy black dog. I turned back, submerged in my misery. The stray dog walked around me, pushed its wet nose into my hands and tried to lick my face. I put my arms around its dirty scruffy neck and pulled it close, feeling comfort from its warmth. I remembered cold nights when Rebecca kept me warm and I cried even harder.

The sun had set and it was now starting to get cold. I finally stood up feeling emotionally drained and walked back to the hotel, leaving my sympathetic friend on the beach. I wished I could take her with me.

I opened the door to our suite to find Paul still sitting on the couch reading the paper. I was amazed that he hadn't moved.

"Paul, I'm sorry," I said through the newspaper blocking his face from mine. I didn't know what I was sorry for, but I just needed him to stop being angry with me. "I don't want to ruin the rest of our holiday." He didn't respond. "Please!" I begged.

He put down the paper and patted the cushion next to him signaling for me to sit down. With his hand on my knee, his voice took on a paternal tone. "I believe you Janine, but you need to understand that your selfish behavior has consequences. You just need to remember that next time and not go off somewhere without your watch."

"I won't ever do that again," I promised.

I realized I would have to be careful never to make him that angry.

* * *

By the end of 1987 I discovered I was pregnant. After the initial shock and surprise, I was simultaneously excited and apprehensive. I hadn't thought I could get pregnant as we were always very careful. I was nervous about all the drugs I had been using, unaware that a new life was growing inside me. My periods were irregular, so it was hard to tell, but I figured I was probably about four weeks along. Paul and I had taken a trip to the racetrack in Monterey a few weeks earlier and we consumed more than our usual amount of cocaine and champagne.

When I told Paul I was pregnant he was elated. He was forty-four years old and this would be his first child. Katie was now almost eight and going to elementary school. This pregnancy started to change my feelings about everything. Whereas in England I had gone through it alone, I now felt supported. Excited about being pregnant, it was easy for me to stop drinking and using. The prospect of a baby brother or sister thrilled Katie. My in-laws were happy and the news spread rapidly. Paul decided to sell the condo in Palm Springs and we made the transition to live full-time at the ranch in Malibu.

Once there, he took on the role of manager at his father's Van Nuys tow yard and subsidized his income by buying and selling cars from the adjacent used car lot. Now the project of leveling the old ranch house and building our dream home became more crucial. Paul negotiated with a combination of professionals, semi-professionals, and con artists who came and went as the house began taking shape.

Paul and his family were definitely more interested in my pregnancy than Clive and his family ever had been. However, Paul continued his party lifestyle whenever he could, meeting friends after work and on weekends. I assumed that since I had stopped using drugs that he would stop too. I had found a vial of cocaine in his soft Italian purse one night. My heart sank in disappointment. I was afraid to confront him so I didn't say anything.

Samantha was born August 2, 1988. I endured sixteen long hours for her to make her appearance, and then finally, with the help of a birthing chair and suction cup, she was pulled from my body. I went through the same unbearable pain as I had the first time, but I wasn't alone and terrified. She was thinner than Katie had been at birth, and had the longest fingers I'd ever seen on a baby. Her head was cone shaped from her birth trauma.

"She looks like E.T.," I said to Paul as we marveled over her.

My mother brought Katie to visit me and meet her baby sister. I was exhausted, but happy to see them. I recovered from this birth experience faster and did not slip into the black hole of isolation and depression.

Paul and I fell asleep on the hospital bed with the baby nestled between us.

Just maybe everything was going to be okay.

Chapter Nineteen

I was filled with love for my family, my baby Samantha, and Katie, who at eight had become my constant companion and helper. As soon as we were home from the hospital she learned how to change, dress, and feed her baby sister whom we called Sam. The next three months were bliss.

Then one night Paul's friends came to visit us and see the baby. During the course of the evening a vial of cocaine materialized. I had not touched the drug in over a year. At first I was angry that they brought drugs to a home with a new baby. I was also angry with Paul for not setting any boundaries with his drug-using friends. I looked over at him as he talked and laughed, all the while saying nothing as his friend placed the vial on the table.

Excuse me but you'll have to leave. We have a new baby and its totally inappropriate for you to bring drugs into our house.

Yet I said nothing. I knew I couldn't resist.

That night I put Sam on formula as I was seduced back for one more dance with the devil. I never even paused to give this life-changing decision a second thought.

* * *

By some miracle my mother had remained sober and now it was her turn to watch helplessly as I continued down the genetic path. The kindling in my brain ignited and soon burned like a fire as it was re-introduced to alcohol and drugs. It only took me a week to start calling Nikki again. I felt like a monster, a freak of nature. What kind of mother would use drugs when she had a new baby to look after? I didn't understand what had happened to my high resolve when I was pregnant, because now my willpower was nonexistent.

Within months I was falling deeper and deeper into the grips of addiction until the madness started permeating all aspects of my life. I was using so much coke during the day that the only way I could bring myself down to sleep at night was to drink vodka. Then I would pass out, but only for a couple hours before needing to drink again. I would binge like this for a week and then go on the wagon, only to fall off two weeks later and start the cycle all over again. I was baffled, I didn't even like the taste of alcohol. I wrote everything down so I wouldn't forget to feed the baby or pick up Katie from school.

I hid my secret well as Paul continued working long hours at the tow yard. Our home was under construction, gradually evolving from a quaint, rustic red two-bedroom ranch house to an almost four thousand square foot house nestled in the hills above Zuma beach. We were confined to cramped living quarters, separated from the rest of the house by a plastic sheet hanging in the doorway of the original two bedrooms. The incessant construction went on around us, accompanied by nails pounding and the screeching of electric chain saws, jarring me awake early in the morning to blinding hangovers.

The pastures now contained an acquired melee of livestock: pigmy goats, potbellied pigs, a mule, a donkey, and a horse. I had rescued the donkey, the mule, and the pigs from a shelter. The horse was purchased from a stable in Malibu; Rebel was a tall chestnut thoroughbred measuring 16.2 hands at his withers. Our three dogs roamed the property during the day and came inside to sleep at night. If Paul had his way they wouldn't come inside the house at all.

As Sam passed her first year, Paul's family became less interested and involved. The novelty of the new baby had worn off. Paul adored her, but still spent the majority of his time immersed at his job at the tow yard and projects around the ranch. Katie was her sister's main caretaker, constantly anticipating the baby's needs and being the mother that I should have been. This freedom allowed me to engage in my addictions.

If I wasn't under the influence, I was chronically hung over, which made me just as incapacitated. I had various hiding places around the house for my alcohol, including glasses half-filled with booze hidden in the back of clothing shelves, the garage, or behind the cereal in the pantry.

Much to my dismay, even though we no longer lived in Palm Springs, we made a torturous weekend trip every month to visit Paul's parents; his sister Sandra was now divorced from Steve and living in the same gated community as her parents.

We invariably arrived late to be greeted at the door by Harriet, arms folded across her chest and disapproval etched on her face. "Vhy are you so late?"

Paul was chronically late for everything, yet his mother continually remained surprised by his tardiness.

I couldn't sneak alcohol into their house without the risk of Paul catching me, so I resorted to stealing from their liquor cabinet when no one was around, including my frequent trips from the dinner table to the bathroom. Harriet and Ernie collected miniature airline bottles whenever they traveled out of the country. I would grab a handful of the little bottles, stuff them into my pockets and take them into the bathroom with me. I wondered if they ever noticed their supply dwindling.

On one such evening we were eating the last of the over-cooked beef, soggy broccoli, and cold potatoes, when Harriet turned to me.

"Janine, are you still considering converting to Judaism?"

I froze, my eyes not leaving my plate.

This subject had come up a couple of times in the past, but I had neatly evaded it. The children were now in the den watching television, and I looked up to see Paul, his father, and sister, all looking expectantly at me.

"Our family is so small," Harriet continued. "And ze child takes the faith of its muzzer. It vould mean so much to us."

* * *

Later in the spare bedroom, fortified by a combination of several different little airline bottles, I told Paul that I felt I was ready to take the classes I had looked into. I had also discussed conversion with the rabbi at the reform temple we sporadically attended.

* * *

The ceremony took place a few months later. Paul's family dressed as if they were attending a graduation. I had sailed through the course, but often in a somewhat fogged state of mind as a result of pre-class imbibing. The classroom was in a building adjacent to the temple. Here discussions on spirituality would illicit passionate ideas and thoughts by the other students. At these times I sadly felt I had nothing to contribute, no ideas of my own. Spirituality or discussions about God had never been expressed in my alcoholically dysfunctional family. Vodka now dulled my senses; that was as close to spiritual as I could seem to get.

The big day came and I had hidden a bottle of vodka in a cubby in the garage. My mother dressed Sam in a striped blouse and plaid skirt, and for a moment, as my clarity returned, I wondered what she thought of my conversion. She had to quit her job at the Sheraton due to worsening symptoms of her fibromyalgia. Paul's parents were very empathetic of her physical ailments and lack of income. Out of kindness they hired her to do light part-time secretarial work at the tow yard, and gave her a little one-bedroom house on the property. It was certainly in my mother's best interest that she preserve the source of these benefits. She probably would have converted herself if they had asked her to.

By the time we left to meet Paul's family for dinner, I was doing my best to maintain my composure and balance. The rest of the evening was indistinct as I started to fade into a black out.

The next morning, I came too, my head pounding and my eyes feeling like they were filled with grains of fine sand. I lay in bed trying to put together the pieces of the evening. I looked around the room for clues. My clothes were piled on the chair, but the outfit was not one I would normally wear. I felt as though I were a detective reading clues to come up with a mental picture of where I had been and what I had done?

I could hear chatter coming from the kitchen downstairs. Dragging myself out of bed, I had to steady `myself against a chest of drawers. My head felt like it was about to detonate, my mouth so dry it was hard to swallow, and my hands had tremors. Holding the banister for support, I made my way toward the sound of people talking.

Paul, his family, and my mother were in the kitchen making breakfast.

Did they all stay the night?

I was afraid to say anything in case I inadvertently gave myself away. Harriet looked up from the kitchen counter where she was preparing lox and bagels, a grin spread across her face. I think it was the first time I had seen her smile.

"And, here she is! Velcome to the family, Hannah."

"Remember?" Paul noticed my confused look. "Your Jewish name is Hannah."

Sam was jumping up and down on the couch. "Mommy's name is Hannah; Mommy's name is Hannah!"

I turned around and went back upstairs.

* * *

The conversion did not cure me of my problems. I was becoming more and more depressed as I attempted to keep my secret hidden. My mother knew things were bad as she was looking after the kids a lot of the time, but even she didn't know how much cocaine I was using. I went and saw a doctor she recommended, but I wasn't honest about my drinking and drug use. He prescribed little pink pills for my anxiety, and yellow and burgundy ones for the depression.

It wasn't long before I started mixing the pink ones with alcohol.

* * *

Thanksgiving came around and Paul decided to invite the family to our house. I had enthusiastically prepared food all day with the help of a half pint of vodka hidden in the pantry behind a bag of rice. I was only taking little sips, trying hard not to overshoot the mark. I felt I was holding it together pretty well.

However, right before we were about to eat, I felt the synergistic effects of the alcohol and sedatives hit at the same time. As I carried a bowl of green peas to the dinner table, I tripped on the corner of the rug and the heavy bowl slipped out of my hands. I stood transfixed when, as if in slow motion, hundreds of little green balls rolled in different directions all around me on the parquet floor. Harriet, Ernie, and Sandra, along with Paul, my mother and Katie watched in silence. Then Sam started laughing, "Look at all the peas Grandma!"

I unsteadily knelt down and laboriously began picking up each individual pea, dropping it carefully back into the cracked bowl. After a moment of uncomfortable silence, everyone at the table resumed their conversations.

I had become the elephant in the living room.

* * *

Some afternoons when Katie was doing her homework, I would saddle up Rebel and ride him in the pasture or cross the road and go a little way down the trail with the dogs. Sam was getting old enough that she often asked to ride with me. This is what my dad had done with my younger half-sister Emily when she was a toddler. I failed to recollect that my sister had fallen off the horse and cracked her skull when she was three.

I pulled Sam up into the saddle with me and we walked the horse around the pasture calling out to Bob and Sylvia, the two overgrown Vietnamese potbellied pigs. As if on cue the morbidly obese hogs came lumbering out of their barn to greet us, followed by a nursery of screaming piglets.

"Piggies, piggies!" Sam shrilled excitedly as she pointed to them. She had the same fearless connection with animals as I had as a child.

My routine was to drink in the mornings and stop around noon. After taking a nap I was ready for a couple more drinks before I picked up Katie from the bus stop. The rest of the afternoon I would try to limit myself to only one vodka and orange juice. Around nine in the evening, Paul's headlights shining up the driveway propelled me into an attempted state of sobriety. Often he didn't even notice that I had been drinking. The cocaine was more sporadic, because of the expense, and Nikki wasn't always available; she was now starting to avoid my obsessive phone calls.

Sometimes I would be so hungover that I would dry heave all day and be unable to get out of bed. On those days I couldn't look after the children and my mother would come to the rescue. This was happening more frequently. I wondered if the children were any safer with her at times, but at least she was sober.

Once she brought Sam back from a weekend stay with her so I could recover from a particularly bad binge. I heard her old car coughing up the driveway and went outside to greet them. I hadn't had a drink in two days, and I was feeling better but still shaky. I couldn't see Sam anywhere.

"Where is she?" I asked, confused.

My mother raised an index finger to her lips, "Shhhhhhh."

She beckoned me to the back of her vehicle, opened the trunk carefully, and there was Sam curled in a fetal position, her face flushed red from the stifling summer heat.

"What the hell are you thinking?"

She seemed shocked at my reaction.

"Well, she asked if she could ride in the trunk," my mother said with indignation.

I dragged Sam's limp, sweaty body out of the over-heated confined space, and carried her into the air-conditioned house until I was sure she was going to be okay.

Even though my mother was sober, she had not been restored to sanity.

* * *

One afternoon I called to Katie letting her know Sam and I were riding Rebel on the trail. Sam was getting more comfortable riding with me and I felt it was time to transition from the pasture to the trail.

"We won't be long," I shouted as I closed the front door behind me.

I caught Rebel and saddled him up as Sam played in the hay by the barn. She stood dutifully on one of the bales, reached up her hand and I pulled her up into the saddle with me as I had many times before. This time though, I pushed myself back from the seat of the saddle and onto the horse's rump so she could have the saddle to herself.

We were no more than fifty yards down the trail when I heard loud buzzing sound and suddenly Rebel spooked. I tried to rein him in, but he was backing up and spinning around. Sam started crying and one of the dogs who had followed us down the trail was barking excitedly at a rattlesnake on the side of the trail. I knew at that moment that it wasn't going to end well. The big horse continued dancing himself into a state of agitation. I tried to control the reins from my perilous position behind the saddle, but I felt myself losing traction as Sam began to slide from the saddle.

In a split-second decision, I grabbed her by the arm, pulled her free, and dropped her to the ground. I heard her scream as she hit the dirt.

At that point Rebel reared up and I lost my balance, falling backward between his thrashing legs. The breath was knocked from me as I struck the ground. The flailing reins were caught up in the horse's front legs which intensified his panic. I was now entangled in his rear hooves and knew I could no longer protect myself. For a terrifying moment I was sure I was about to die and curled into a fetal position, my arms covering my head. Then the pain as the horse's weight crushed my abdomen and compressed my rib cage tore through me.

I could hear Sam screaming. She sounded like she was somewhere far away as I struggled to regain consciousness. I tried to lift myself to my knees, only to collapse again. The urgency of Sam's crying compelled me to keep trying, but it was no use, I couldn't get up. I heard one of the dogs whining and I could feel it licking my face.

Then everything went black.

Chapter Twenty

Sometimes the saving of a life can be measured in seconds. A man driving the canyon road noticed the rider-less horse trotting across the road. He could have kept on driving, or perhaps called the incident into the local Sherriff's station. He didn't make either of these choices. Instead he pulled into a turnout on the isolated road. It didn't take him long to catch the nervous animal since he had grown up with horses, as had a lot of people in the area. The man looked around and called out a few times, hearing nothing, he led the trembling animal up the conifer-lined driveway to a nearby house.

A girl standing on the porch recognized the horse and ran down to greet the man.

"Where's my mother?" Katie was already crying.

"Is this your mother's horse?" the stranger asked.

"Yes, she went down the trail with my sister. Where are they?" Her voice rose to a scream; she knew something bad had happened. She watched as the stranger led Rebel into the pasture and then they ran down the driveway together, Katie leading the way.

They found Sam sitting on the edge of the trail screaming, her face covered in dirt. I was lying on my side not moving. A dog was lying close to my head, whimpering.

"You need to go back to the house right now and call 911. Run as fast as you can," the stranger shouted at the scared girl.

She ran fast as her eleven-year-old legs could carry her.

Katie waited out on the street while the stranger stayed with us trying to comfort Sam. As soon as the paramedics arrived, she led them down the trail. There was no visible trauma but my blood pressure was dropping fast. I was put into a compression suit to reduce possible internal bleeding. Consciousness came and went, as the commotion around me brought neighbors to the location. I could feel the paramedics pulling off my boots and I wondered briefly if anyone might see my bare breasts as my clothes were cut from my body. The pain was now dissipating and I was getting cold.

There was a brief exchange of words between the emergency crew members. I couldn't understand what they were saying, but I could sense the urgency in their voices. Then I felt myself levitate off the ground.

For what seemed like an eternity I drifted through the air, until finally I felt the ground beneath me once again. I could hear the whirring of helicopter blades. As a paramedic attempted to load me inside, I grabbed his arm.

"No, not the helicopter, we can't afford a helicopter," I pleaded, afraid of what Paul would say when he saw the bill.

The paramedic leaned forward so I could hear him and reassured me that we would not have to pay for the rescue units.

Where was Sam? I couldn't hear her crying anymore.

As the helicopter rose up, blackness enveloped me again. Then I heard a woman's voice. "I don't think she's going to make it."

I couldn't communicate and didn't know how to let her know I was okay.

Was there another injured person in the helicopter? Someone in worse shape than me?

I needed to let them know I wasn't going to die.

We arrived at Westlake Hospital at the end of the day when most of the medical staff were changing shifts. My nurse later told me that a gastric surgeon and a hematologist were apprehended in the parking lot and a group of doctors and nurses hurriedly assembled to make up an emergency surgical team. Katie had called Paul and my mother immediately after she dialed 911. Paul left work and was on his way to the hospital. My mother headed to the ranch to take care of Katie who had gone to one of the neighbor's houses. Ernie and Harriet were driving from Palm Desert.

The surgery lasted eight hours as a team of twelve worked to save my life.

I had suffered a lacerated liver, several cracked ribs, and a collapsed lung. During the procedure I was given seventy-two units of blood through transfusions, my liver losing the blood as fast as they were trying to get it in. If there had been alcohol in by bloodstream, nobody said anything.

Following the surgery, a nurse emerged from the operating room and informed Paul and his parents that they had done all they could. Her suggestion was that they seek spiritual guidance because there was nothing more that could be done for me medically. The outcome was out of their hands.

I was told later that I regained consciousness that evening in the intensive care unit. I was intubated for three days, which could have been three hours or three years as far as I was concerned. I had no awareness of time as I drifted in and out of a morphine haze, hearing only the "whoosh whoosh" of the respirator and beeping from the intravenous towers. When finally alert enough, I tried to communicate with a little chalkboard and a piece of chalk. "Is Sam okay?" I wrote. The nurse reassured me that Sam had suffered a fractured collarbone and she was at home with my mother.

I was unable to move, more than fifty staples held my midsection together. Numerous IV lines hung all around me, tangled like spaghetti. My life was now dependent on the fluids dripping into my veins through a central line just below my collarbone.

On day three I started to run a fever. By the time it hit 104 degrees, I was placed on a refrigerated bed, fans blowing on me from all four corners. I lay there shaking and begging for blankets that no one would bring. I found out later that in the frenzy of the blood drive, two units of blood coming from Nevada had been mismatched. My blood was now at war with itself. Within twenty-four hours I was stabilized, yet still in critical condition.

A few days later when I was off the respirator my mind gradually began to clear; I remembered that Nikki had said she would be mailing me some coke on the morning of the accident. I imagined Paul opening the letter hand addressed to me, a little paper packet inside revealing my dirty secret. During my pain and suffering, I detoxed from the alcohol. One substance was replaced by another as I pushed the morphine button every twenty minutes.

I told the nurse I needed to see my mother. A short time later my she materialized at my bedside, leaning in close to hear what I was trying to say. My voice was hoarse and I struggled to talk.

"You have to bring me the mail, anything that's addressed to me. Please Mum!"

"No, no, darling," Mother reassured me, patting my hand.

"You don't need to worry about that now, you need to get well."

"I need the mail," I insisted with all the force I could muster.

Concerned that stress would impede my recovery and figuring a distraction might be good for me; she assured me that she would bring my mail the following day.

True to her word, the next day she returned with a handful of letters. I weakly took them from her and waited until she had gone. I leafed through the junk until I found the familiar cursive. I had planned to throw the unopened envelope in the trash, but the urge to look inside was so powerful I gave in, tearing it open.

I just need to make sure it's there.

A small packet slipped out and fell to the floor by my bed.

Shit!

Now the evidence of my secret was on the floor next to me and I had no way of getting to it.

"Nurse!" I called out weakly.

A young nurse approached my bed.

"I think I'm ready to try getting out of bed and sitting in the chair."

I motioned to the big armchair next to my bed. A nurse had encouraged me earlier to try the chair, but I had been unwilling to go through the pain of moving.

She called over another nurse, and together they were able to slowly sit me up. Wrapping me like a cocoon in a blanket, they lifted me out of the bed and eased me gently into the chair next to the window. I felt like I was going to pass out.

"Thank you," I told them breathlessly. "I think I'll be okay now."

I winced. I was sweating and the pain was excruciating.

"You sure you're okay there?" One of the nurses asked me.

"Yes, I'm fine thank you. It feels good to get out of that bed for a minute."

"All right," she said. "Well, you just give us a call when you're ready to get back in here." She rearranged the pillows and they both returned to the nurse's station.

I waited until they were busy and began looking around on the floor for the packet. I eventually spotted it, lying next to one of the wheels of my bed closest to the chair. In agony I reached down, shards of pain ripping through my abdomen. I managed to pinch the packet between my fingertips and gradually return to an upright position. I could feel perspiration running down my back. Holding the packet in the palm of my sweaty hand, I pushed my call button, desperate to get back in the bed.

Over the next two weeks I worked my way through the gram of coke, a little at a time.

Was I insane? I was in the ICU, for God's sake! What was wrong with me?

The power of choice no longer existed. I didn't know it at the time but one's willpower is virtually non-existent when it comes to addiction. The drug embodied survival. My defective brain told me I would die without drugs.

The nurse frowned over my jittery disposition as she read my vitals. I smiled weakly at her and hoped she thought that my physical pain was indicative of the stress that she saw on my monitor. By the third week I was finally transferred to the hospital ward.

I was now able to get out of bed by myself, so I shuffled over to the mirror above the sink and saw my reflection for the first time in weeks. I didn't recognize the person looking back at me.

My face was so bloated that my features had virtually disappeared. I was told that this was from liver damage and a diet of intravenous fluids. My skin color had a yellowish hue and my yellow eyes had sunk into my face. I looked down sadly at the trunk of my body, it would be a long time before I would be able to stand up straight again. I had four drainage bags hanging from small portholes in my abdomen; I could see they contained various levels of murky looking liquids. I sighed heavily and made my way back to the bed. Paul would be here any minute. He had told me he wanted me to help him by writing the checks for the month's utilities, so he was going to bring the bills to the hospital for me to sort through. My initial resentment was replaced with the thought that perhaps I wouldn't be so depressed if I were distracted.

One more week and I was finally told that I was strong enough to go home.

Chapter Twenty-One

Paul came to fetch me from the hospital in the old pickup he used to transport feed for the livestock. I wished he had brought a more comfortable vehicle, but he obviously killed two birds with one stone by picking up bales of hay on route. On the drive home to the ranch, I looked out of the window and marveled at the sky. I had been in the hospital so long that I had forgotten how blue it was.

Back home I was in for a long period of recovery. I was very weak, hardly able to walk or stand up straight. I would get out of breath easily and small tasks like getting dressed were incredibly hard. Paul was back to his old routine in a matter of days and I saw that my life-threatening accident hadn't changed anything for him. He was either in Van Nuys at the car lot or working outside on the property. I looked out of our bedroom window and saw Rebel innocently grazing in the pasture. I found that the opiate pain pills I had been given by the surgeon took the edge off everything, as well as numbing my senses to the pain. I wasn't used to pain pills and I was using them unaware that I was quickly developing a tolerance. Sam had recovered from her fractured collarbone and was eager to tell anyone who listened how she almost got "trampled up" by a horse.

By the end of the second month I was feeling a little stronger and my depression was lifting. The only tell-tale sign of the accident was the angry vertical scar that ran the length of my torso and small indentations at locations where the drainage tubes had been placed in my abdomen.

I had gradually started drinking again. Before being released from the hospital, the kindly GI surgeon had told me I should have a glass of champagne with my husband to celebrate my miraculous recovery. His words played like a jingle I couldn't get out of my head. At first a harmless glass of wine, which soon became two, and then a bottle. I knew I was lucky to be alive and that I shouldn't drink with a compromised liver, but the urge driving me was stronger than any logic. Once again, I was hiding bottles of alcohol in the pantry, the laundry hamper, and in the garage. I was now mixing the pain pills with alcohol.

I wanted so badly to be helped, but I was afraid to ask, afraid that Paul would send me somewhere far away and take the kids if he knew how bad it was.

How could he not see that there was something terribly wrong with me?

He came home late at night to invariably find me asleep on the couch and his cold dinner left out on the kitchen counter. I would wake confused around two o'clock in the morning, get up to quench my parched throat, and climb into bed next to his snoring body. The next day he would get up out of bed and go about his business. I wished he would ask me what was wrong, force me to tell him, assure me that I could trust him to help me. But he never said a word, so neither did I.

Sometimes I felt on the verge of telling him, but was unable to utter those three simple words that could potentially save my life. By this time, I knew I had lost control and I had a resigned feeling that my end, whatever that looked like and in whatever form, was getting closer.

I had stopped using coke since the hospital, but I would still occasionally see Nikki socially. She respected my decision to stop using after the accident, however she was unaware I had a problem with alcohol. She called me one evening and asked me to join her and some friends at a bar in Malibu. It had now been four months since my accident. Paul was still at work, so I left Katie and Sam with the couple who lived in our guesthouse.

I was already drinking vodka at home, not thinking I would be going anywhere that night. I figured I could go just for a couple of hours and probably still get home before Paul.

Paul's Porsche and Mercedes were in the garage as he had taken the pick-up truck to work. The black European Mercedes was his pride and joy. I knew he was hesitant for me to drive it as I had a habit of getting into accidents. Nevertheless, I reversed the Mercedes out of the garage and set off down the hill.

Less than a couple of miles down Mulholland Highway, I took the tight left curve onto Decker Canyon as I had so many times in the past. However, this time I entered into the curve a little too fast. In what seemed like slow motion, I lost control for a split second and the car left the road. Executing a perfect dive, the vehicle plunged off the hillside. There was a three second delay as I desperately tried to process what was happening. I realized, when the wheels finally hit dirt, that this was probably the end.

After bouncing about fifty feet down the hill the car lurched and turned sideways, slamming into something solid and stopping our descent to the bottom. Shaken up and stunned to be alive, I looked out the window and saw only branches and thick shrubbery. I was glad that even in my drunken haze I had remembered to fasten my safety belt.

Then I noticed a flicker from a flashlight penetrating the foliage that encompassed the car. A distant voice was calling.

"Hello! Is there anybody down there?"

I unbuckled my seatbelt and with great difficulty pushed open the heavy door, the brush scratched at my arms and legs as I pulled myself out of the car. I was now slipping and sliding on the loose dirt, compromised by liquor and a steep, rocky terrain.

"I'm okay, but can you help me get the car out of here?" I yelled.

I felt my question to be perfectly logical. I was worried about Paul seeing his car in such a condition and knew I was going to have to race against time to get it back to the ranch and cleaned up before he got home.

"I don't think so, lady," the stranger said, his voice closer now.

He was making his way down the slope to toward me.

"You sure did get yourself into a mess," he said running the flashlight over the car and shaking his head. Then he turned his attention to me.

"You been drinking?"

"No, I have not!" The lie escaped my lips before I could think.

I heard the wail of sirens faintly in the distance, getting louder as the man's neighbors came to the canyon's edge pointing flashlights at us. By the time the stranger helped me scramble to the top, the fire trucks were parked and the paramedics had come down to meet us and helped with our ascent. I appeared to be unharmed, other than minor bruises and scratches from climbing the hill.

The car didn't fare so well. Looking down at the dented vehicle nestled in the rugged chaparral below, I felt a sort of seasickness in the pit of my stomach and for a moment thought I was going to faint.

What was Paul going to say when he saw his precious car?

I felt panic coming on just as I saw a police cruiser pull up alongside one of the fire trucks.

The cop walked up to us, shined his flashlight in my eyes, and asked me the same question.

"Have you been drinking this evening, ma'am?"

"No, I haven't," I insisted, hoping he would take me at my word.

Of course he wanted proof, so I followed his direction, priding myself on how well I was executing his commands. As I was touching the end of my nose with my index finger, I thought I saw Paul's truck slowly pass by. I watched frozen in horror, as the truck stopped and the reverse lights came on. I opted out of the field sobriety test and wailed miserably, "That's my husband. He's going to kill me!"

The truck continued backing up and then came to a stop next to us.

Paul rolled down the window.

"What is going on here, officer?" he asked, smiling insincerely.

He kept his eye on me the entire time the cop was describing the accident. Paul politely explained that I was his wife, we lived close by, and could he not just take me home to sleep it off?

The cop shook his head, "I'm sorry sir, there was a call. I have to take her in."

At that moment, we all turned to watch the heavy-duty flatbed tow-truck haul the almost unrecognizable Mercedes over the crest of the hill and back onto the road.

The once sleek foreign car was pummeled with dents and scratches, brush was jammed in the hubcaps, and the windshield was caved in as if an elephant had sat on it.

* * *

That night I sobered up in jail, the reality of the evening sinking in. I couldn't even imagine what I was going to have to face the next day. There was no way I'd be able to beg myself out of this one.

Fear gripped my stomach when I realized that Paul would be arriving soon to take me home.

The following morning I was taken from the cell into the main station. I saw Paul waiting for me holding Sam's hand. I couldn't believe he had brought her with him.

We drove home in silence, Sam chattering in the backseat about wanting to be a cop when she grew up.

Paul left the battered Mercedes in the garage for weeks.

"I'm not going to cover it," he said. "I want you to think about what you did to my car every time you walk past it."

* * *

I was initiated into the protocol of the DUI world: suspended license, court fees, SR-22 insurance, DUI classes, and AA meetings. Sitting in one of my DUI classes one night, I looked around at the rest of the group, noticing all the differences and none of the similarities between myself and the other members.

What the hell was I doing here?

The counselor came over to my desk. He looked like what I felt an alcoholic should look like: craggy pitted face, deep sunken eyes, and a couple of missing teeth.

"What's your story?" he asked, whistling the "s" in story.

I entertained the group with my recount of driving the car off the cliff. I felt it was a pretty good story, all things considered. When I finished he looked at me and shook his head.

"You'll be back. I'll bet on that."

* * *

It was not until I sincerely tried to stop drinking that I realized I couldn't. I was now continuing to drink alcohol despite my license being suspended and being in DUI school. The harder I tried, and the harder Paul tried to control me, the more I drank; and the more I drank, the sicker I became. I was no longer the elephant in the living room. If there was ever a way of sneaking off to buy alcohol, I would find it. Even though my license was suspended, I still drove the truck down to the store while Paul was at work. I had an extra key he wasn't aware of. He would drop me off at an AA meeting in the evening while he and the girls went for dinner; I waited ten minutes and then snuck off to the store to get little half pints of vodka I could hide in my handbag. One time I even stole all the change out of Katie's piggy bank to get booze.

I felt it was God's cruel joke that my mother was sober and now I was the drunk. A couple of years previously when I had gone through all the legalities for my citizenship, I had taken offense when asked if I was, or had ever been, a habitual drunkard. In the box where I had marked an indignant "no," I could now check "yes."

Katie was thirteen, Sam was five, and Paul and I had been married for eight years. The pain of knowing that alcohol had replaced my love for my children was acute.

Despite the fact I drank through DUI school, I wasn't caught, and after a couple of months I had a restricted license and was able to drive legally again. I wondered what Paul was thinking when he let me drive the kids knowing I couldn't stay sober. I sat in my car outside Sam's school, not daring to get out in case one of the other mothers approached me. I no longer knew how to talk to people. I was pushing myself further and further into a realm of isolation. My mother was starting to care for the kids more than I. She lived so close that she could be at the ranch within the hour whenever Paul or Katie called her to come to the rescue.

I went to my court appointed AA meetings early in the morning and hopelessly endured the hour as members gratefully spoke of the gifts of their recovery. I couldn't understand the language of emotional honesty they were sharing with each other, and I would leave feeling worse than before. I was able to stay sober in a meeting for an hour, but what was I to do with all the other hours in the day? Paul was at work, the kids were in school, and I was alone with my thoughts. As busy as I tried to be, taking care of the house, the pets, chores and errands–I could never shut off my brain.

On the way home from the meeting I had no choice but to stop by a liquor store and pick up a half pint of vodka, fooling myself into thinking that I just needed enough to calm my nerves. As paranoia set in, I started using different liquor stores to avoid the possibility that a cashier might realize I had a problem.

"There goes that woman again. She was in here buying vodka yesterday morning. Can you believe it?"

Members of the local AA meeting were getting to know me. I was afraid if I shopped at the market I might bump into one of them. I would furtively walk the aisles, scanning for anyone I might recognize. In my feverish mind I preferred risking markets than being seen coming out of a liquor store. It was dangerous living at the ranch and driving the canyon roads while fading in and out of blackouts. I could remain sober for a week, maybe two, scaring myself straight after a blackout, only to relapse again. Horror and despair became my constant companions, as I fell deeper and deeper into the abyss.

Chapter Twenty-Two

Sadly, by now my alcoholic life felt normal to me. Lack of judgment due to drinking, coupled with free-range livestock was a dangerous combination. I was a constant accident waiting to happen as I stumbled around the barns at feeding time. I had been caring for two pigmy goats belonging to a girl I had met at one of the meetings. The goats were housed in a pen next to the pot-bellied pigs. On one occasion I was carrying a bucket of pellets out of the barn and into their pen. Excitedly the goats crowded me, pushing me, and almost knocking the bucket out of my hands. I kept nudging them back with my knee, but the billy goat was relentless. After closing up the pen I looked down and noticed blood seeping through my jeans.

I ran my fingers over the warm stickiness and felt a hole in the denim. Limping back in the house, I peeled off my pants only to discover a gaping inch-long puncture wound in my leg just above my knee. The billy goat must have gored me and I didn't even feel it. I wrapped some gauze around my leg, pulled on sweatpants, and drove myself down the hill to the closest emergency room. I was numbly surprised that none of the nurses seemed to notice I was intoxicated, even in my altered state I knew I probably smelled of the tequila I had been drinking. I hoped none of them recognized me from the horse accident. I was given a tetanus shot and a young doctor stitched my wound.

A couple of hours later I made my way home with the added benefit of a bottle of pain pills in my purse.

Chemicals did for me what I couldn't do for myself: they made me feel better. I tricked myself into believing that everything was okay. Reality became distorted and I mostly inhabited a world of alcohol-fueled delusion.

Paul ultimately noticed that I wasn't getting any better and the AA meetings were not keeping me sober. Instead of berating me and lecturing me as usual, he suggested I check myself into treatment.

Our health insurance didn't cover inpatient, so with new resolve I transferred some of my money in England to my US account. Hopefully if I paid for the treatment myself, I wouldn't screw it up. A month seemed pricey, so I opted for the two-week fast-track.

Everything that had happened to me from birth to this point in time was now coming to the surface. Symptoms of my childhood traumas were manifested by a paralyzing fear that I could not overcome. Anxiety coursed continuously through my veins like electrical currents. If I wasn't drinking or using pills I couldn't talk to people or do the simplest things like make a phone call.

I went through the two-week process of treatment in a state of fogged emotional numbness. I left the facility not understanding myself any better than when I went in. I was discharged with a bottle of ninety Klonopin the psychiatrist prescribed for my anxiety.

In less than two weeks I was drinking again.

Once again, I tried AA. The members watched me arrive intoxicated. I knew they were shaking their heads and wondering what it was going to take in order for me get sober. It was even worse for me to watch people around me get sober and stay sober, but somehow the phenomenon of sobriety was elusive to me.

What was it going to take to make me stop? The horse accident? The car accident? Going to jail? Putting myself in treatment?

Nothing seemed to make any difference. Family and friends were baffled, but none more than me. My mother couldn't help me; well-meaning friends I had made in the AA program had come to my house several times trying to talk sense into me. I got a new sponsor every month. Katie had to constantly call Paul at work, begging him to come home.

"There's something wrong with Mum again," she'd say, as I was passed out and non-responsive on the floor.

The couple who lived in the guesthouse had moved on. This just gave me another location to drink. I could hide vodka in the guesthouse kitchen and drink while Paul was out working on the property. I peeked nervously through the small kitchen window as I drank; making sure I knew where he was at all times. I emerged from blackouts confused and afraid, unsure of what was going on, or how I got where I was. My mother would pick up the kids from their schools, give them dinner, and wait for Paul to get home. Often she spent the night as Paul was now hiding from me just as much as I was hiding from him.

Once I came out of a blackout in a grocery store, pushing a cart down one of the aisles. Looking down into my cart, I saw a random collection of items I must have pulled off the shelves. Abandoning the cart, I walked unsteadily out to the parking lot. Searching frantically around the lot I finally saw the little white pickup truck. Already covered in dents from ranch work, I didn't think Paul cared too much what I did to it. I opened the unlocked door. The car keys had been left casually on the passenger seat. With shaking hands, I got back in the car and made my way home, the groceries long forgotten.

Following that incident, I found a local therapist who specialized in eating disorders and addictions. I also decided to go back to the gym in order to get healthier. I felt if my body were stronger, perhaps my mind would be too. My new-found resolve would last less than a month, but I never gave up trying. I went to the gym in the mornings after dropping the kids at the bus stop; I knew it was a trigger for me to be home alone. After the gym I went to the noon meeting and then lunch with some of the sober women I was getting to know. These activities would fill the hours and give me a better chance of staying sober the rest of the day.

The same women I tried to avoid everywhere else were at the gym: women in matching workout gear, long hair pulled back in ponytails, and three carat diamond studs in their ears. I noticed they didn't sweat; or if they did, only little beads of perspiration gathered on the temples of their smooth brows. I watched them exercise and wondered what lives they lived and what thoughts went through their heads. I was sure they weren't struggling with the need to buy booze on the way home like I was.

One morning I was on the StairMaster when an attractive woman on the machine next to me struck up conversation.

"Hi," she said, exhibiting whiter-than-white teeth as she flashed me a smile, "I can see you do a pretty good workout!"

"Thank you." I looked back down at my magazine, not sure if I wanted to talk to her.

"I come here to make up for all the partying I do," she said giggling.

I looked at her again. She was about my age, her thick, blond, shoulder-length hair bouncing up and down as she worked the machine. I envied every woman with thick hair; I kept my thin hair tucked under a cap as it looked ridiculous in a ponytail. I liked how direct this woman was; I felt I didn't have to hide from her as I did the mothers at Sam's school. Within fifteen minutes I knew her name was Wendy, she was going through a divorce, and hiding her "partying" from her ex-husband.

"He won't let me have shared custody of my son if he knows I'm drinking again."

The fact that she said drinking "again" made me feel like she could have a problem like me.

"Where do you live?" she asked.

I told her and suggested that maybe sometime she make the drive up the canyon and we could have tea together. I really didn't have any friends other than Nikki.

* * *

A couple of weeks later Wendy showed up at the ranch. The doorbell rang and there she was on the threshold holding a bottle of wine in each hand.

"I thought this might be better than tea," she said giggling as she handed me one of the bottles.

I wondered what had happened to my new resolve as I stepped back and let her walk past me into the house.

A couple of hours later we had finished both of the bottles of wine.

Wendy reached into her spacious purse and pulled out a pint of vodka and a bottle of pills. "How about some shots and Vicodin?"

The last thing I remember was getting up to get us some shot glasses.

* * *

It was dark and I was laying on the grass in one of the pastures. All the lights were on in the house and I wondered if I had come outside because I had forgotten to feed the donkeys. I could see their silhouettes outlined by the moon as they stood side by side under a tree. They were watching me curiously, probably as confused as I was. My head was now pounding from the combination of pills, vodka, and wine. I felt like I was going to throw up. I rolled over onto my knees using the fence for support as I unsteadily got to my feet. That's when I noticed the shotgun propped against the three-rail fence. I vaguely remembered Wendy leaving and I was feeling depressed and hopeless about relapsing. I must have taken the shotgun out of the garage, but I had no memory of doing so. I had often had thoughts that everyone would be better off without me, but hadn't taken this kind of step to make it happen.

Did I seriously intend to shoot myself?

I must have gone into the pasture so the kids wouldn't hear the sound of the gun blast. I couldn't figure what had happened after that. I grabbed the cold metal barrel of the weapon and made my way back to the garage.

Passing out that night had saved my life.

* * *

Two days later Paul came home during the day as I wasn't answering the phone. He found me in the guesthouse trying to cut my wrists with a kitchen knife.

That was it. He had had enough.

Carrying me to his Porsche as if I were an unruly child, he tossed me roughly in the passenger seat and pulled the seatbelt tight.

I fought him pleading, "Please don't send me away, please don't send me away!"

I had hit my head on the door when he pushed me into the car and a painful knot was already forming on my temple; I cried and begged him to give me another chance, but to no avail. He was focused on the solution at hand. As he drove I finally fell asleep, exhausted from crying and the effects of alcohol. I woke up to find myself being wheeled into the ER of a big unfamiliar hospital. Paul was nowhere to be seen.

After my stomach was pumped with a charcoal solution, a police officer materialized at the side of my bed.

"How did you get this black eye?" He asked me coldly, his pen poised above a small black notepad.

I wasn't aware that I had a black eye.

"My husband and I got into a fight," I told him, forgetting that I hit my head on the car door.

I was stabilized a few hours later and told that my blood alcohol content had been at 0.40 percent, a level that could lead to coma or possible death due to respiratory arrest.

"You are lucky to still be alive young lady." The nurse gently touched my hand.

Lucky to be alive? Who was she kidding?

The next day I was moved to a different ward of the hospital. I looked around the room to see patients either sitting on the sides of their beds or in chairs like zombies. I tried to sit up and realized that my hands were bound to the bed with leather straps. Confused and scared I started to cry.

A young nurse approached me.

"How are we doing?" she asked kindly.

"Why am I tied to the bed? Where am I?" I asked, bewildered and getting panicky.

"You're in the psych ward at Olive View Hospital in Los Angeles."

The psych ward? Why did Paul bring me all the way to Los Angeles?

"You're tied down so you can't hurt yourself," she said. "Did you know you tried to kill yourself?"

She undid one of the straps and lifted my hand to show me my bandaged wrist.

Did I do that? I didn't remember trying to cut myself.

"You've been sleeping the past two days," she explained as she cinched the strap back in place. "We need to keep you safe."

* * *

The next few days were a blur. I found out my nurse's name was Anna. My family had abandoned me, or so I thought, as Anna told me my husband had instructed her that I was not to come home.

"We need to get you into a thirty-day rehab," she told me.

"I don't have any money," I said forlornly. "What am I going to do?"

"Don't worry. We'll figure something out," she assured me.

"Can I call my husband and ask him if he can help me?"

"Unfortunately, honey, we already tried that. He said that this time around he wasn't going to be able to help you out."

"But…" I protested.

"Shhh," she said, stroking my forehead. "We'll figure it out. The most important thing right now is you getting well."

I still had some of the money left in England from the house. Besides, what choice did I have? I couldn't stay in the hospital and if I left, I'd have nowhere to go.

"Can you help me contact my bank in England? I still have some money there."

The following day the transaction between banks was complete and I now had several thousand dollars in my U.S account. Anna arranged to get me into a rehab and they were going to come and pick me up from the hospital.

When the driver from the treatment center arrived, I found Anna and hugged her good-bye; she pulled back and held me at arm's length.

She looked into my eyes with sincerity. "Don't give up, Janine. I know you can do this," she said squeezing my hands. We hugged once more and I tearfully walked out of the unit.

The driver of the white van said nothing, as he drove for what seemed like forever, but it was maybe only a half hour. I was so nervous about where we were going that I didn't want to talk to anyone. I knew for a fact that I was going to be miserable for the next month. I also felt completely deserted by my family. Even my mother wouldn't rescue me this time.

I stared out of the window as we passed unfamiliar street signs and buildings.

"Here we are." The driver finally broke the silence. "Underwood Treatment Center. Your new home for the next month."

Chapter Twenty-Three

I was led into a small, sparse waiting room and spent the next couple of hours tediously filling out admittance forms. I looked out through the office window and noticed that most of the "inmates" appeared to be having fun. I went into a bathroom to do their regulation urine test and looked at myself in the mirror. My hair was tangled and unwashed. I still sported a blood-shot black eye. I looked down at my wrist: crosscut red surface scars revealed my pathetic attempt to end my life.

What had happened to me?

I tried to piece together the events of the past week but kept coming up with nothing other than a vague memory of Paul trying to force me into his car. I was shown to the women's dorm, which had bunk beds lined up against either side of the room. I was reminded of being the new girl in a boarding school, only these weren't kids.

I sat on the bottom bunk that was allocated to me by a disinterested staff member, and noticed a girl on the bunk across the room knitting what looked like a scarf. I saw that she had swastikas tattooed around her neck and quickly looked away. The only belongings to my name were a wash bag that Anna had put together for me and my handbag. Anna also had the clothes washed that I had been wearing when I was admitted to the hospital. I looked around at the other bedside tables and saw that most of the girls had pictures of their kids or husbands to remind them of home, someone who was waiting for them, people who loved them.

I had nothing to put in my drawers and no pictures of my family to set on my bedside table. I felt abandoned.

I had felt alone when I was fourteen and hitchhiking to Edinburgh, but at least then I felt I had made that decision. I had hopes that something good might have come from my journey. This place seemed to be the end of the road. I had no idea what I was supposed to do after I completed the thirty days of treatment. I fell into a deeper depression when the routine pregnancy test came back positive. I had no idea that I could be pregnant.

What was I going to do?

I wondered if Paul would take me back if we had another baby.

He came to visit me at the end of my first week. We sat out on the quad and he showed me his wrists.

"Do you see this?" he asked me calmly.

I could see angry red welts and asked him what they were.

"The police arrested me. Apparently the hospital thought I hit you."

I looked down, disgrace gripping my gut and making it hard for me to breathe. I didn't want to ask him how he got out of jail or if he faced any charges. I didn't want him to tell me anymore.

"I'm pregnant," I said softly, looking up at him.

Looking down at his hands, he said nothing for a while. Then he sighed and met my gaze.

"I'm sorry, I can't deal with that Janine. You can't come home if you're going to have a baby," he said flatly. "It's bad enough as it is, you need to get an abortion."

* * *

The month at Underwood seemed to last forever, every minute felt like an hour. I battled morning sickness as I went to groups with my peers. I would yearn for my grandmother in those dark moments, her lavender scent and her gentleness. She was too old to come and visit me anymore and it had been so long since I'd seen her.

Most of the clients were addicted to heroin or meth. There was a large demographic of young people who were HIV positive, and here

I was, the alcoholic housewife from Malibu. A lot of the addicts had been in and out of the treatment center multiple times, trying to evade jail sentences. They seemed apathetic and used to the routine.

I was in the infirmary one day getting some anti-nausea medication, when the nurse beckoned to me and whispered, "If you get an abortion, I can guarantee that your baby will be waiting to reckon with you when you're dead. You won't get away with this you know."

She took a step back, head tilted and a twisted smile as if she were an authority from God himself. I rushed out of the infirmary and shut myself in the hall bathroom. Feelings of hopelessness and anxiety overwhelmed me. My future looked so bleak and frightening. I lifted my shirt and put my hands on my stomach. I knew I had to have the abortion, even if Paul hadn't said what he did, the odds that I had done damage to the fetus were too great.

"I'm sorry," I whispered to my unborn child.

I touched the soft skin of my stomach as tears began to well in my eyes. "I'm so sorry," I said again as I dropped to my knees on the cold tile floor. Right then as I cried I craved alcohol more than ever and longed for the numbness that I knew would come instantly as the liquid burned my throat and settled in my stomach, radiating ease and comfort, taking away all of my pain. But instead there was nothing, just the indifferent institutional walls around me and the sound of voices talking excitedly outside in the hallway.

* * *

It was Mother's Day when Paul finally brought Katie and Sam to see me. They were holding hands and looking around nervously as I approached.

"Mummy!" they yelled in unison and ran to me. "Happy Mother's Day, Mummy!"

Sam's big trusting brown eyes looked up at me. I could see that Katie was uncomfortable and I immediately felt ashamed.

I sat down on a bench and took both their hands in mine. It had been years since I had really looked at my children, really seen their innocent faces. I was so entrenched in my sickness and self-pity that I hadn't been able to see them anymore. I felt grief wash over me and I swallowed hard so as not to cry in front of them. I hadn't been able to take care of them, to listen to them, to watch them grow up.

I was embarrassed that they had to come and visit me in such a place on Mother's Day. I led them over to the quad and a fellow client came up to us and offered her blanket for us to sit on.

"Wow, this really is a family isn't it?" Paul smiled sarcastically, motioning to the sign on the quad wall, which read "We Are Family."

He sheepishly handed me a wrapped gift.

I unwrapped it and opened the box to find a soft, leather wallet.

What was I supposed to do with a wallet in here? We weren't allowed money.

I asked him if he could bring me some clothes on his next visit. All I had was what I was wearing and some underwear and socks a staff member had given me.

After they left I felt more depressed than ever. There was no way I was going to risk losing my children. It was then that I realized that they were my life and the only thing worth living for. I had to fight for them.

The next two weeks dragged. My last weekend I was allowed to go home on a pass for the day to see how it felt being around my triggers. I asked if I could take somebody with me for moral support, but in reality, I was afraid of being around Paul by myself. I knew he had a lot of anger toward me.

One of my dorm mates was glad to get out of the treatment center for a while. Paul came and picked us up and we drove back to the ranch in relative silence. Once there, I realized how anxious I felt. Everything was a trigger for an upsetting memory. The couch I would pass out on, the medicine cabinet where pills were kept, the kitchen pantry where I hid booze, the stairs I once fell down, the list was endless.

The kids were at school, so Paul went back to working on a project.

Nothing had changed.

The girl that came with me was awed by the opulence of the house. We went outside to visit the horses, donkeys, and pigs. The pygmy goats had been returned to their owner.

With little to do, I found myself looking forward to getting back to the familiar surroundings and structure of the rehab where I had finally settled in and found a few women with whom I could talk and relate. We had promised to stay in touch when we left. I was told that the rehab held a weekly meeting for alumni, and I could attend if I wanted to.

Back in my dorm, I looked through the pictures of Katie and Sam that I had brought back with me. I knew having them on my bedside table would help me get through the rest of my treatment.

* * *

On my last day, I sat in the center of a circle of clients who took turns telling me I would be missed and how it was now time for me to embark on my new life. I thanked my peers and the counselors and made my way out to the front of the building. A counselor had told me that ninety percent of the clients who graduated came back. I was determined I wouldn't be one of them.

Paul was sitting in his Porsche, talking intently into his phone. He didn't even look at me as I opened the door and pushed my small bag of belongings onto the back seat.

As we pulled out of the parking lot, I looked out of the rear window and was thankful to be leaving the facility and released into the world once more. I put my head back and closed my eyes listening to the throbbing of the car's engine and Paul's voice as he talked business. I was suddenly startled out of my reverie.

"Janine." Paul was looking at me intently.

I sat up and saw that we were in a small auto strip mall in front of a tire shop.

"I need to go in here to talk to someone. I'll only be a few minutes."

"Okay."

I put my head back again and started thinking about all the things that had happened to me in the past year.

What was it going to be like when I got home? Would the children forgive me? Did the neighbors know? How about our friends?

I was sure Paul had painted himself a nice little picture of being the loving tolerant husband, stuck with a crazy, alcoholic wife. Did they know he had introduced me to drugs? I looked down at my watch. He had now been in the tire store for thirty minutes. I decided to get out of the car and walk around.

Over an hour later he came sauntering out of the store, seeming oblivious that he had left me waiting so long.

"What were you doing in there for so long?"

"Listen, Janine," he snapped, "this is what I have to do if you want to keep living in a nice house and having the nice things you have. You just need to deal with it."

I was shocked and stunned by his anger. It was my first day out and I had only asked him a question. Tears stung my eyes.

The rest of the drive was silent. He didn't see the tears behind my sunglasses, but even if he had I was sure he wouldn't care. We finally approached the ranch driveway and as we got closer I could see Katie and Sam standing at the front of the house.

"Mummy!" they both yelled as I got out of the car. Dogs were clambering on top of one another in an effort to be the first to greet me. Katie and Sam ran up to the car, and I hugged them, holding them tight. My mother stood on the porch smiling.

Chapter Twenty-Four

A week later I had the abortion. Paul was supposed to take me to the doctor's office, but he got held up at work. I drove myself down the hill to the gynecologist and sat in the waiting room, my heart racing and my stomach doing cartwheels. Paul arrived after everything was finished so he could drive me home. We could leave my vehicle in the parking lot, he said, and he would take me down the hill the next day to pick it up.

"You understand this is for the best don't you?" He glanced at me as he drove us back through the winding canyon.

I just looked straight ahead, still numb from the sedatives.

I was now staying sober but felt just as miserable as when I was drinking–only more aware of it. I felt everything now. Life was sharp and real, and the embarrassment and guilt I felt for all the things I had done tortured me every minute of every day. The anesthesia for coping was gone and I felt like I was going insane. I didn't know how to care for myself, let alone look after two kids, and meet the needs of a demanding husband.

I was trapped and could see no way out.

* * *

Yuma was my dog. Paul had wanted a guard dog but Yuma was more interested in sleeping than guarding. She spent her days on a long chain attached to a doghouse at the top of the driveway. At night she was allowed to roam the property, but she usually slept by the front door. Paul was adamant that dogs do not belong in houses.

"They're dogs," he would remind me, "not people."

Yuma's house was painted the same sky blue as ours, and she would lie, chained to her house, as I was chained to mine. She passed the long summer days napping in the shade of a tree, oblivious to her purpose. She nonchalantly ignored cars approaching the house, yet pulled the fierce guard dog routine when they tried to leave; blocking the entrance to the driveway and barking ferociously.

Yuma had a penchant for anything with wings. She liked to bark at birds flying overhead and the murder of crows that landed in the pastures drove her crazy. She was blissfully happy in her uncomplicated world, until the ducks arrived.

One afternoon I arrived home from a shopping trip carrying an incubator I had rented from a feed store. I was talked into the idea of hatching ducklings by Jim, the owner's stepson.

"Hey look," he said, pulling the incubator off the shelf, "you should get one of these for the kids, they'll love it!"

I had only gone into the store to buy a bag of pig pellets. Now I was laughing as Jim held the odd contraption in front of me. I felt at ease with Jim. I was going to AA meetings and I would sometimes see him there. A few members talked about him, laughing and judging him because he "couldn't get it." I identified with his struggle to stay sober. A couple of weeks prior he had returned to the meeting after a relapse, looking sheepish, minus his moustache and eyebrows.

"What happened Jim?" his peers asked laughing.

He explained to them that he was drunk when he tried to light the barbeque with his face too close to the grill. As others laughed at his story, I felt sad for him. I knew what it was like to continuously fail at staying sober.

Now I was looking at the metal contraption he held in front of me.

"What is it?" I asked.

"It's an incubator for duck eggs," he said. "It's cheap to rent, and I can give you a couple of duck eggs."

He set down the incubator, returning a few minutes later with an egg held gently in each hand.

"Here," he said, passing me one.

I held the warm fragile egg in my palm, surprised at how heavy it was. Jim pulled a marker out of his shirt pocket and carefully drew an O and X on either side of the egg.

He handed me the marker. "Do the same with yours, then remember to rotate the eggs four times a day."

He packed the eggs carefully into a small box and carried the bag of pellets out to my car.

"Four times a day, don't forget."

"I won't," I said and smiled at him.

* * *

When the kids got home from school, I led them into the garage and showed them the incubator. I had already added water and plugged it into an electrical outlet. Carefully lifting the lid, we looked at the two eggs in awe.

"Oh my God!" they both shrieked.

"When will they hatch?" Katie asked, gently touching an egg with her finger.

"About a month," I said. "They will live with us on the ranch."

Paul had excavated an area alongside one of the pastures and filled it with water. There was even a makeshift dam with a culvert and wood bridge spanning a narrow section of the pond. The ducks would have their very own habitat.

The girls turned the eggs religiously every day. Then one afternoon I heard squealing and yelling coming from the garage.

"Mom come! They're hatching! The babies are hatching!"

We watched in mesmerized silence as the little beaks worked through their shells. Jim had been right; it was a great experience for all of us—a wonderful distraction, an anticipation of something good, fun, and exciting. Mostly it had been an escape from all we couldn't control in our lives.

The ducklings grew quickly, and it wasn't long before they acclimated to the pond. They imprinted Sam as their mother and waddled behind her as she played a game of trying to hide from them.

* * *

Early one Sunday evening the four of us returned from a trip to Paul's parents in Palm Springs. We immediately noticed something was odd because Yuma was not standing in her usual position at the top of the driveway. My stomach dropped as I thought of the ducks. The only thing that prevented the ducks being attacked by Yuma was her steel chain. We pulled up to the front of the house as Yuma came loping up from the pond, tongue flopping out of the side of her mouth and covered in feathers. I knew then that she had killed one of the ducks, if not both of them.

Sam started crying and I told Katie to take her into the house. Paul and I walked down to the pond, and there, on the other side of the fence, we saw both mangled ducks about five feet apart in the grass. They had come to a violent end, murdered by the guard dog that preferred to kill ducks than protect our home.

I looked on sadly at the depressing culmination of the last couple of months of joy. Paul roughly grabbed Yuma's collar and dragged her back to the doghouse. She knew she was in trouble and her four legs locked, leaving a furrow in the gravel behind her. I watched helplessly as he yelled, spit spraying out of his mouth, screaming incoherent words at the cowering dog. It wasn't her fault—one of the workers must have let her off her chain.

But Paul wasn't finished; he planned to teach Yuma a lesson. I tried to reason with him, but then his rage turned on me.

"Get the fuck away from me Janine and go in the house!"

I made the kids some hot chocolate, reassuring them that the ducks had not suffered, Yuma had been driven by instinct and killed them quickly. I returned to the porch in time to witness Paul walking purposefully across the lawn, one of the dead ducks dangling from his clenched fist. In his other hand he carried a ball of twine. He then grappled with the petrified dog as he wrapped the duck around her neck with the twine.

He finally stood back, red faced and sweating.

"See how you like that!"

When he came in the house, I begged him to unwrap the twine from her neck.

"It can strangle her!" I cried.

"An old ranch hand told me that's how you stop a dog from ever killing again." Paul explained that the stench of the decomposing duck around Yuma's neck was a negative reinforcement tactic.

Over the next few days the odor emanating from the decomposing duck wafted constantly toward the house, affecting all of us. I begged him every day to let me take the duck off her neck. I was sure his psychological intention was lost on the poor dog.

Finally on day five he let me cut the rotting fowl from her neck.

* * *

A phone call from my mother a few days later was just what I needed. It was now a month since I had left treatment.

"Why don't you visit Pete?" she suggested.

My brother Pete was now living in Connecticut and working as a gardener.

"I don't know. I really don't feel like going out of town right now," I said, curling the telephone cord around my finger as I paced back and forth in the empty kitchen.

I was used to the routine of going to my meeting every morning and I knew she was relieved I was staying sober.

"I think it would be good for you. Just to go somewhere different and get away from everything. I know Pete would love to see you. He says he never hears from you."

Here came the guilt trip.

"You know he's really made quite a life for himself out there."

"He's a gardener, Mum."

"Yes, I know, but he's a very good one. I'm so proud of him."

"Yes, you're always telling me how proud you are of him," I mumbled.

"Pardon?"

I immediately regretted my passive aggressive comment.

"Nothing. Look, I think you're right. Maybe I will go and see him. I could use a change of scenery. I'm going to go discuss it with Paul. I'll speak to you later. Bye, Mum."

"Good bye, darling. Don't forget, you can find a meeting anywhere. I love you."

I cringed, not wanting to give her the response I knew she was expecting. Why was it so hard for me to tell her I loved her?

"Me, too," I said instead.

That evening I discussed my mother's idea with Paul. Surprisingly, he agreed and said he'd leave work early every day to pick the kids up from the bus stop and help them with homework.

* * *

A week later I was on a plane to Connecticut.

It was now over three months since I had checked into rehab. I felt proud of myself for passing the ninety-day marker. I knew that a lot of people didn't make it that far without a relapse.

On the plane I was seated next to a woman in a smart burgundy and brown coordinated business suit, her perfectly painted burgundy nails tapping on the fold down tray in front of her. I wondered who she was and where she was going. I contemplated what it would be like to have an important job, motivation to dress up, and an expectation to fulfill responsibilities. People must be counting on her.

While mulling these thoughts over, the airline stewardess approached and asked her what she would like to drink.

"Oh, I'll have a white wine please," the businesswoman replied.

The stewardess turned to me and smiled, "And for you?"

"I'd like the same please."

As she walked away, I was shocked by what had just happened. *Did I just ask for a glass of wine?*

I waited in anxious anticipation for the stewardess to return, knowing that I could tell her I had changed my mind. The businesswoman got her wine first, and I watched as she innocuously opened the bottle and poured the amber liquid into her glass. She raised the glass to her painted lips and drank with impunity, replacing it on the table with a sigh.

"Miss!" I turned and the stewardess was patiently trying to hand me a glass and miniature bottle of wine.

"Oh, sorry!" I reached out and took them from her.

As if pre-programmed, my hand unscrewed the cap and emptied the wine into the glass. I then guided the glass toward my mouth and raised it to my lips. Trance-like, I drank from the flute until I had drained its contents and then placed the empty glass back onto my tray.

Then, just as suddenly as I had gone into the trance, I was snapped back to reality.

I hurriedly left my seat and headed to the bathroom. I pushed the door closed behind me and locked it. In the cramped inconvenience of the bathroom, I bent over the toilet bowl and willed the wine to come up. I didn't have any trouble vomiting into the bowl, its acrid taste burning my throat and smell filling the small space. I rinsed my mouth with cold water. I looked at myself in the small mirror.

I didn't drink the wine. I got rid of it before it even touched my blood stream.

I repeated this over and over accepting the logic of my lie, but somewhere deep inside I felt there was going to be a price to pay for what I had just done.

Chapter Twenty-Five

The week with my brother was relaxing. I didn't drink again; instead I hung out with him and his friends and enjoyed his uncomplicated life. I realized while I was there, that perhaps I had never completely adapted to living in Southern California. I struggled making friends and missed Lindsey and Nina and the British camaraderie. Paul liked to remind me that I didn't need friends, as he had enough for both of us. I did love being at the ranch, where I could have animals and free space, but a lot of the time I was bored and lonely. With Pete and his friends, I now enjoyed the easy-going banter, the pool bars, and the low-key lifestyle that comes with minimal responsibility. There was no one parenting or micromanaging me. No one was trying to be in control of anyone else. They drank their beer and I had my Sprite. I wasn't tempted and the incident on the plane was almost forgotten.

I came home a few days later feeling rested and resolute. When I went back to meetings, I was determined to make more of an effort to make sober friends this time. I knew I had to build a strong sober community around me that I could feel a part of. I always had a hard time trusting women, but if I didn't at least try to do the things I was supposed to do, I knew I wouldn't be able to change my life. I appreciated the support and understanding that the members gave me. I felt it was the one place where I could be myself and not have to pretend I was okay. I could screw up and in return be met with unconditional love and support. Paul had written me a letter while I was in treatment saying that he couldn't understand why someone with my strong willpower couldn't use that same willpower to overcome drinking.

Where was my willpower when I lifted that wine glass to my lips?

I had stopped binging and purging since the accident. My weight had settled at 125 pounds. Someone in the meeting who had overcome an eating disorder suggested I not have a scale in the house. The last time I was weighed was at a doctor appointment. After the life-saving surgery, I suffered several intestinal obstructions due to scar tissue and had to be very careful to eat little but often. If the accident had cured my eating disorder, why couldn't it also cure my alcoholism?

By now I had come to understand and accept that I had an illness called alcoholism and that illness made me drink alcohol even when I didn't want to. No amount of willpower would ever fix that problem. It didn't matter how strong my willpower was in other areas. Paul could not grasp that concept. It was the same way he thought about the homeless.—why didn't they just get a job?

Through the stories of others, I learned a lot about myself. I realized I had had problems since I was a young child. I looked for negative attention. I stole because my needs were never met, I didn't feel loved or accepted, so I couldn't love myself. I lied when it served me better to tell the truth. And I would run rather than face my problems. Ultimately, I became addicted so I wouldn't have to feel anything at all.

When I started using drugs and drinking I turned into a person even I didn't recognize. I was alternately aggressive, emotional, uncaring, impulsive, and erratic. Each day I woke from the horrors of the day before. I hurt the ones I loved the most.

How could I have done this to my kids?

Finally, the day came when I realized that I had become my mother. I was doing to my children what she had done to hers: abandoning them for alcohol. I remembered the time Clive and I watched her through our living room window as she stumbled up the steps of a bus, the look of disgust on his face, and my shame for being her daughter.

For years I told myself that I wasn't as bad as she, but I knew this was no longer the truth.

When I was sober, reality was sometimes too sharp and painful to bear. Shame and guilt were always with me despite the meetings and friends I was making. I suffered frequent flashbacks of humiliating things I had done. Sometimes driving the freeway, I considered how easy it would be to end it all by colliding with the center divider at high speed. All I needed was to pull the steering wheel ever so slightly to the left. Everyone would think it was an accident. Sometimes I felt so close to making it happen, but always something pulled me back.

* * *

My attention turned to a handsome new man in my meeting. His long legs stretched in front of him; a cowboy hat rested at an angle on one knee. I loved the way his thick salt and pepper hair fell forward whenever he bowed his head. He wore light blue denim jeans and scuffed cowboy boots. I would covertly sneak glances at him from where I was sitting and imagined him smiling back at me.

One morning his blue eyes did catch mine and I quickly averted my gaze, feeling the heat rise up my neck to my face. I had been staring at what looked like a tribal tattoo wrapped around his left bicep. He was wearing short sleeves and I hadn't noticed it before.

My new secret was Marlboro Man and my giddy feelings for him. I was desperate for his attention. I wasn't obsessed with alcohol or my shame anymore; I had just become fixated with a less dangerous substitute.

I started hanging out with a small group who went for coffee and bagels after the morning meeting. One day Marlboro Man joined us and I found out more about him. His name was Greg and he had been sober for eight years. His father had been an actor and his mother was a beautiful socialite who had succumbed to alcoholism in her fifties. Greg was a musician and an artist. His handsome craggy face told of a life of rock and roll, drugs, and cigarettes. I was smitten.

He told me more about his mother. She had abandoned Greg and his brother for alcohol when they were adolescents. It had been years since Greg had seen her, and then one day he was in a store in

Marina Del Rey, when he recognized her in one of the aisles. She was disheveled and it was obvious she was homeless. She hardly resembled the mother he remembered, but he knew it was her. Greg told me he hid from her, not wanting her to see him. He left the store quickly and that was the last time he saw her. She died a few months later. I listened to him with tears in my eyes; I had never felt so connected to another person at such depth. He was sharing with me at such a gut level that I fell in love with him that day.

Back home Paul seemed unaware of my distance and preoccupation. It wasn't long before Greg and I started an affair. As I watched Paul through the windows of the big remodeled ranch house, I thought up excuses of how I could sneak away and be with Greg.

As usual Paul avoided the obvious problems in our relationship by working constantly, either at the tow yard, the car lot, or the ranch. On the weekends he immersed himself in all kinds of projects on the property. He was absorbed in whatever he was doing, bent over, his T-shirt and shorts covered in dirt and debris, maniacally digging a trench or fixing water pipes. He could easily pay contractors to do the work, but as he liked to say, he could save a buck and do it himself. Sam had become a tomboy and followed him around trying to help, carrying her miniature tool belt, bolts and washers in her pockets. Katie was usually in her bedroom. Her method of coping with her dysfunctional family was by isolating, unless she could be at a friend's house. She would watch television, read, or teach school to her dolls. I'm sure it wasn't comfortable for her to invite friends into the tension of our home.

After being sober for over six months, it was clear to me that I could no longer stay married to Paul. I tried to talk to him a few times before meeting Greg, hoping he would accept at least partial responsibility for what had happened to us, but he wouldn't hear it. He would get immediately angry and defensive. "Don't you try to make me the scapegoat!"

I was afraid of leaving, afraid that he would use the DUI and the time I spent in rehab against me. I was terrified that the judge would see what an unfit mother I was and award Paul full custody. I couldn't bear to lose the kids. My mother encouraged me to at least go and talk to an attorney.

My relationship with my mother was changing at this time, and although the roles were reversing to healthier ones, I was still struggling with years of built-up resentments toward her. I didn't need her to come to my rescue anymore. She had always been available for the kids, but now we were okay without her. Neither Paul nor Katie were calling her at all hours saying they needed her help. I hated when she told anyone who would listen about how she had to raise the children because I was such a disaster. I felt angry with her for finding it necessary to remind everyone, including myself about how incapable I had been as a mother. When I was drunk I was unable to function, but now I was sober and I wanted to take back my responsibilities. I was trying to make sense of everything that had happened the last few years, and I could feel myself displacing my self-loathing onto her. I was convinced that my alcoholism was because of my dysfunctional childhood, the fact that she and my father abandoned me as a child, how she sent me to boarding schools, allowed my stepfather to abuse me, kept me away from my real father, and forced me to live in hotel rooms with her drunk most of the time. Growing up the way I did gave me no coping skills to deal with life.

Our relationship had become so entangled, or maybe it always had been. I was looking for ways to break free now and I took offense at her influence on our lives. But what I hated most was that there were still times when I needed her. Now she was sitting next to me in the attorney's waiting room. I was terrified that Paul would do something crazy if he knew what I was planning. The attorney listened to me while my mother interjected with her perceptions of how I had been mistreated by my husband. He kindly leaned in toward me as if he were going to divulge a secret that he wished only to reveal to me.

"Janine," he said softly, "this is America. This isn't a country where, as a woman, you have no power. I can see how scared you are, but you need to know that you have rights."

He continued by telling me what it was that I needed to do. I would first have to leave the house, because it was obvious that Paul would never do that. I didn't care about the ranch anyway, I just wanted my freedom. I remembered when Paul told me about his ex-wife and how she had wanted the house in their divorce. He had gathered all his friends to divulge her drinking problem and destroy her character in court. I knew she had been degraded and left with nothing. I was afraid of the same thing happening to me.

* * *

One afternoon in mid-July 1996, the children were away at a two-week summer camp; and Paul and I were alone in the house. I mustered up the courage to confront the issue. After looking for him in all the usual places, I realized he must be in the bathroom. I tried to calm the butterflies in my stomach as I walked through the master bedroom and into our bathroom.

Paul had a peculiar ritual of doing business while sitting on the toilet; when the house was built, he specified a wall phone within arm's reach. Reprimands and commands were often executed from this throne. Whenever we couldn't find him, this is where we looked.

I took a deep breath, anticipating his reaction.

"Paul, I want a divorce." I was surprised I was so direct.

"You want *what?*" he looked up at me incredulously, setting the open newspaper down on his bare legs.

I focused on his feet, poking out from beneath crumpled pants.

"I can't continue in this marriage, I feel like I'm suppressed by a tyrant and I can't stand it anymore. I want a divorce."

"You can't *just decide* you want a divorce," he said. "Not after all I've done for you. It doesn't work that way, Janine."

I realized how ridiculous it was to be having a conversation about ending our marriage with my husband sitting on the toilet.

"I've already talked to an attorney and I'm planning to be out by the end of the week."

I turned and walked out of the bathroom.

* * *

With my meetings, new friends, and Greg, I could stay busy during the day and just go home to sleep. I sold the engagement ring I hated and diamond studs to a jeweler in order to pay a retainer to the attorney.

During my last few days at the ranch Paul tried to alternately plead with me to stay, or threaten me if I left. He told me that I wouldn't get anything out of him and therefore, I'd never be able to survive.

"Are you seeing someone else?"

His question caught me off guard.

"No, I'm not," I said, fearful that the slight hesitation would give me away.

* * *

I had been sleeping in Katie's room during the time she was at camp. I wasn't afraid that he'd hurt me physically, because he never had, it was just his verbal tirade, insults, and threats that would wear me down.

A kind old widower at the meeting had offered the kids and me his house for two weeks while he was out of the state visiting his family. I knew he was retired and spent a lot of his time doing service work. I was told by others that I could trust him.

I was getting anxious as moving day approached. I wanted some sort of guarantee that my life would get better if I left Paul, but I knew this time I had to put hope into the uncertainty of the future. I envied my friends who believed in God or a Higher Power. As an agnostic I could only trust the wisdom of the collective group, as anything else was too uncertain. I now had counsel from people who knew my triggers and helped me develop a plan with the best possible outcome for my continued recovery. Starting a new relationship in early recovery wasn't recommended by AA and I wasn't divorced yet, but there was no way I could give up Greg.

It had been arranged for a couple of guys from the meeting to bring a U-Haul truck up to the ranch so that I could take the things I really needed, like a bed, television, a chest of drawers, clothes, and the kids' stuff.

I picked the kids up from camp, telling them what was happening on the drive home.

"Where will we go?" Katie's voice trembled.

"We're going to stay at this really nice person's house for two weeks and we'll look for a place to rent. It's going to be so exciting!"

"Can I bring Doggy?" Sam asked.

"Of course you can," I said, smiling at her in the rearview mirror.

Doggy went everywhere with Sam. His floppy ears were now threadbare from rubbing against her cheeks when she was falling asleep. Her innocence made me want to cry.

"Soon after we get home Grandma is going to come and pick you guys up and take you back to her place," I reassured them. "I'll come and pick you up tomorrow. It'll be like an adventure."

I wondered if I was seriously crazy to go through with this. I was going to walk away from the only security and safety I knew. I failed to heed the warnings of old-timers not to make big changes in my first year.

As I packed up the last of my belongings into boxes, Paul followed me around reminding me that I'd never make it without him, I'd be sorry, and I'd soon be back with my tail between my legs.

I instructed Katie to take Sam back to her bedroom and help her pack up some toys and clothes.

"You can't leave me. Not after all the hell you've put me through!" Paul yelled after me.

The doorbell rang and he marched over to fling it open. My mother stood in the doorway in a peach floral sundress with a wicker handbag loosely swinging on her arm. She looked like Mary Poppins.

"What the fuck are you doing here?" he snapped at her.

I stared in disbelief as she pushed him aside as if he were a bothersome child. "Oh, do shut up you puffy little man."

Her contemptuousness made me giggle out loud. It was the same feeling I had when Lindsey had told Clive to shut up!

Oh sweet bliss, I was soon going to be free.

After the kids left with my mother, Paul decided to turn his frustration onto one of the guys loading the U-Haul. He strode over.

"Paul!" I shouted at his back. "Leave him alone, he didn't do anything."

"Get the fuck off my property. Now!"

The mover looked helplessly at me over Paul's shoulder.

Abruptly, Paul seemed to come to his senses, stopped in mid stride, turned, and stormed back toward the house.

I took the little Ford pick-up that he told me I could keep and followed the U-Haul down the driveway. When I got to the road I stopped and looked in my rearview mirror one last time. I couldn't see Paul anywhere and figured he must have gone inside the house.

"Goodbye to the past," I said softly to myself, as I turned onto the road.

Chapter Twenty-Six

Three weeks later the kids and I were renting a modest family-style home in a town close-by. As part of the divorce agreement I needed to find a house no further than twelve miles from the ranch. Sam was going to have to split her week between the two of us. I knew that Paul adored her. His relationship with Katie however was fraught with tension and conflict; he had always been so hard on her, not understanding that she was more sensitive than Sam. She just wanted him to love her. After all, he was the only father she had known since she was three.

I borrowed $2,000 from my uncle who lived in Palm Springs. Uncle Tom was my father's only sibling and had built himself a success story in the entertainment industry. He had left England for the States when he was still in his teens, and after working at Disney for twenty years, he started producing his own films and shows. I knew my father envied his younger brother because he made sarcastic remarks to me about him being their mother's favorite son. In later years Tom would pay for Vincent and Audrey to go on vacations with him and sent them money so they could pay their bills.

Despite Tom's wealth, I felt uneasy asking him for a loan. I had never asked anyone in my family for financial help. Combining this loan with the money I got for my jewelry, I had enough to pay the attorney's retainer and the two-month deposit I needed to move into the house I found. These were very grown-up things for me to be doing and it felt good.

* * *

Our new home was close to the shops and schools; the seclusion and isolation of the ranch was replaced by small town hustle and bustle. Katie was now fourteen and Sam was six. I knew they were enjoying freedom from the dysfunction caused by my drinking and Paul's obsessive need to control us all. The kids could now ride bikes to their friend's houses and invite them over to ours. They could feel secure that when they returned home from school in the afternoon, their mother would be the same as when they left that morning.

They could finally begin living like normal kids.

Nevertheless, I now lived with a different kind of fear: the constant dread of having no money. Although Paul was paying alimony and child support, I had nothing to fall back on and no savings. I obsessed that any moment he could get angry about something and withhold my next support check.

I enrolled Sam in elementary school and Katie began her sophomore year at a nearby high school. Paul picked Sam up from school two days a week and she spent alternate weekends with him. She got used to the schedule quicker than I did. He started reaching out to Katie too, taking her for dinner and shopping. I was happy he was making an effort to become closer to her.

I had wanted for so long to be liberated, but now I wasn't sure how to maintain my independence. I needed a decent paying job so I could pay my own bills, rent, and have a car in my name. Those were my long-term goals, but right now I just needed to get *a job*. The last time I had worked was at the Metropole Hotel in Brighton. That was twenty years ago!

A couple of women I knew suggested I look into cleaning houses. They said I could make good money and at least I'd be doing something instead of just worrying. Through an ad I posted in the local paper I was soon able to secure four houses that I would be cleaning every week. I had acquired my first income.

I swallowed my pride and made my weekly source of cash with my bucket of cleaning supplies. As I scrubbed the grimy bathtubs and toilets, I reminded myself that I was doing whatever necessary to make it on my own. This was the first time since I was sixteen that I didn't have a man to depend on. I knew I had to do something with my life, I just didn't know what yet. I was scared, but excited simultaneously.

Despite having an attorney, things did not turn out the way I hoped they would. Paul was not going to let go of any portion of his wealth without a fight. I feared him keeping me in court for the next few years with the sole purpose of making sure that I didn't get one penny more than he thought I deserved.

I toyed with the idea of threatening to expose our wild nights of drugs and alcohol to his family, letting them know he was the one that introduced me to cocaine. But then I knew I couldn't use blackmail to get what I felt I deserved, not when I was trying to stay sober and live an honest life. This meant taking advice from my sponsor and practicing the ethics of the program. Ultimately, I knew I had to do what was right.

As our divorce progressed, I found out that there was no community property, even though we had been married eleven years and had a child; everything still belonged to Paul. I knew his pride had been severely bruised by my leaving. He had stuck with me through the hospitals, accidents, and institutions. Now, I was finally sober and he was not going to be able to benefit from the new and improved me. When I felt guilty, I reminded myself that he was unable to admit that he had constantly sabotaged my sobriety when we were together: The times I would come home from a meeting and he had been drinking or smoking pot. The cocaine I found in his bag. The New Year's Eve when we were in a café toasting each other with cappuccinos and he said, "I guess this is as good as it's ever going to get." How he made fun of my sober friends or chastised me for wanting to call my sponsor when I was upset or scared.

"We are trying to figure out your husband's paper trail and where it leads us," the forensic accountant said as he continued the laborious discovery process through endless boxes of paperwork. But the paper trail lead nowhere, it was just frustrating everyone and increasing the hourly charges for disclosure. I finally settled for a cash sum to put a down payment on a house and get a decent car. I decided not to fight for more.

The kids liked the neighborhood and didn't want to move again, so I bought a nice little house on the street where we were renting. It was perfect for the three of us. This was the first time in my life I was about to own my own home. I was not going to hold on to resentment; I didn't want to be the ex-wife holding onto a lifetime of bitterness.

Now I was able to date Greg openly. He had given me the time I needed to get through the divorce and the children settled into their new schools and home. I was happy in a relationship for the first time. I was free of my eating disorder, sober, and enjoying life. We spent time together when I wasn't working or needing to do something with one of the kids. He still received royalties which paid his bills and gave him the freedom to paint and play music for fun. He was often immersed on a wood carving project or painting, and when he wasn't we would go hiking, to a meeting, or visit one of his artist friends. Every now and again he was asked to play music at a café or club and I would go along and watch. One time he even wrote a song for me which I felt was the ultimate display of romance. He had a son and daughter in their teens who lived in New York with their mother. They would periodically visit during school holidays and stay a few weeks. Even the kids got along well.

Although my mother claimed she was happy I was no longer with Paul, I knew she had been negatively impacted by the divorce, losing her source of income and her home.

"Don't you worry about me," she reassured me. "Your old mother always finds a way to make ends meet."

Time passed and I was blissfully unaware that Greg suffered from untreated bi-polar disorder. I had never known anyone with a mood disorder, so I wasn't able to identify the subtle signs. I was in denial that the charming hypo-manic individual I had fallen in love with also had a seriously dark side. In the year we had been together he had not suffered a depressive event.

On the anniversary of our first year I noticed his attitude start to change, and for the first time he was mean and purposely hurtful to me. He was always sarcastic and cynical, but now there was something more sinister to his comments. He slowly started to withdraw, criticizing and fault-finding everyone around him. He would leave our bed in the middle of the night and smoke cigarettes in front of the embers of the living room fireplace, mulling over the insignificance of human life. He didn't want to socialize anymore and his handsome face no longer lit up when he saw me. I tried to talk to him and remind him of all the good he had in his life, such as his sobriety, his kids, and us. But it was exhausting; everything I offered as a solution, he rejected, until I felt as hopeless as he.

As Greg distanced himself from me, I spent more and more time with Jim from the local feed store. Jim had been our third wheel for as long as Greg and I had known each other. Greg and I jokingly called him "Feed Store Jim," as he always had random sprigs of hay in his hair from living at the feed store. Poor Jim was still relapsing and often needed saving. One late evening he called me and told me he was drunk and needed help. I hadn't heard from Greg in two weeks and he hadn't been answering my messages.

"Okay," I said. "I'll come and get you."

Twenty minutes later I pulled up the driveway of the feed store; I scanned the darkness, silhouettes of stacked bales of hay creating an eerie atmosphere. Then I spotted him sitting on the dirt leaning back against one of the bales. He must have heard my car and tried to pull himself up, but failed, plopping back down like a baby learning how to walk. I parked the car and walked over to him. I could smell booze as I reached down to help him up.

"I love youuu," he slurred into my neck.

"I love you too, Jim."

I somehow managed to support him as he stumbled to the car and collapsed into the passenger seat. I had already prepared the couch as a bed for him. I left him there and went to bed myself.

The next morning, we sat at the breakfast bar laughing at his story from the night before. He suddenly stopped and looked at me.

"Janine, I need to tell you something."

I looked at him already knowing what he was going to say.

"I've fallen in love with you."

He leaned forward and I let him kiss me.

What was I doing?

I told him about Greg and how it was getting harder and harder to deal with his negativity.

"He just wants to be alone all the time and he's not willing to see a doctor or therapist," I said sadly.

"I know what you mean," Jim said looking down into his coffee and nodding his head reflectively. "He's been a real asshole to me lately."

"I can help you with this house," he suddenly said, excitedly looking around. "You need all kinds of things done. I'm very handy and I promise from this day forward I'll stay sober."

And that's how it started. I never bothered to tell Greg I was dating Jim, as I felt he had already abandoned our relationship. Then I heard through the AA grapevine that Greg grew suspicious about us when he saw Jim's truck outside my house one night. Apparently, after nine years of sobriety, he had taken a bottle of Jack Daniels and a shotgun and driven himself to some remote area to end his life. I'm sure that his friends must have intervened because I saw him at a meeting a couple of weeks later. He gave me a nasty look and then strode over to Jim who was sitting a few seats away and kicked his foot. I couldn't hear what Jim said, but I saw him get up and push Greg. The next thing I knew a group of guys had gathered around the two of them. A commotion started and then Greg picked up one of the metal folding chairs, yelled something inaudible, and threw it at Jim before storming out of the room.

I had entertained a fantasy of two men fighting over me, but two alcoholics in a meeting was more of a reflection of the drama that was once again developing in my life.

Jim was not as sober as he claimed. His stepfather accidently let it slip that a pain management doctor was treating him for a back injury. Jim had told me he once had a major problem with pills, but he also told me that he quit a long time ago. The truth was confirmed early one morning when I went out to his truck while he was still in the house sleeping. Heart pounding, I looked through the glove compartment and the center console until I found a bottle of prescription pills.

I checked the label, *Percocet*. I had heard that Percocet was a lot stronger than the Vicodin I had been taking after my accident. I tapped three of the round white pills into the palm of my hand, leaving enough in the bottle that he wouldn't notice. While crossing the street, I hesitated, I could still turn around and put them back, but within seconds I had rationalized that I had been hiding a slip with the glass of wine I drank on the plane a year and a half ago. No one had known about that secret, so no one needed to know about this one either.

I had set myself up that day on the plane. I thought about the AA saying "you are only as sick as your secrets" and realized I had kept my secret a long time now. The burden of my secret was my sickness. I thought I was recovered, but it was all a delusion. I was still hiding the "me" I wanted no one to see. My recovery had really been for everyone else.

It wasn't long before Jim found out that I was into his stash. Taking three or four had turned into a handful.

"Why didn't you just ask me? I would have given you some if I had known you were in pain."

How could I tell him I wanted them all?

It didn't take long for us both to begin drinking "harmless" amounts of beer with the pills. My need to use more pills had been triggered and I secretly secured my own supply from an understanding doctor. I had developed plantar fasciitis in both feet from years of jogging on cement sidewalks. This was the diagnosis I presented, being sure to tell the doctor that over-the-counter medication did not work. It didn't take long to manipulate him into prescribing me narcotics.

My tolerance quickly increased and in a short time I was hooked once again.

My mother also gave me some of her pills if I whined enough about my physical aches and pains. She had been taking them for years for her fibromyalgia and I knew she always kept some in her bag. I would track her handbag whenever she came to the house to visit. All the addict behaviors had returned. I knew that if she went upstairs to use the bathroom she wouldn't take her heavy bag with her. She'd leave it on a chair in the kitchen. I figured I had about four minutes to get into the bag, unzip the little side compartment, grab the pill bottle and empty some of its contents into my pocket before I heard her flush the toilet.

I hated who I had become again. I didn't even have time to try to figure out what had gone wrong, or what had happened to the happy sober girl who was starting her life over? My days were now dictated by securing pills. I didn't even know how I was going to get sober again. I had stopped going to meetings because I was too ashamed and embarrassed. The kids didn't seem to suspect, or at least I didn't think so. They were busy with school and their friends. I shuddered at the thought of Paul finding out.

I did my best to justify and rationalize the lengths I would go to get my fix, rationalizing that my mother knew I was taking her pills but hadn't confronted me in person made it okay to keep stealing from her. She never asked me how I was managing to get into her apartment. She didn't know that I would leave the window screen loose for easy access. Thank God her apartment was on the ground floor. She was now on disability and, with the help of the system, acquired a ground-floor apartment with a little garden for an extremely low subsidized rent she could pay with her disability and social security. I helped by giving her money whenever I was able. Giving her money eased my guilt.

I could pull myself together for a couple of weeks at a time, but the physical and mental torture would be too much—and then once again, I'd fall back into the same old trap. Sometimes I did wonder if I was lying to myself about the kids being unaware.

One time Sam had found an empty bottle of beer I had hidden in my bedside cabinet. The cabinet latch must have been weak and unbeknownst to me the door swung open while she was jumping on my bed.

"What's this?" She inquired as she climbed down off the side of the bed and held the bottle in front of her for me to inspect.

"Oh, that's non-alcoholic beer." The lie escaped my lips.

Then I watched in horror as she turned the label around to face her and began to read.

"Doesn't say its non-alcoholic," she said, looking back at me.

I felt like I was the child being busted by the parent. How I hated myself for what I was doing to her. I felt like such a wretched mother, hiding from her and Katie the true nature of who I really was and what I was doing. They had been my biggest supporters when I got sober. I couldn't bear for them to know I had relapsed.

For the first time I prayed to God to help me.

Chapter Twenty-Seven

I dropped down to cleaning two houses a week when I secured a job at a pet store. The owner was an overweight, balding man in his mid-fifties named Bernie. I had shopped in his store when I was married to Paul. From comments he made, I believed Bernie was probably a misogynist. Yet the store was conveniently close to my home and carried the supplies I needed for the menagerie I had gradually accumulated. In addition to my little Scottish terrier, I had kept from the ranch, we now had a Chihuahua, a Dalmatian, and two kittens from the local shelter. Sam had become obsessed with snakes and lizards and was collecting them as other little girls collected Barbie dolls. I figured at least I could buy pet food at cost if I worked at the store. I just needed to make sure I kept my boundaries with Bernie. I had to start somewhere.

"I can only pay you seven-fifty an hour. You have to be here at eight-thirty in the morning until we close at six." He told me when I asked if he had any part-time work available.

"Okay," I responded nervously. "When do I start?"

"You can start tomorrow."

"I'm so happy you got a job at the pet shop," Sam said later that day. "Now you can get me stuff for my lizards!"

I had never in my life worked a cash register and was feeling really nervous about this next phase of independence. I would get to work early in the morning, open up the blinds and play with the frenzied puppies. Living in a plexiglass container and having no human contact during the night, the pups were beside themselves to see the first visitor of the day. The reptiles' nightlights had to be replaced with the warmer day ones and they all needed food and water. I was also in charge of the cricket buckets.

There were three different sizes of crickets: small, medium, and large. The crickets lived amongst pieces of broken up cardboard egg cartons and were used to feed lizards and turtles. I had to gingerly reach into the container, pick up a section harboring dozens of the little critters hanging on for dear life, then shake them gently into a baggie while simultaneously attempting a head count as they fell into the bag which carried them to their final destination. A few sometimes managed to escape, either running up the inside of my sleeve or scurrying across the floor to freedom under a shelf unit.

I felt sad for the breeding mother mice; after giving birth to a heap of little squirming pink bodies, they helplessly watched their children disappear one by one. I concluded that in the event of reincarnation, a person would have to have done something really bad during their life to come back as one of these baby mice or "pinkies." Pinkies were sold solely as food for the larger reptiles and snakes.

I reached into the warm, squirming pile of little translucent bodies and carefully extracted one. I squeezed my eyes shut as I dropped it into the terrarium. The lizard, mouth agape, eagerly anticipated its breakfast. Because I felt sorry for the mice and their fate, I was always mindful to spend extra time with them. I kept their cages nice and clean and brought them treats from home. I wondered if they knew that their short lives were without hope. I wondered if I had the hope of ever getting sober again.

Bernie often reminded me to make sure that the lizards didn't escape. "Keep the terrarium doors closed at all times, unless you want to pay to replace one of the reptiles."

On the hourly wage I was making it would probably take me months to pay off the cost of a bearded dragon.

Sometimes Bernie barricaded me behind the cash register when we didn't have customers. Placing both hands on either side of the counter, he blocked my only exit. I backed up as far as I could until I felt my back press up against the cash register.

My only escape would be to climb over the counter, which I felt was a little dramatic, so instead I looked down at my shoes. He saw this as his opportunity to share sexually inappropriate or bigoted jokes with me.

"Hey, did you hear what the prostitute said to the Arab?"

"No Bernie, I didn't and I don't want to!"

I turned away from him, but I could still feel his beady eyes boring into my back.

How I hated him. I hated that I had to work for such a creep.

Just then a surgically enhanced woman came into the store looking for diet food for her Chihuahua. Bernie instantly turned on the charm, getting her to buy his most expensive product. I quickly moved into a safe zone. As she was leaving the store he turned his attention back to me.

"Boy, did ya see the rack on that one?"

I wondered if he could see himself as I saw him, stomach straining at the buttons of his shirt which was stained from today's lunch, pasty white face that would sweat profusely at the smallest amount of exertion, little eyes set back into pockets of fat, and wispy hairs that he attempted to comb over his shiny bald spot.

If I bought anything for one of the dogs or Sam's lizards, he charged me the regular price, only subtracting the tax. With prices three times that of any other store, this was hardly a good deal for me.

My solution was to do my shopping before Bernie got to the store. I had a routine about once a month of pulling my car up to the back door and opening the trunk. Within five minutes I had enough pig ears, chew bones, and lizard vitamins to last a couple of weeks.

Bernie was sporadic in doing inventories and I just hoped I would never get caught. I felt I deserved the perks for putting up with his behavior and being paid such a crappy wage. My honest living had gone out the window with my sobriety.

He'd also make me lie for him. Pitbull-mix puppies would be sold as purebred lab mixes.

"Are you sure this is a Lab?" the young woman asked holding the puppy up for inspection.

"Yes, it is," I assured her. "They are Labrador and retriever mix, only six hundred dollars."

One morning as I went about my daily routine, I noticed one of the terrarium doors was partially open. My heart skipped a beat as I realized the lizard could have escaped at any time during the night. I started looking around the store, under cabinets and between the cans of dog food on the shelf.

Where the hell was it?

I had to find the escapee before Bernie came in.

Just then I heard the key turn in the lock and the door to the pet store swung open.

"Hey Janine! Everything okay?"

I kept my back to him.

"Yes, everything is fine," I said, trying to sound calm.

I closed the glass door of the terrarium and prayed that he wouldn't come to the back of the store. As the morning went on I was continually scanning corners, shelves and under cabinets for the renegade lizard.

Around the middle of the day, Bernie was waiting on an entitled housewife who was complaining that her Pomeranian had earwax. Out of the corner of my eye I saw something slink under the fridge where we kept the frozen dog food.

I got on my hands and knees and reached under the fridge as far as I could without attracting attention to myself. The lizard tried to escape by darting past my hand. I grabbed his long, scaly tail and was horrified when he dropped the part I was holding in my clenched fist. I pulled myself back out from under the fridge, shoving the writhing four-inch tail in my sweatshirt pocket.

I could still hear Bernie explaining different brands of eardrops to the customer at the front of the store. The tail wriggled in my pocket as I desperately searched for the rest of the lizard. I saw it scurry back toward the shelves. I threw myself in its path and grabbed it with both hands.

Gotcha!

I hurriedly placed the struggling reptile back into the empty terrarium, throwing his tail in with him. I prayed if Bernie noticed, he'd think the lizard caught its tail on something in the cage during the night.

* * *

Katie had her first serious boyfriend around this time. I didn't know how to talk to her and felt embarrassed that I was in a relationship with a chronic relapser like Jim. I didn't think she knew about the pills, but she would see Jim and I drinking together, and I knew it scared her. Sam was lost in her own little world of reptiles and magical thinking.

What if Katie tells Paul I'm drinking again? What if he cuts me off? What if he takes the kids?

My fears and obsessive thinking kept me hooked in the cycle of my addiction as I tried to deal with all the "what if's" in my life. As I struggled to maintain control of the pills, alcohol, my job, and being a single mother, deep inside I felt it was only a matter of time before everything would come crashing down around me again.

But at the moment I was still functioning.

I avoided talking to Paul if I could. If I came home and saw the red light flashing on the answering machine, I'd have to take a drink or a pill before I could hear what he had to say. My heart felt like it would beat out of my chest when I pushed the button and heard the sound of his voice.

"Janine, it's Paul. You need to call me."

What I needed was a couple more beers and three pills before I could do that.

It was usually something about Sam. He would remind me of what he felt my responsibilities were. I felt like a child as I was held hostage by his diatribe. It wasn't fair; I knew he was dating questionable girls. Sam had come back from a weekend with her father to inform me that his new girlfriend was a "special" dancer.

"What do you mean by special?" I asked her.

"She wears really weird outfits," Sam said giggling. "She dressed me up in one of them and taught me some moves."

Upset, I went outside and complained to Jim who was busy skimming the pool.

"It's not fair. He gets to do whatever he wants and I'm constantly the one in trouble."

"Don't worry," Jim said, grinning at me. "Maybe it's time for a trip to Mexico!"

Jim loved taking trips down to Mexico. His favorite spot was Rosarito where he used a local family-run pharmacy to buy sheets of pain pills. He paid the pharmacist a small fee to consult with a doctor sitting in a back room of the store. Jim told me the doctor was probably a family member, like an uncle, who had an online degree. I had gone on these trips with him a couple of times. On those occasions, we'd hang out in the town like normal tourists, looking through the stores and buying furniture for the house. We drove back across the border, the pills conveniently popped into prescription bottles we had brought with us, and the furniture packed up in the back of his pickup truck.

This time we took Katie, her boyfriend, and Sam along with us. We decided to stay in a hotel overlooking the beach with an infinity pool. It felt like a real family vacation. The kids were excited about an overnight trip to Mexico.

The first afternoon at the hotel Jim went out to run a couple of errands. He came back a few hours later with newly filled prescription bottles and his arms loaded with grocery bags. He was grinning from ear to ear like a little boy who had just won a trophy. He set the bags down on the coffee table in front of me.

"What the hell are all these?" I said, rifling through the grocery bags that were filled with cardboard tubes and individually wrapped packages with cartoon bombs on them.

"Fireworks, baby."

"And how old are you?" I asked, looking up as the goofy smile on his face slowly subsided.

"Aww c'mon! We can take them down to the beach tonight and set them off. It'll be so much fun!"

Later that evening we all piled into his truck and headed down to a deserted beach. Jim excitedly pulled the fireworks out of the back of his truck while Katie, her boyfriend, and I looked on nervously. Sam was jumping up and down on the sand. "Light the fireworks! Light the fireworks!"

The tide was out and the waning moon reflected a dim light off of the ocean's dark surface. There was no one around. Jim rolled up his pant legs and waded out into the shallow water with a couple of Roman candles tucked under one arm. When he was satisfied with the depth, he stuck the remaining candles in his back pocket and turned to look at us.

Grinning and arching his eyebrows he yelled, "Check this out!"

He lit the end of one of the candles and we watched as intermittent rockets blazed out of the other end, briefly lighting up the night sky before making their slow descent into the waters below. As the last one fizzled out he turned to face us.

"Yes!" he shouted, punching his fists into the air. "That was awesome!"

His head appeared to be glowing, and for a minute I was confused until I heard Katie shout from behind me, "Jim! Your hair is on fire!"

He began walking toward us unaware that the top of his head was ablaze, small flames licking at his unruly curls.

"YOUR HAIR IS ON FIRE!" Katie yelled again.

"JIM!" we all chimed in, "YOUR HAIR'S ON FIRE!"

For a moment he looked puzzled and then, realizing what was happening, he ran back into the water, bent down, and frantically dunked his head into the cold ocean water. We all collapsed onto the sand, laughing uncontrollably.

Chapter Twenty-Eight

Inevitably it wasn't long before cocaine came back into my life. People in the meetings had warned about relapses getting progressively worse. So many warnings I failed to heed. Always thinking they didn't apply to me. It had been six years since I last used, but my midbrain knew neither time nor reason.

One night I suspected Jim was on something stronger than pills as I watched him staring intently at the television and grinding his jaw.

"Have you taken anything?" I asked, the last word catching in my throat.

"No!" He angrily turned and looked at me. "Why would you ask?"

"I don't know. You're so tense and weird."

"So, I guess that means I'm on drugs right?

He got up from the couch and angrily walked out of the room.

We did not speak for the rest of the night. I knew his primary addiction had been to speed. I had never used it, but I knew it was a stimulant like cocaine, and I knew coke made you super focused and grind your teeth.

I took Sam to school the next morning. As I walked back into the kitchen, Jim was standing at the counter, nursing a cup of coffee.

"I have a confession to make," he said in a small voice. "I did get some speed. I saw one of my old friends yesterday. I'm sorry I lied, I was scared you'd be mad with me."

As upset as I was, the next day I asked if he could get me coke. I was already on a journey of self-destruction with pills and alcohol. All my natural instincts were compromised by the obsession to use harder drugs. The dismal costs from ending up in jail to losing my kids were pushed aside for a temporary rush. A rush for which I was willing to trade my life.

Now Jim would get speed for himself, cocaine for me, and pills for both of us. I was functioning pretty much at a base level during the day, four days a week at the pet shop and two days a week cleaning houses. Thankfully Katie was self-sufficient and Sam spent half the week with Paul. I had to do my best to hide my lack of sleep and declining cognition while working at the shop, however when doing my cleaning job I used drugs to help me get through the monotonous back-breaking work.

Didn't all cleaning ladies do drugs?

One particular Friday I was cleaning a house belonging to a family who lived in a luxury gated community in Topanga Canyon. I cleaned this house every week and usually the wife was home hovering around me. She made me feel uncomfortable, talking to me in a condescending manner, and pointing out what I needed to do. When her children were home they threw their candy wrappers on the floor right in front of me, so they could giggle as I bent down to pick them up. This week the woman had left me the code to the gate as the family was going to be out of town until Sunday night.

Fortified with a fair amount of the cocaine I had brought with me, I let myself into the house and got down to the business of cleaning. Driven by the endurance and strength of ten people, I maniacally pulled out beds, sofas, and armoires. I was tireless, and the hours passed rapidly as I cleaned and rearranged. Until I realized I had run out of drugs. All of a sudden I felt myself crashing, the energy draining from me as if I were a raft with a puncture. My brain was shutting down and there was nothing I could do to re-boot.

I made a call. "I need more Jim. I've run out and the house is upside-down."

A couple of hours later, during which time I paced back and forth, he called me back and told me there was no way he could get it tonight.

"Come home and we'll figure out something tomorrow."

So I left the house looking like it had been ransacked by burglars.

The next day was Saturday and we were still not able to score. I was on the verge of panic all day. The family was due back soon and I had to straighten the house before they returned. I was relieved that Sam was with Paul and Katie was with her boyfriend, as I could no longer hide the symptoms of withdrawal.

At the eleventh hour, Jim called me from the feed store. "Got it!"

I sighed with relief. I felt my body and brain returning to a state of homeostasis even though I hadn't as yet ingested any drug. Just knowing it was coming made some of the symptoms of the withdrawal sickness dissipate.

"I'll come by and pick you up in a few minutes."

We went to some guy's house who worked with Jim at the feed store; I think he was one of the drivers who delivered hay. I watched from the truck as they did the deal in the dim light of the man's doorstep. My stomach churned. I hadn't eaten or slept in over forty-eight hours, my mind was racing, and I was experiencing really uncomfortable involuntary muscle twitches.

After what seemed like an hour Jim got back in the truck and handed me a small baggy. I used the cap of a pen and inhaled a little of the white chemical powder. Immediately I could feel the neurons in my brain fire in sequence, energy once again running through my veins.

We got to the gated community only to realize that I had left the piece of paper with the gate code in my car.

"I don't care, I'll find a way in," I told Jim. "Just be back here in four hours to pick me up."

I watched his taillights disappear down the dark canyon road. With determination over-riding feelings of total terror, I set off into the hillside next to the homes. It was a pitch-black night with very little moonlight, and I was fighting to see my way around the outside of the tall fence. It was a struggle to stay upright on the steep shrub and brush-choked incline. I slowly made my way around the fence, trying to gauge where their house was. I was slipping and scratching my bare arms and hands on the prickly growth as I grabbed branches and whatever I could to maintain balance. The night sounds were scaring me and I wondered if there were coyotes or rattlesnakes anywhere close by.

I finally recognized the green striped awning on the rear deck of the house. With all the strength I could muster, I pulled myself up the steep slope and grabbed hold of the railings. Inch by inch I climbed the seven-foot fence, blindly stabbing for footholds, until I was finally able to drop down to the other side. I winced as I landed on the soft grass. At any moment I expected to be illuminated by a spot light and given the amplified command to "stop" through a police bullhorn.

What would I tell them? That I was breaking into this house because I needed to finish cleaning it before the family returned home?

Luck was on my side however, and it seemed I had not been observed by anyone. The back door was unlocked, and in a few seconds I was in the house. I finished cleaning up and putting everything back in less than four hours. As I walked to the main entrance, I saw Jim's truck parked across the road. He revved the engine, swung around and pulled up alongside me. I let myself out through the pedestrian gate.

"Did you finish?" he asked as I opened the passenger door and pulled my dirty, battered body into the truck.

"Mission accomplished," I replied as he handed me a cold beer.

* * *

The friends I had made during the year I was sober with Greg were now gone. I felt alone and rejected, but the truth was that I had turned my back on everyone to return to a life of self-destruction. I felt a deep sadness for all that I had lost and wondered how I could ever get it back. It seemed so impossible now.

After dropping Sam off at school one day I took a detour and drove past my old meeting. It had just ended, and I saw the member's congregating outside, small groups having meaningful conversations. I recognized certain people and yearned to reach out and ask them for help. I could just pull into the parking lot and get out of the car and walk up to someone. But instead I drove home.

I was going to need something or somebody to stop me before I died. I was putting my life at risk engaging in more and more dangerous behaviors, such as going to Mexico by myself to get pills, or the time I discharged a shotgun when I had been drinking. Katie and Sam were at school and Jim was at work. I hadn't gone to work because I had overindulged the day before and was suffering from a debilitating hangover. I took a couple of shots of vodka from my hiding place under the sink—I was now even concealing how much I was drinking from Jim. I just needed enough to stop the strong electrical currents and tremors from coursing through my body in the mornings.

As the alcohol dulled my senses again, I pulled out an old French cookery book from the bookshelf in the kitchen. It was one of the few belongings I had brought with me from England. I nostalgically ran my hand over the picture of the quaint French village on the cover. My eyes filled with tears as I read the *Recipes from Provence*. I flashed back to the happy times in Le Lavandou when I was a young child, climbing on the rocks at Les Balaines and looking for crabs in the tide pools. That was before everything changed at the age of twelve. I sat at the kitchen counter leafing through the pages, my vision blurred by tears. I stopped at a picture of a wild rabbit casserole, and remembered the 12-gauge shotgun in the garage I had brought from the ranch.

I pulled the heavy cold metal gun down from the shelf and searched on the shelf until I found a half empty box of buckshot cartridges. When Paul bought me the gun, he had wanted me to practice using it to get familiar with the powerful kick-back. I had a perfect opportunity one day at the ranch when I saw a huge rattlesnake on the lawn. I grabbed the dogs and put them in the house. I loaded the gun, just as I had been shown, raised it to my shoulder, aimed, and was knocked back by the unexpected recoil. The pain in my shoulder was soon forgotten when I looked up to see the obliterated snake on the lawn. As I walked up to what was left of the reptile, I realized that one of Paul's vehicles was parked in the driveway about twenty feet beyond the snake. The entire side panel of the truck was peppered in buckshot.

After taking it into work the next day, he was teased and tormented by his employees. "Hey Paul, did your wife try to kill you?"

They all thought it was hysterical. It was common knowledge amongst the employees at the tow yard that the owner's son's wife had a drinking problem.

Now, back in the kitchen with the shotgun loaded and deep in my alcohol fog, I decided it was time to hunt some of the rabbits that overpopulated the hillside behind the house and cook one for dinner. Going through the gate at the end of the back yard, I started to make my way down the steep dirt trail of the hillside, which was a challenge in my Uggs. All of a sudden the shotgun discharged. The unexpected boom threw me on my back. I lay there, confused for a moment before I realized the safety must have been off. As the effects of the alcohol diminished, pain seared through my brain. I looked down, expecting to see one of my legs missing. Instead, the side of one of my Uggs was sprayed with pellet holes.

I struggled to my knees and limped back to the house using the rifle for support. Once home, I painfully removed my boot and peeled off the bloody sock, wincing as I assessed the damage. Now completely shocked back into a sober state of mind, I was afraid that one of the neighbors had called the police.

Crazy woman in pajamas and Uggs seen shooting at rabbits on residential hillside.

I was afraid to go to the ER and have to explain a shotgun wound, so I carefully removed what remained of the little lead balls from the side of my foot with a pair of tweezers. I was lucky that the main blast missed my foot and the lead balls had not gone too deep. Wincing from the sting, I flushed the area with hydrogen peroxide several times, before wrapping my foot with gauze.

"What the hell happened to you?" Jim asked when he came over after work.

"Oh," I said looking down at my bandaged foot, "I was going down the hill in my flip flops and I slipped. I got gravel in it. It's no big deal."

* * *

My inevitable intervention finally came in the form of the police after a night of clubbing and after-hours joints. Jim and I had both been drinking copious amounts that night. Vodka and tequila had now replaced the harmless beers. Jim had recently consumed a handful of his Mexican Percodan and I was high on cocaine. We had already started to party at home and decided to go out dancing and have some fun. By the time we were able to focus enough to get out of the house it was after midnight. I hid my little baggie of coke in my make-up bag and Jim stashed his pills in the console of his truck.

We drove into the city and stopped at one of the clubs on the Hollywood strip. The place was packed and music blared from speakers surrounding the dance floor. Pushing our way through the crowd, we ordered a couple of drinks from the bar and then hit the dance floor. Jim wasn't much of a dancer so after a few songs and some minimal hip movement, he wound up back at the bar ordering more drinks as I danced the night away.

On a trip to the bathroom I sat on the toilet and rummaged through my purse until I found my make-up bag. I emptied the remainder of the white powder onto the mirror of my compact. I was putting my make-up bag back into my purse when one of my tampons tumbled out and rolled onto the floor. It came to a stop next to my boot heel and as I reached down to pick it up, I was struck by an ingenious idea. The club was equipped with a spectacular lighting system; blue, red, and white lights strobed to the beat of the music and illuminated the couples on the dance floor.

Unwrapping the applicator-free tampon, I unraveled the string and let the bullet shaped cotton dangle from my pinched fingertips. Now I just needed one more. Setting the opened tampon on my lap, I rifled through my purse until I found another and unwrapped that one as well. Using the strings, I attached each tampon to the laces of my ankle boots. Kicking my legs out in front of me, I watched the tampons sway back and forth. I was ready to dance.

I left the bathroom and made my way back out onto the dance floor. Fueled by the music and high on coke I found an empty spot on the floor and watched in a hypnotic trance as the glowing tampons spun around like pinwheels while I turned and stepped in rhythm to the beat.

Sweating and out of breath, I found Jim back at the bar and we began to argue. He accused me of flirting with other men on the dance floor. It was around three in the morning when I stormed out of the club and started staggering down the street. I had now run out of cocaine.

With nothing left but an empty plastic bag, I suddenly realized what a bad idea all of this had been.

"Janine, where are you going? You can't just walk off. Come back!" Jim shouted from behind me.

I was dressed only in a long T-shirt and the tampons now marched in an angry beat to the heels of my ankle boots. I knew I looked ridiculous, but I didn't care. A girl in the club bathroom had said she wanted a pair of pants just like mine. Without a second thought, I pulled them off and drunkenly handed them to her as she stared at me in shocked disbelief.

I continued walking down the street wearing only my shirt and heard the heavy rumble of Jim's engine as his truck pulled up alongside me.

"Janine, get in the car, God damn it! You're gonna freeze out here without any pants on!"

I looked at his stupid, exasperated face and realized I was enjoying tormenting him. He kept shouting for me to get into the truck, until I finally resigned and climbed into the passenger seat. We continued to argue on the drive home. I was sick of his possessiveness and jealousy and told him so. My resentments came spewing out as I unleashed onto him all the anger and disgust I felt for myself. As we veered off the highway onto the canyon road, he pulled into a gas station to get some cigarettes. As I sat in the car feeling the intense depressing crash from the mix of drugs and alcohol coming on, I noticed a police car in the shadows of the parking lot.

I had a crazy idea that maybe I could get Jim out of my life if he were arrested. I knew he had a slew of DUIs on his record from various states. In fact, he was currently driving on a suspended license. I pulled a crumpled piece of paper out of my purse and with some bright red lipstick wrote the words "Help me."

They would think he was holding me hostage. I was going to get him back for being such an asshole. In my sick mind I blamed him for my relapse. As we pulled out of the gas station, I dropped the paper nonchalantly out of the open window.

A minute later, the lights of the police car illuminated the rear-view mirror.

"Shit, shit, shit!" Jim yelled, hitting the steering wheel.

We pulled over and I heard the crunch of gravel as they came to a stop behind us. I sat silently as the cop came up to Jim's window, his hand resting on his gun. I noticed a female officer standing a little way behind him.

"Evening, sir. Any idea why I pulled you over?"

He glanced at me and I quickly looked away.

"You two been drinking tonight?" He asked, shining his flashlight into Jim's eyes.

Jim looked at him sheepishly. "I've had a few beers," he admitted.

"Step out of the car please."

The cop took a couple of steps backward as Jim opened the door, trying as hard as he could to appear sober. I watched as the three of them walked up ahead of our vehicle. Instead of a roadside sobriety test, I noticed Jim explaining something to the officers and waving his arms around descriptively. The cop had his hands on his hips and was nodding his head as he listened.

What the hell was going on? Thank God I had removed the tampons from my boots.

After a few minutes the two officers walked back, this time to my side of the truck. Jim stayed where he was.

The woman officer approached. "I need you to step out of the vehicle, Miss."

I stepped out. She reached up and pulled me down onto the road. She then grabbed my right wrist yanking my arm sharply behind my back.

"Ow, that hurts!"

I tried to pull away, but she just held on tighter and pulled my other arm behind my back. I felt the cuffs snap on.

I stood and watched helplessly as they opened my purse, pulled out my make-up bag, removed my compact and opened it to reveal the empty baggie coated in residue.

"Well, what do we have here?"

They both looked at me, and then the male officer motioned to Jim.

"Come on you two, we're going for a ride."

He took the keys out of the ignition of the truck and locked it.

I sat cuffed in the backseat of the police car as Jim sat next to me softly pleading.

"Give me your credit card, I'll bail you out."

I ignored him and stared straight ahead, my eyes burning with tears. Whatever was going to happen next was beyond my control. I felt a relief in knowing it was all over. I knew Jim had turned me in because they knew exactly where to find my stash.

"Give me your card," he whined again as we approached the station.

I was pulled roughly out of the car, and then the cop turned to Jim.

"You'd better call someone to give you a ride back home. You can pick up your truck from the impound yard tomorrow."

As Jim was released, I was taken into the station.

* * *

The early hours of the morning came too soon. My mind was spinning and my body was going through withdrawals. My head throbbed and my lips were covered in blisters. I was taken into a bathroom stall and asked to pee into a cup as a female uniformed officer stood and watched over me unsympathetically. I was weak and dehydrated, alcohol and drugs had taken precedence over the normal things people do to keep their bodies functioning properly.

"I can't go with you watching me," I informed her miserably.

"Well then, we'll just have to stay here until you do, won't we?" She responded matter-of-factly, arms crossed in front of her ample chest.

Later in my cell I felt myself flooded by such intense depression. I couldn't think who to call for help. I didn't want anyone to know what had happened to me.

What's going to happen now? My thoughts were repetitive and never ending and I prayed desperately that someone would come and save me, but by this time I had pushed everyone out of my life.

Chapter Twenty-Nine

Later that morning I was brought a breakfast of cold toast and powdered scrambled eggs, but I had no appetite. All I wanted was water or juice to quench the burning in my throat. My question of what was going to happen next was answered soon enough. I was taken out of my cell, handcuffed again, and then led outside to a white van with blacked out windows. The sunlight hurt my eyes and I had to look down at the sidewalk.

I stepped into the van where five men sat handcuffed and looking about as depressed as I felt. I turned and sat in the front row of seats, directly behind the metal grate separating us from the driver. The doors closed and we pulled out onto the road. I had no idea where we were going and was afraid to ask. I wasn't even sure if I was allowed to speak. I listened as the driver and his buddy talked about their sons and baseball. My life was unraveling—I had spiraled out of control into a complete and utter nightmare, and they were discussing something as normal as the Dodgers.

About an hour and a half later we arrived at our destination and I was informed that it was the women's section of Twin Towers County Jail. I was placed in a holding cell with what appeared to be about twenty other women. I looked around and realized that other than a girl sitting in the corner crying, I was the only white woman. It was as cold as a hospital and I was dressed only in my T-shirt and underwear. I shivered, my teeth chattering as I now waited for whatever was going to happen next.

The boredom was momentarily suspended by the intermittent delivery of bologna sandwiches. The bologna was still partially frozen and I couldn't have eaten it even if I were hungry. There was a freestanding toilet in the cell and prisoners would use it seemingly unaffected by the lack of privacy. I realized most of them must be used to ending up in this sort of situation. Not me. I had been arrested for that DUI in Malibu five years prior, but it was nothing like this. I had no idea what the protocol was or how long I might be held in this dismal situation. I looked around at my cellmates. They were a mixture of women ranging in age from early twenties to grandmothers in their late sixties. I was going to deal with this as best I could, and I would accept total responsibility, unlike the girl who was still crying in the corner.

The women's stories were all very similar. I met a woman in her forties who was arrested for heroin. She and her husband would deal out of their house. They had two kids in junior high school. She was involved in the PTA and her husband coached the son's basketball team. I was amazed as she went on to explain to me that they had never both been imprisoned at the same time. Whoever was at home would look after the kids. Jail was just a sporadic reality. She claimed to use her time incarcerated to catch up on sleep and I watched as she slept through everything, only to wake up for more bologna sandwiches.

Then I spoke to a grandmother who told me she had ten grandchildren, but she couldn't give up the crack pipe. Her teeth were just about all missing, and the remaining ones were ground down to yellowy brown stumps. Her face was cracked and sunken by the toxic smoke. Her lifeless eyes showed that she knew she would do this until she died. Her brain so fried that this life had become normal to her. Mothers, daughters, and grandmothers, all suffering from a common curse, often passed down helplessly from one generation to the next. They cared for me with tender words and a woman took off her sweater and gave it to me because I couldn't stop shaking. At least five of them donated their orange juices to me as I was obviously so dehydrated. They could tell I was new and they comforted me with a kindness in the midst of this dehumanizing experience.

I went through the booking process and the showers. I stood, degraded and naked in front of guards, men as well as women. I looked over to the woman on my left. I felt my eyes drawn toward her legs, which were as hairy as a goat's. A female guard broke me out of my reverie.

"YOU!"

I looked up.

"Yes, you! I know you. I've seen you here before."

"No, you haven't," I responded. "I've never been here before."

I buckled as her bully stick unexpectedly jammed into my gut.

"That's bullshit, I know you. I've seen you before, don't lie to me!"

This time I cried from the pain as well as from the humiliation.

I was assigned an orange jumpsuit, and was just happy to finally have a pair of pants to wear. I was now on day two and I had managed to get in touch with my mother. She was at my house, Katie having called her when I didn't come home. I realized I needed a lawyer and so she had contacted my divorce attorney to see if he could send someone to help me.

That "someone" arrived the next day in the form of a criminal attorney. I explained to him how I had used all the cocaine and by the time I was arrested there was nothing left in the bag but residue, and how my boyfriend had turned me in. He assured me that he'd be able to help me and told me to just try to ride out my time, while he worked hard on his end to get me out of jail.

I had started talking to the girl who had been crying when I first arrived. Her name was Stephanie; she told me she went to college and lived in Laguna Beach. She had gone to a crack dealer's house that was under surveillance. It was the first time she had ever gone out and bought the drug herself. She told me that she didn't even get high, because the cops arrested her as soon as she got back in her car. She was so scared, scared of her parents finding out, scared of the arrest ruining her life. I reassured her and told her that if this was her first time, they would go easy on her. I realized then that I hoped the same held true for me. I looked up at the television playing a Jerry Springer episode. I wished I could be at home, watching television like a regular person with my family.

* * *

It was just past midnight a week later, and I had been tossing and turning in my usual fashion trying to fall asleep. Two guards came to the door and one of them called my name through the intercom.

"I'm Janine Fox," I told them, wondering what was going on.

"Well it's your lucky day lady, you've been bailed out."

Walking between the two of them, I was led to a place where I traded my orange jumpsuit for the clothes I was wearing when I was arrested.

I was handed a pair of men's jeans, five sizes too big and caked in dirt and dried blood.

"These aren't mine," I said looking aghast at the rancit-smelling pants.

"Well, they are now if you want to get outta here. You don't leave here without pants."

I hesitantly stepped into them as I was handed my purse along with my watch.

Not used to the discharge system, I had no idea what was to happen next. Did they take me to a waiting lounge where maybe I could use the phone and see if someone could pick me up? I had no money for a cab fare and was wondering whom I could call. I determined that Jim was out of my life forever.

I was taken down a flight of stairs and through two heavy metal doors and then turned out onto the street and into the hostile darkness. I had no idea where I was or how I was going to get home. I didn't even know north from south as I had been transported in the van with blacked-out windows. I squinted at the face of my watch. It looked like it was now almost two in the morning. I had to hold up the pants to keep them from sliding down my legs. I saw a payphone and rummaged through my purse, pushing around crumpled up bits of paper, balls of Kleenex, and broken cigarettes looking for change. In the dim light of the streetlamp, I punched in a number on a card with a women's name that had been handed to me months ago. An answering machine came on and I hung up. Looking down I was startled by a three-inch cockroach climbing over my shoe. I screamed and kicked my foot back, hurling the monstrous insect into the darkness. Now filled with trepidation, I walked close to the edge of the unfamiliar sidewalk in an attempt to avoid the creepy crawlies lurking in the shadows The streets were devoid of daylight activity and the night dwellers claimed their posts. I could just make out the shapes of the homeless bunkered down for the night, when I noticed a group of three men round the corner and begin walking toward me. I felt the cold grip of panic in my gut.

What if this is where my life ends?

I shifted into survival mode and crossed to the other side of the street. I kept my head down and walked briskly, I wanted it to appear like I was angry with someone. I was wearing the oversized pants covered in dried blood; maybe they would think I had killed someone.

I heard one of them call out.

"Hey you!"

My heart stopped.

Please don't let them come over. Please.

I broke into a shuffling run and turned the corner of the dark street. Once under a street lamp I slowed down and listened. I couldn't hear them. I didn't think they followed me. I stayed under the lamp for a couple of minutes until my heart slowed down and I could catch my breath. There was nothing else to do except call Jim and ask him to come and pick me up.

He told me to wait for him and directed me to a nearby Denny's. I walked through the door, self-conscious of my appearance. I knew I most likely looked homeless, but I figured that the staff were probably used to seeing drifters. A waitress came over to my table and I looked up at her haggard washed-out face. Everything about her told me that she had given up a long time ago. Maybe she had been young and pretty once, and someone had been in love with her. Now she just waited to get an order from a disheveled, unwashed woman in a pair of blood-stained jeans.

"I'm just waiting for someone," I told her.

About an hour later Jim walked through the doors.

"I've been so worried about you," he said breathlessly.

Yeah right.

I knew he had turned me in to save his own skin.

Right now I had to keep my mouth shut because I needed a ride home.

"Come on, let's get out of here," he grabbed my arm and pulled me up. "We can find a hotel room so that you can have a shower and get some sleep."

We stopped at a drug store and Jim went in to get me sweatpants, underwear, a new shirt, and some toiletries. That night as I lay in the bed next to him, I couldn't sleep. My body was clean but the rest of me felt as soiled as it had ever been.

* * *

The next morning Jim drove me back home. I knew how the kids felt about him by then, so I told him to drop me off at the park below my house.

"When will I see you?" he whined.

"I don't know," I said. slamming the door behind me.

The low throttle of the truck revved angrily as he pulled away. I walked up the hill, anxious with the anticipation of seeing my mother.

What was I going to say?

My heart was pounding from exertion and apprehension as I approached the gate to the back yard. I walked around the side of the house and could see her through the kitchen window. I realized the girls were at school.

I opened the back door and she turned from washing dishes to look at me.

"Oh, so you're back now, are you?" She shut off the faucet and looked me up and down. "When are you going to do something to pull yourself together, Janine? You can't go on like this. It's killing the girls."

"Not now, Mum!" I sobbed as I ran past her.

I sat on my bed and thought about all the legal consequences yet to come. I dropped my head into my hands and cried. I curled into a fetal position on my bed and cried for so long I finally fell asleep.

I woke in the middle of the night. It took me a minute to remember everything that had happened. I felt wretched. I was terrified of seeing

Katie in the morning and telling her what had happened. For a moment I wished I would die and then I would never have to face anyone again. I changed out of my clothes and slept fitfully on and off the next few hours.

I decided not to come out of my room as I listened to the bustle of my mother getting the kids ready for school. I just couldn't face them yet. When she came back from dropping them off I told her I didn't want to leave my room, and that I would talk to the girls when they came home from school. She made no argument and I was grateful for that. Depression clothed me like a dark and heavy cape.

I called the girls up to my room when they got home. They both stood at my bedroom door looking too scared to approach me. I patted my bed for them to come and sit with me and told them about the arrest. Sam was eight and I felt she was old enough to know. I felt like the scum of the earth as I looked at their confused faces. I cried and they tried to comfort me through their own tears.

"What'll happen to Jim?" Sam asked.

"I don't know," I told her. But I did know he wasn't coming over anymore and he was out of my life forever.

* * *

I returned to meetings once again. Familiar faces smiled and welcomed me back. My shame dissolved a little due to their unconditional kindness. Everyone was happy to see me, and no one was shocked or disappointed to learn that I had relapsed and been arrested for possession. I learned from them that I had a progressive illness and unless I remained abstinent, it would just continue to get worse.

Jim hadn't even tried to call me after he dropped me back in my neighborhood. He knew that I had figured out he was the one who turned me in and, being a coward, was afraid to face me. Most days I was either feeling anxious or depressed. Any time I was alone the depression would intensify. As I slowly came out of the fog and reality set in, I couldn't believe I had sunk so low. My attorney told me we were due in court in two weeks.

I was in the shower one morning when suddenly all the feelings I had pushed down for years came to the surface and I felt myself flooded with emotion so intense I dropped to my knees. This was not the foxhole "get me out of this mess" prayer that I was prone to use in times of desperation.

"God, if you exist, please help me." My prayer came from the deepest part of my soul.

Chapter Thirty

My court date came and went. I was sentenced to continue going to AA meetings, hefty court fines and diversion. I had to check into a location in the San Fernando Valley every week and meet with my counselor to submit a urine sample. I was also placed on probation for three years. This meant that I couldn't be around anyone using drugs or in any location where there were drugs. I was determined to change my life. I was almost forty years old and this crap just had to stop.

Katie was wrapped up in her life with her boyfriend while trying to graduate high school. She couldn't make it though and had to get her diploma through a continuation school.

Now sober, the guilt was hard for me to face. I felt responsible that Katie had struggled in school and I hadn't been available to help her. I had been so selfishly consumed with my own fears and addictions. I had no coping skills or source of wisdom to tap into with which I could help her. I was foundering just taking care of myself while she was struggling to graduate.

Sam was slowing transforming from a reptile-loving tomboy into a fashion-conscious preteen. She was eager to be accepted by the "populars" at her school who made fun of her baggy clothes, her unstyled hair, and her love of reptiles.

"They call me Snaky Sam," she said forlornly when I picked her up from school one afternoon.

"I've decided I'm not going to be a tomboy anymore. Mom can we go and buy some dresses today?"

I could tell she was serious.

I felt sadness at losing a unique child to the desperation of fitting in. At least she was seeing a therapist.

"Okay, Sam, but what about all of your reptiles?"

She thought for a moment.

"We can give them away to kids who want them," she said with satisfaction.

Sam not only turned into a girl, trading oversized pants, shirts, and caps for dresses and tank tops, but she also joined a competitive cheerleading squad.

I was amazed at her determination once she set her mind to something. She had once been the only girl on an all-boy's ice hockey team and scoffed at people who wondered why.

"I'm as good as any boy!"

Oh God, I wished I were more like her.

* * *

I quit cleaning houses and working for Bernie. I needed to find a job that made me feel good about myself. If I felt good about myself, I was more likely to stay sober. In the back of the pet store was a small dog grooming business run by a young woman named Maggie. I had no training, but was pretty adept at bathing and clipping the nails of my own dogs.

Maggie had approached me one day. "I need help with my grooming business. I can pay you cash, it'll be about two hundred dollars a day, and you'll probably only work three days a week."

She smiled and I at once felt attracted to her openness and enthusiasm. She knew Bernie didn't treat me with any respect and she would often make me giggle as she called him names under her breath.

"I'll give Bernie two-weeks notice," I told her.

Everything seemed to be going surprisingly well. I still had the legal fees to stress over, but I knew I could pay them off over time. The kids didn't discuss my arrest and they didn't ask me any more questions. They were just happy I wasn't with Jim and I was staying sober.

I would sometimes think about the broken girl who binged and purged all day. I had now read books about anorexia and bulimia and how hard eating disorders were to treat. Yet without treatment, I had somehow experienced a natural remission. I was sure that crossing to cocaine, alcohol, and then pills had just transferred my self-destructive drive from numbing with food to numbing with chemicals. Maybe I would have been a heroin addict when I was sixteen if someone had offered it to me. Food had been my first easily accessible source of comfort. It felt like I had some sort of internal liberation I'd never experienced before. Even as a child I ate chocolate until I hit a sugar high. Now I could eat when I was hungry and stop before I was full. I was no longer driven to feed my brain to sedation. I was finally feeling happier and looking forward to a future.

Paul's financial support was going to come to an end soon, and I needed to be ready to take care of myself, the girls, and our home. I was so proud of having a bank account and credit cards in my name. I also had my own car now, as opposed to driving one of Paul's. Most importantly, I had hope.

Sometimes I was overwhelmed with all the new responsibility, but it was worth it because I felt such pride in myself for the first time. I believe that self-esteem and healthy pride in oneself are essential to recovery. My resiliency was back and I was looking ahead with a new optimism. That was a high in itself. A life high.

I often missed my grandmother. Granny had died the year before and I was filled with sadness that I wasn't with her when she passed. She had been such a constant source of love and wisdom in my life. I was lonely sometimes and afraid that I would never find a healthy relationship with a man, but I remembered her words, "for every pot there's a lid," and I wondered if my "lid" was out there somewhere. I realized the truth of what I had always known but never taken the time to think through; it's far easier to get into a relationship than it is to get out of one. I needed to learn to trust my gut more.

I had decided I would not date for at least a year from my sobriety date. I would learn about myself before I explored what a healthy relationship looked like. I had never taken the time or had the desire to invest in self-discovery. It was time for me to find out who I was and what I liked doing. Why, I didn't even know what my favorite color was or what ice cream flavor I liked the best. I yearned to experience life through my eyes, not anyone else's. I felt empowered by the choices I was making for myself.

I was excited to finally get to know the woman I had been trying to kill for so many years.

Chapter Thirty-One

My life now was going to meetings, the gym, work, and then coming home, doing household chores, and taking care of Sam. I planted flowers in the garden, and bought things for the house. I took the dogs on hikes where we enjoyed the beauty of nature. I went to see movies by myself, sitting in my solitary seat with a bucket of popcorn, completely immersed in the movie. I looked after Sam as I felt a good mother should, making her lunches every day and taking her to her cheerleading practices and games. I was also making sober women friends and going on coffee or hiking dates.

I didn't need my mother to do my job anymore. She had known I was trying to stay sober, yet she never confronted me when she knew I was taking pills from her. To me it felt like she was trying to sabotage my recovery. She knew how weak I was and she knew if I got "bad" again she would be able to reclaim her position as the children's caretaker. I was sure she felt guilty for all the years that she lost being a mother to myself and Pete. My kids gave her the opportunity to feel needed, wanted, and loved. Now that I was able to do these things myself, I didn't need her to take care of them anymore.

It would be another year before I could take responsibility for my own behavior and work through the barriers I erected against my mother. I was so conditioned to blaming her and not looking at how I manipulated and used her to get what I wanted.

I was desperate to talk to Katie but didn't know how. There was so much unsaid between the two of us. I would sometimes stand at her bedroom door, willing myself to turn the knob and walk over the threshold, but I never could. Fear always held me back. I wanted her to have a life outside her room. She had started college, but then dropped out shortly thereafter. She had a night job testing video games which meant she spent the days sleeping. Her relationship with her boyfriend had ended when he went off to college and I knew she was depressed. I just didn't know how to help her.

Even though I was sober and keeping myself busy, I was still always in financial fear, projecting to the day when Paul would no longer help me.

I realized that I had been in financial fear my entire life, not just because money would come and go, but perpetual anxiety that however stable I felt right now, it was surely not going to last. The other shoe would always drop.

My dependency on others for my security was the problem.

Then one night I woke from a dream. I couldn't remember the content, but as I lay in the dark, I realized that perhaps I wasn't as stupid as the messages I had received and internalized all my life. I was so tired of hiding my inadequacies and trying to pretend I knew how to live when I didn't. Even the simplest of life's problems often seemed incredibly difficult for me to solve. I had to stop running. If I put the same effort into facing life as I did into running from life, perhaps, *just perhaps* I could do the unthinkable. It was three o'clock in the morning and for the first time I was experiencing hope and excitement for a future career. What if I were to get my GED and go to college?

I thought back to my childhood school reports. "Janine lacks concentration" was noted on every one of them.

My childhood had been a blurred timeline of twelve different schools. I was always confused and lagging behind the other girls in my class. Once at the convent, I gave up even trying. I would sit in class staring vacantly out of the window. There was no one to care anyway, so why should I?

The thought of going to school seemed both exciting and terrifying at the same time.

* * *

I began to talk about my idea to people at my meeting whom I knew would encourage and support my goal. It wasn't going to be easy to let go of a lifetime of self-defeating beliefs about myself and try something new. I wondered if I was too old, but I got so much positive feedback from people that the idea became more and more of a reality.

I yearned for routine and craved a life where I could work nine to five and be able to pay my own bills without help. I longed for the day I would be able to help my kids with their homework and not freeze when they showed me something from one of their school textbooks.

I bought myself a large third grade math book. The book had an illustration of a dragon on the front cover. The dragon's mouth was open wide and he was hungrily eating an array of numbers. I felt as hungry as the dragon, hungry to start learning all I had been avoiding since I left school twenty-four years ago.

I had always suffered math anxiety. When I was thirteen and living for a few months with Uncle George, he sent me to a math tutor in the village to see if I could be helped. The tutor was a priest from a nearby Catholic church. He and I would sit for hours at his dining table littered with sheets of paper covered in numerals. His sister thankfully interrupted our sessions with freshly baked cupcakes. As I sat and stared at the problems, my brain shut down. I could never make sense of what the tutor was saying; it was as if he were speaking another language, one I didn't and never would be able to understand. I unconsciously fed myself with baked goods from the tray, numbly dropping the crumbs down the front of my shirt and onto the math papers. After a month, the tutor called my uncle and told him it was useless trying to help me, and apologetically informed him that he was wasting his money.

Fear of math was the main reason I never even dared consider going back to school.

Then I had the idea of asking Sam if she could help me; she was a natural at math and at least I would be comfortable working with her. We scheduled a time in the evening three nights a week.

"Okay Sam, I'm ready!"

I stood in the doorway of her room, holding my new workbook and pencil. We climbed onto her bed and she gave me an hour lesson on multiplication and division, then she gave me homework assignments and graded them at the end of each week.

"You're doing really well Mommy!" My ten-year-old encouraged me as she corrected my work. "Only two wrong today!" She smiled at me.

* * *

Sam was dealing with her own problems when she was at Paul's house. He still hadn't come to terms with the injustice of me getting sober and then leaving him. Sam was the only vehicle for resentment that he had left and he would complain to her about me whenever he could.

Paul and I rarely spoke, events of the past weighed heavy on both of us and we had bottled up our feelings of blame toward each other. We were like two magnets whose opposing poles would not allow us to communicate.

Katie's relationship with him seemed to be slowly improving. I knew how she craved his approval. She had already been abandoned by her biological father. After leaving England when she was four, she had only seen Clive three times. He failed to stay in touch with her and instead created a new family for himself in Hong Kong.

Paul had wanted to adopt Katie when we married, but Clive had refused to consent. "I'm not going to have the same thing happen to her that happened to you!"

I knew he was referring to how my stepfather adopted me when I was about the same age as Katie and then abandoned me when I was twelve.

During my active alcoholism my eldest daughter had cared for Sam and covered up for me. She must have feared for her life and her little sister's as I drove them home from school under the influence. She had to call paramedics when she couldn't rouse me, and then call Paul to come home because "there's something wrong with Mum."

She couldn't bring friends home from school for the same reason I couldn't bring friends home when I was a kid: the embarrassment of everyone seeing that her mother was drunk.

So now Katie was adrift in a matrix, off course, without guidance or direction, and I didn't know how to help her or motivate her to go back to college. Within the following year she would move out of the house and into an apartment with her new boyfriend. This transition was fraught with resentment on her part, and guilt and shame on mine.

* * *

A year and a half had passed since my arrest. This time I had a new attitude about my recovery, and I was at last willing to take responsibility for myself and step up to the plate.

I decided it was now time to be brave enough to take my GED.

I discovered there was an adult school nearby, and I built up enough courage to walk into the registration area one day. There I was greeted by the warm, smiling faces of women in the office. They reassured me and encouraged me to take the practice test.

"What have you got to lose?" a middle-aged woman asked, smiling kindly.

If only she knew I had everything to lose.

I took the practice test expecting to fail miserably and was surprised that I passed all subjects, except for math. Sam and I stepped up on the lessons and I would spend hours in bookstores looking for anything else that might help.

After taking my GED, I spent the next couple of weeks preoccupied about my score. If I failed at least I had tried. But what if I passed? If I passed, then the next step would be going to college. Just the thought of that made me nauseated. I wasn't sure that I was ready for such a huge commitment. I knew I would have to take math classes and know how to use a computer. I didn't even know how to turn on a computer.

I informed the office staff that I would pick up my results from the school; I was worried that if they were mailed to me, I would have a harder time handling the bad news. I didn't want to be caught off guard. I could deal with bad news, as long as I was ready for it. My dogs accompanied me to the school; they were always my calming agents and loved going for car rides. I left them in the vehicle as I walked across the parking lot to the school office, feeling like my heart was going to give out.

A few minutes later I returned to the car carrying the sealed envelope; I was feeling so incredibly anxious about opening it that my hands were shaking. Once in the car, I tore open the seal and stared in disbelief at the results. Elation ran through me, the ineffable feeling for which I had always longed.

"I passed! I passed!" I cried from within the confines of the car, tears of joy running down my cheeks.

The dogs barked applause as I bounced up and down on the car seat like an excited child. I couldn't wait to call my sober friends who had become my surrogate family. I had finally achieved something because of my dedication and the willingness to face my own fears.

That night I lay in bed and realized for the first time that maybe my father had been wrong. I knew I had certainly brought a fair amount of my pain and suffering on myself, but I had never had a goal, a vision, or a personal cause that I could realize into an outward reality. My continual relapses reinforced my feelings of helplessness. I represented the poor souls who could not stay sober no matter how hard they tried.

I called my father the next day. I was apprehensive but wanted to hear what he had to say when I told him my news. He picked up the phone on the third ring.

"Hello?"

"Dad, guess what?"

"Who's this? There's a strange person calling me Dad. I don't have any children."

"Dad, *please!*" I was frustrated as always with his stupid jokes.

"Oh dear! This child seems a little upset. What is it you want little girl?"

"I'm going to college, Dad. I passed the GED!" I said, excitedly.

He laughed and I could hear my stepmother's voice in the background.

"Who is that Vinceeent?" The last syllable of my father's name was drawn out.

"Dad!" I said again, annoyed that they had to act out their repartee every time I called. "I said that I'm going to college!"

"Oh, good Lord, what *are* you talking about?"

He was now sounding irritated.

"I've decided I'm going to go to college and get a degree," I persisted.

"You were stupid when you were a child in school, what makes you think anything has changed?" I heard him guffaw at his own joke.

I heard Audrey's shrill voice, "What's she saying, Vinceeeent? Did she say she's going to college? She's not serious, is she?"

I angrily hung up the phone.

"Screw you," I snapped at no one, feeling that I *was* a stupid girl to ever get the idea of calling him.

Screw both of them. Why did I call?

I should have known better. I had set myself up once again. I could still hear his voice. *"Stupid girl!"*

I sat down on the step at the bottom of the staircase; the dogs offered me their wet noses as a source of comfort.

This time his words didn't stop me as they had in the past. The pilot light that had been ignited within me was too strong to be extinguished and I could not get the idea of college out of my head. I decided then that I was willing to take the risk of failure. I had to find out if I could do it.

A wise old-timer took me aside one morning after the meeting. "Why do you think what your father says is true?" he asked me, having heard some of my story. He looked intently into my eyes, waiting for me to answer.

"I don't know." I realized then that I had never even thought of questioning the truth. For the first time, I considered that I had been raised on a lie.

* * *

I sat at home in the solitude of the kitchen nursing a cup of tea. The phone rang and I saw it was Katie. We had started to talk more often since she left home. We would meet every couple of weeks for a movie or for lunch. She and her new boyfriend Tim were living in an apartment in Woodland Hills. I realized that knowing I had let her down so terribly, made loving her even more painful. I told her about what I was planning to do.

"Mum, if you're going to go to college," she seemed to hesitate, "then I want to try to go back too. Maybe we could go together?"

I couldn't believe what I was hearing. She confided that she had been afraid to see her transcript as she had dropped out of classes.

"I've always been afraid of speech class," she admitted.

"I've always been afraid of math."

We giggled.

It was at that moment that I recognized my truth. I understood the question the old-timer had posed to me. Everything that had happened up to this point in my life culminated in this moment.

"Okay," I replied. "Let's do it then Katie. Let's go together."

Chapter Thirty-Two

I woke up excited, as today was the day I was celebrating eight years of sobriety. It was the first year I was asking the girls to give me my cake at a meeting. I had felt so much shame and guilt that I couldn't bring myself to ask them before.

I went into the spare room and could just make out Sam's head under the covers.

I pulled back the blanket, "Come on Sam, we only have a few minutes to get ready."

I left her light on as an incentive for her to get up and went back in my room to get dressed. Barry was already out of bed.

"I'll let the dogs out and feed them." He said, whistling to the three dogs from the top of the staircase.

It was 2011, and somehow I had managed to beat the odds. Barry had come into my life in 1999 and Granny was right, I had found the lid to my pot. His family was from Philadelphia and they were very close and loving—the opposite of my crazy, dysfunctional family. They quickly became my family and I finally knew what it felt like to be part of a loving system. He had two young sons and we all moved in together about a year after we started dating. His sons attended the same elementary school as Sam; it didn't take long for us to become a happy blended family.

Less than twenty minutes later, Sam and I were in the car. Katie was going to meet us in the meeting parking lot. My phone chirped, announcing that I had a text. I looked down and saw that it was from Katie.

"I think I'm where I'm supposed to be. There are people standing around outside drinking coffee and smoking cigarettes."

I smiled to myself. It was six-forty in the morning, and anyone who had ever been involved in the program knew that this was the sign of a nearby meeting.

I pulled into the parking lot next to Katie's car.

"Thank you so much for coming, Kates."

We hugged each other tightly and then she pulled back so she could look into my eyes.

"I wouldn't miss this for the world, Mum."

Sam, Katie, and I walked through the double doors and into the long hallway.

The room was spacious and already starting to fill with people. The community is fairly affluent, and members consisted of professionals, members of the community, housewives, and kids still in college. Some were high functioning, whereas others had lost everything; some on disability or unemployment; and others living in sober-houses because their families didn't want them home. Alcoholism has no social boundaries, no preference for whose life it destroys. Addiction is the great equalizer.

I saw Barry and waved him over to our row of seats. I looked around and realized more than a hundred people filled the room. As the hands of the clock on the wall approached seven, the room fell silent as if by some unspoken command.

The preamble was read and then it would be time for the chips which were milestones in every member's recovery. The collective support of the group helped the chip takers to achieve an accumulation of time where they were not drinking alcohol or using any drugs. I looked up at the birthday board and saw my name with the number eight next to it.

It had been eight years since the end of my last relapse.

I let my mind drift back as the leader's voice faded into the background.

Katie and I had gone to college together. In 2001 she transferred to California State University, Northridge (CSUN), and I was quietly struggling again. The terrifying cycle had gradually started with innocuous amounts of non-alcoholic beer, which I thought were safe, and then graduated to wine coolers, which hadn't existed when I got sober in 1996. Within three months I had lost control again and was drinking vodka. My secret was out when Barry came home from work to find me passed out and unresponsive.

I had been sober for over four years before the relapse. During that time, I had accumulated enough support that many rallied around me as soon as they knew I was in trouble again. Nevertheless, it still took me over two years of trying before I was able to accumulate sober time once again. I realized that it was much easier to stay sober through difficulties, than it was to try to get sober again after relapsing. Even with so much support, the demons had been awakened and would not retreat so easily. Someone once said it was like dancing with a gorilla: you weren't done until the gorilla was.

Being sober when I met him, Barry had never seen this side of me. He was confused, angry, and afraid. He reached out to my sober friends for help, and painfully watched me go through a detox, only to start drinking again with the Librium I was prescribed to help the withdrawals.

Who was this person? He no longer knew the woman with whom he had fallen in love.

The inevitable end came when I was pulled over just a block from my house. A concerned citizen had called the police informing them that I was driving erratically. Another night spent in a jail cell, dry heaving for hours, hoping daylight would never come. With daylight came all the questions and consequences that I would have to face.

Barry paid my bail and told me he expected me to pay him back. I couldn't believe this was happening again. We drove home in silence, a terrible painful silence. I felt that anything I said would be worse than not saying anything. All I could do now was do everything in my power to make sure I didn't relapse again. At the first meeting I attended after the DUI, I asked a woman to sponsor me and guide me through the process of the Twelve Steps. I had never completed them in my past sobriety, always balking at the challenge of the fourth step. I had never been willing to take on the workload that the steps required, but this time was different. I had a fear that I would be the only person who didn't change after going through the process, but then the only way to find out would be to do it.

I had to work a lot harder; just going to meetings wasn't enough.

The determination to not quit college pulled me back from the brink. I lost my driver's license for a year, but refused to let this deter me. I researched and found that I could legally ride a moped without a license.

"You can do over forty-five downhill," the salesman pitched.

My little red moped got me to and from college, my afternoon job, and my Twelve Step workshop for the next year. After that I transferred to a two-year addictive disorders program at Pierce College while Katie was at CSUN graduating with honors in liberal studies.

Katie now worked as a teacher at a reputable private school.

I looked over at her profile, my heart swelling with pride.

In 2005 I completed my training and internship hours, passing the state test to get my license as a drug and alcohol counselor. I found a job volunteering at a small treatment center. Within two years the owner died from an aneurism and I stepped up to run the program for the next four years. The center became very successful and I was asked to open and run a new facility in the community. I was made the program director and hired a clinical team.

What had happened to that scared girl who thought she couldn't make it on her own?

Sam had moved out when she was nineteen choosing a career in acting. She was now living in Venice with her boyfriend.

Barry and I married in 2007.

A few months after my relapse, I had hesitantly asked him, "Will you ever love me again the way you used to?"

I felt I needed to know the extent of the damage from my relapse. His simple response was, "I don't know."

I was surprisingly thankful for his honesty and I knew there was absolutely nothing I could do to make him trust me again. Words meant nothing. I was going to have to show him.

My only sadness was that my brother Pete continued to struggle with depression and alcoholism. The lost child had become a lost man living a transient lifestyle. I would hear from him when he was suicidal, or just got out of treatment or jail, and then he would disappear again for another few years.

Just then I heard the leader's voice switch from the preamble to announcing days in increments of thirty. I pulled myself out of my daydream and brought my attention back to the room. A sobriety birthday is always a time for reflecting on the past.

"Does anyone have thirty days?" He looked around the room. "Sixty days? Ninety days?"

At that moment a woman stood and raised her hand. She was one of my sponsees.

"I have ninety days."

The room erupted in applause as if she had crossed the finishing line in a race.

The leader handed her a colorful token and hugged her.

She turned to face everyone and shyly expressed her gratitude to the program, and to her sponsor who had helped her achieve this milestone. I smiled at her with tears in my eyes, if only she knew that she probably helped me more than I helped her.

As she returned to her seat, the leader continued, "Six months? Nine months?"

"Well I know we have one birthday for Janine, and it's for eight years."

I suddenly felt like my heart was pounding in my throat, I nervously turned to the girls. "Come on, you have to come up with me."

The freshly baked cake was held in front of me topped with a blue and yellow candle shaped in the number eight. Katie and Sam each held the base, and as everyone sang "Happy Birthday," I took a breath, closed my eyes and blew out the candle.

As I walked to the front of the room, I could feel the emotions welling up inside me. For a moment I couldn't speak, and the room fell silent as I attempted to find my voice.

"I can't believe it's been eight years," I said, looking up to see my girls and Barry smiling proudly. I scanned the room recognizing

275

members who had tried to help me since the early 1990s. They had never given up on me. I thanked them and I thanked my daughters for always loving me. I was so proud of the women they had become.

Katie and I had been working on this book for over three years. It brought us close in ways neither of us had ever thought possible.

"We should write a book about writing a book together," I had joked after a particularly emotional stint at her apartment.

As I made my way back to my seat, I saw Katie raise her hand. "Hi, my name is Katie." Her voice sounded small and shaky.

"Hi, Katie," everyone responded.

"I never realized how many lives my mother has touched until today. I want to thank you all for helping her to get better too." I watched her, wanting to capture every word, every facial expression. I wanted to remember this day for the rest of my life.

She started crying and couldn't go on.

My arms were around Sam who was sitting between us and we were all crying now. I could also hear other people in the room weeping softly and knew Katie was touching the hearts of alcoholic parents who hoped that maybe someday their relationships with their kids could also be healed. As we rose to join hands, I felt the sensation of having arrived. It was perfect. Nothing had ever been this perfect.

I smiled to myself.

There's no way it could ever get better than this.

Chapter Thirty-Three

The call came on a Sunday afternoon; it was now January 2012.

"Janine, this is Charlie." Charlie was my half-sister Sarah's husband. They lived in San Diego with their two young sons. Sarah and I had remained close; she moved out to California about eight years after I did. Charlie's voice had a sense of urgency.

"What is it?" I asked, thinking something awful had happened to my sister and remembering she had cancer when she was living with me while I trudged through finalizing my divorce to Paul.

"It's your dad," said Charlie.

I knew Dad had been in bad shape as he suffered from a degenerative brain disease the last few years. He had been getting progressively worse and falling more often.

"Your dad had a stroke today and he's in a coma," Charlie continued. "Sarah's flying out there tonight."

My sister had spent a lot of time flying back and forth to England the last couple of years. I justified it was because she had more money than I did. But the truth was that I had not wanted to go – being around him was still so painful.

Sarah and I texted a few times before she boarded her flight, she insisted that I come as soon as possible. I decided not to make a decision until the following day which was a Monday.

It was almost impossible for me to concentrate at work that day, so at ten in the morning I called Barry.

"I think I need to get a flight out to England as soon as possible."

Within minutes he had called me back. "There's one at seven or nine tonight."

"I'll take the seven," I said, surprised at my eagerness.

* * *

Once on the long flight east, I sat back and began thinking about my dad. The last time I saw him was in 2010. Barry and I had gone on our first trip to England together and I had wanted to see people I hadn't seen for a number of years. I also wanted Barry to meet my friends like Lindsey and Nina, my old convent buddy.

We had decided to stop for a brief visit with my dad. By this time, he and Audrey were both in wheelchairs. Sarah had kept me informed, letting me know when Dad had falls and Audrey had to have a leg amputated due to peripheral arterial disease. I cringed at the thought of her with only one leg. She had always been so stylish, and I wondered how she coped with being an amputee.

I hoped this visit might be the time that I got to talk to Dad alone. Perhaps I could ask him questions? I wondered what sort of questions I would want to ask. Do you love me? Are you proud of anything I've accomplished?

No, that just sounded stupid.

I always wanted to experience what it would be like to be alone with him, without my stepmother present. Maybe he would be the one to say something to me. The only time she hadn't been with us that I could remember, was the time he picked me up from the convent after I was expelled. We had travelled back to Woodlands in silence. I felt that time didn't really count.

At Heathrow Airport I was met by my old friend Lindsey. She had been a constant in my life from the time I had met dad and Audrey. Lindsey wrapped her arms around me and I felt like I had come home.

"Are we going to the nursing home?" Lindsey enquired once we were in the car.

"Yes," I replied bleakly.

The car was filled with our voices as we caught up on the past two years and reminisced about my dad.

"Your father was such a character," Lindsey said, keeping her eyes on the road.

"Do you know he used to chase me and my brothers around the garden at Woodlands with his hunting whip?"

"He called us bloody varmints, and we would scream and run from him as he cracked the whip at our heels."

"That certainly sounds like Dad," I replied.

I wondered if other fathers would terrorize their children's friends in such a manner.

An hour and a half later we arrived at Tall Trees Nursing Home. The rambling house was nestled in the picturesque countryside of Oxfordshire. Behind the stone walls, the helpless aged waited to die, the autonomy of their former lives just a faint memory in their mostly delusional minds.

I saw two men in deep conversation in the parking lot and recognized them as my step-brothers John and Adam.

Lindsey pulled her mud splattered Range Rover into the parking space next to them.

After greeting my stepbrothers, the four of us walked the long hallways, passing bedrooms with the names of the occupants printed on the doors. I wondered about Paddy Gilroy or Rose Treckleman; I speculated who they might have been before they ended up at Tall Trees. All the patients appeared to be encapsulated in their own little worlds; maybe it wasn't so bad after all?

We were almost at the end of the hallway when I saw "Vincent Wellington" in bold print on the last door on the right. My stomach did a summersault.

I then noticed Sarah and my other half-sister Emily as they poked their heads out from around the door.

"Nini," they both shouted in unison.

"Daddy's been holding on for you!"

I felt that was an improbability, but as I hugged them I realized I was happy I made the decision to come. I rarely saw Emily; she lived in Scotland with her husband and two small children. I followed them into the room and saw my dad stretched on a narrow bed. At any other time, he would have put his hand to his forehead, and exclaimed, "Oh my God, what on earth are you doing here?"

This time he didn't say anything.

He lay motionless, the sound of his breathing amplified in the small room. I found myself distracted by his unruly hair. His combover was usually perfect, but now the long thin strands were asymmetrically strewn here and there on top of his head.

Audrey was also in the room, her small frame hunched forward in her oversized wheelchair, sparse red hair pulled back in a large grip. She was impeccably dressed and I unconsciously felt my eyes pulled down to her legs. She was wearing slacks, her left leg ended at her knee where the material was tied in a knot. I noticed a pack of Marlboro Reds and a lighter nestled in her lap.

"Hello Chah-neen." Her familiar voice held the heavy inflection of a class of which she was no longer a part. "It's so good of you to come to see daaadeh."

I smiled awkwardly at her Cheshire cat grin and tried to avoid her eyes; she had greeted me as if I were stopping by their house for a cup of tea. I walked over to my father on his bed, oblivious to all the activity going on around him. Looking down, I watched his chest rise and fall with each laborious breath.

"He waited for you to get here."

I turned, and Sarah smiled kindly at me.

"It's really important to us and to him that you are here," Emily added.

Tears welled up. For years now I had made the decision that if Dad died or was dying, I would get the date for the funeral and fly over for that, nothing more. I had never planned on this. I had never planned on the intensity of the emotions rising in me now. I swallowed hard.

"Where are you guys staying?" I asked Sarah.

"We're staying at The Dog and Fox in Burford, but last night I slept here with him."

I looked around the small, cluttered room, wondering where on earth Sarah could have made a bed for herself.

"The chair turns into a bed," Sarah said, seeing my confusion.

"Where shall I stay tonight?" I asked, just wanting to take direction from them as I really didn't know what I was supposed to do.

"You can stay wherever you want," Sarah said, stroking my arm gently. "You can stay here with Dad if you like. We call the chair the three-thousand-pound executive seat."

Sarah and Emily both laughed.

"It's actually very comfortable," Sarah added. "His room costs three thousand pounds a week, and luckily it's being covered by his insurance plan from the stock market."

I had wondered how my dad was able to remain in a private nursing home. The days of wheeling and dealing stocks, charming clients, and jet setting with Audrey all over Europe on expense accounts had fizzled out a long time ago.

At that moment, Lucy came into the room. She and my step-brother John were still married thirty-three years later. I knew they had two sons, as I had received pictures over the years of little blond boys becoming tall men with beards. We hugged each other, and Lucy's hug felt good. She held me a little longer than I expected, and I didn't pull away.

"Are you okay?" She pulled back and hald me at arm's length so she could look at me.

"Yeah, I'm okay," I said. "I only got about three hours sleep on the plane though so I'm pretty tired."

I turned to Sarah. "I think I'll sleep here tonight."

Did I really just say that?

Everyone started to gather their belongings so they could leave and have dinner, or maybe just be able to breathe outside the claustrophobic room. I went out looking for Lindsey. She hadn't wanted to come in and I didn't blame her. I found her in the lobby, and we walked back to her car to get my luggage.

"I've decided to spend the night." I told her. "I'm finally going to be alone with him."

"Isn't that what you always wanted?" Lindsey smiled and gave me a hug. "Let me know when you want me to come back and get you."

I watched her as she pulled out of the parking lot; it was so good to see her again.

I took a deep breath and walked back inside the nursing home.

I couldn't sleep. The light was always on because the staff would come in and check my dad every hour. I lay watching in the pulled-out executive chair as two caregivers rolled him over and moistened his mouth with swab sticks. I turned my head as they changed his diaper. He was like a rag doll, flopping from side to side as they moved him this way and that at intervals throughout the night.

In one instance, after the caregiver had left, I got up and pulled a chair close to the side of his bed, facing him and less than a foot away.

"Dad," I said, as close as I dared get. "Can you hear me?"

There was no response.

Someone once had told me that people can still hear when they are in a coma. I leaned forward and gently kissed his forehead, he still felt so warm. This was the first time I had ever kissed my father. I knew if he were awake he would push back in mock horror, saying something like, "Aggghhh, someone help me! She's trying to kill me!"

I felt sad that he was so uncomfortable with any sort of intimacy. I thought of Barry and my girls and how relaxed we all were with hugging and expressing ourselves. Of all the experiences my dad had achieved in his life, he had missed out on the greatest one.

His breathing now sounded more strained, tears ran down my face and fell onto his sheet. It had been three days since the stroke. The doctors had given him one to three days and he was still hanging on. His advance directive specified no medical intervention, only morphine if he was in distress. The caregivers had assured us he felt no pain. This was the end of his third day with no food or water. I wondered how much longer he could go on without water.

I managed to sleep an hour or so before I heard the door open and my sisters came in.

"How's he doing?" Sarah asked.

"He's still holding on to life. His breathing has been pretty regular, but he feels really hot."

"He could have a chest infection," she said concerned. "The doctors said that might happen." She walked over to him and gently rested the palm of her hand on his forehead.

"Oh God, his breath smells." She wrinkled her nose and stepped back.

She picked up a bottle of his cologne from the window ledge.

"I gave this to him for Christmas," she noted, looking at the bottle.

She sprayed little bursts of the fragrance in the air around his bed.

"No," I said, waving my hands in the air. "That's way too much. He'll smell like a hooker!"

We burst out laughing and I immediately felt guilty that he had been the butt of our joke.

"I think Dad knows you're here," Emily said to me.

"I know he loved you very much."

"I always thought he didn't," I said, beginning to cry.

"I wonder if he can hear what we're saying." Sarah whispered, looking over at him.

For a little while we talked about Dad, about his sense of humor, his eccentricity, and his antics.

"I think we all have Dad's personality in us," I said.

"Thank God!" Sarah replied.

One thing the three of us could agree on is that we would rather be more like our father than our mothers.

Just then his breathing began to make a gurgling sound. We looked at each other and got up.

"I think this may be it," Emily said as she stroked his forehead. His respiration was slowing down and where he had previously felt hot, he now felt cooler. I wanted to hold his hand, but I was unsure of reaching under the covers without his permission. I gingerly pulled back the sheet, felt for his hand and pulled it out onto my lap.

As I held it in mine I looked up and noticed that Sarah, Emily, and I were positioned at three corners of a triangle, and Dad was in the middle like the magnet holding his three daughters together. Then he stopped breathing. At that moment I felt the three of us stopped breathing too.

Was that it?

Then, unexpectedly, he took another breath and we almost jumped off the bed.

"Oh God, Dad," Sarah wailed, tears streaming down her cheeks.

He would stop and start breathing until finally he didn't take a breath for about a minute.

We waited on edge.

But he didn't breathe again.

There was no sound now other than the three of us weeping. It was finally over. He was gone. My dad had died and in doing so had brought myself and my sisters together in a way I had never imagined.

* * *

On the flight home I tried to get comfortable curling up on the two seats I had managed to secure, but I couldn't sleep. My mind kept playing over the events of the last week. The memory of watching my dad die seemed surreal. I had never watched a person die. I pulled myself up on my knees and looking behind my seat, I could see Sarah about five rows back. I settled back into my seat again, glad that Barry had managed to get us on the same flight back.

My thoughts drifted to my dad's service. Sarah, Emily, and I had gone to the funeral home the day after he passed. I had been sitting on the couch in the cozy waiting room while Emily discussed arrangements with the director. I noticed that the decor created a warm and inviting environment in which to discuss the recent death of a loved one. I could hear Emily drone on about the financial package Dad had put together in preparation for his funeral.

Bored, I picked a catalog off the table. Thumbing through the brochure, I realized I was looking at themed coffins. There was a coffin designed as a colorful garden, or a cricket match, or a beautiful African safari at sunrise. Excitedly I kept turning the pages, until I found what I was looking for, a horse-racing themed coffin. Perfect. I got up and waved the catalogue at my sisters.

"We have to get him this," I said excitedly pointing at the racing scene.

They burst into laughter.

"How much extra is it?" Emily asked the director.

"Ohhh, let's see…" The woman with the blonde beehive hairdo took the catalogue out of my hands as I almost choked on her heavy perfume.

"It's another two hundred and fifty pounds."

"Does Dad have enough money put away?" I asked Emily.

"Yes, he does," she responded, "and he would love it."

* * *

The coffin looked perfectly inappropriate as it was carried up the aisle of the small seventeenth-century Catholic church. I smiled to myself as I remembered the stifled giggles coming from the pews as the garish coffin came to its resting place in front of the alter, flanked by my dad's saddle, racing colors, and a pair of binoculars adorned with the tags of every race he had ever attended.

I didn't know it but Emily had prepared a speech. As she stood up next to me, I moved my legs to one side so she could get past.

"You're coming too," she said, giving me a gentle nudge to get up.

I hesitantly rose to my feet and followed her. Sarah, John and Adam joined us and the five of us stood together in front of Dad's coffin facing the congregation.

Emily read a eulogy she had written on the life of Vincent Aubrey Wellington. At that moment, I realized that this was my real family. I knew that I would probably never have to see Audrey again, but the gift of my sisters and step-brothers was the family I had always wanted.

* * *

I curled up in my airplane seat again, happy I was going back to the life I had created for myself, the life I never thought I would have. I had a feeling that being with my dad when he died would probably change my relationship with my mother for the better. I hoped something would happen as I still struggled with lifelong resentments making it impossible for me to feel the freedom of forgiveness toward her.

I was almost at the point of admitting that my parents actually did the best they could with the limitations they had. I had to forgive them and more importantly, I had to forgive myself. I always thought that I didn't care about them, but that wasn't true, I cared very deeply. I had just told myself I didn't care my whole life so I wouldn't hurt as much.

I was thankful that I had the chance to be with my dad at the end, and I was glad that when I got home I would still have the opportunity to tell my mother I loved her.

I closed my eyes and drifted off to sleep.

Epilogue

My father's passing profoundly altered a lifetime of resentments I had carried toward my mother. Resentments that went so deep I didn't think they could ever be removed.

It began very gradually, such as the time she told me a story from World War II that I had heard a hundred times before, yet this time I heard the story differently, as it were for the first time. I found myself asking her questions about her life and being interested in her responses. I laughed because she said something funny. When had I ever thought my mother was funny?

I took her to the shelter and helped her pick out a little Chihuahua mix and six months later I found her a kitten. I started calling her weekly and then every other day. I would ask her about the pets, and she would tell me how they brought so much joy to her life. I listened to her stories from AA and how much support the members offered her. I stopped judging her.

On visits I noticed she needed new towels and bedding, so I started buying things for her apartment.

"You're so good to me Nini. I don't deserve a daughter like you."

If only she knew, she deserved so much better.

* * *

One afternoon while driving her to an appointment, I took a deep breath and asked her if she knew that I had stolen pills from her before I got sober.

"Of course I knew darling. I would try and hide them in different places, but you always found them." She didn't seem the least bit angry.

"I'm so sorry, Mum. I feel so terrible about doing that to you. You needed them. I seriously couldn't help myself. I hate myself for stealing from you." I started to cry.

"Janine, darling, if anyone knows what that struggle is like, it's me. You have come so far, look at you now, running a treatment center. Your life's work is helping people."

I realized then that I had always been seeking some kind of redemption. It had now been thirteen years since I had to feed my addiction. So much had happened in the last three years alone. After my dad died, my stepbrother Adam also died detoxing from alcohol. He had struggled in and out of recovery for many years. He went on a final binge, suffered a seizure and fell, hitting his head on the corner of the kitchen counter.

Then Audrey passed from complications from gangrene in her remaining leg shortly after Adam.

The one I wasn't expecting was Paul. He had married again and seemed very happy. He was doing some amateur car racing in Monterey when he suffered a massive heart attack. Sam called me and told me she couldn't reach Katie.

"Dad's had a heart attack and we need to go to a hospital in Monterey." It was hard to understand her as she was crying and speaking so fast. I told her to sit tight, I would find Katie and call Barry to book their flights.

It took me talking to several people at the school where Katie worked before she was located in the cafeteria. I told her what had happened and to meet me at her apartment.

We were packing her bag, and I was reassuring her everything would be okay, when Sam called.

"We're not going anymore."

"What do you mean you're not going anymore?" I asked, confused.

"Dad just died." Sam was on speaker and with those words Katie dropped to her knees, letting out the most primal wail I had ever heard.

"Nooooooooooooooooo!" she screamed, sobbing.

288

I sat on the floor of her apartment and held her in my arms rocking her as she cried. I could hear Sam crying on the other end of the phone. Never was I more grateful to be sober. I could be completely present and available to help my girls through this terrible tragedy. Barry left work, picked up Sam and brought her to our house. I knew she and Katie needed to be together as soon as possible.

The year that followed was hard on the girls. Barry and I married in 2007, and although they accepted him as their stepfather, they now began to lean on him more. They both received an inheritance after going through the arduous process of probate. Paul hadn't left a will, but his widow had been gracious in not trying to cut the girls out of their share. Katie and her boyfriend moved to a quaint house in Woodland Hills, and Sam continued to rent with her boyfriend in Venice.

* * *

It was 2015, two days after my fifty-seventh birthday, when my cell rang at work. I looked down and saw it was Katie.

"Hi Kates! What's up?"

"Are you busy?" She knew it was always busy at the treatment center.

"Never too busy for you."

We both laughed.

"I wanted to call you with your birthday present."

There was a long pause.

"I'm pregnant Mum, you're going to be a grandma!"

I couldn't speak.

"Mum, are you there? I'm going to have a baby and you're going to be a grandma," she repeated.

"Oh my God, Katie," was all that came out of my mouth before I started crying.

"I wish Dad were here so I could call him too," she said sadly.

She told me that I was the only one who knew and I needed to keep it a secret until she felt it was the right time to go public.

"Oh God Katie, that's going to be so hard. Are you saying I can't even tell Barry?"

"No Mum, not even Barry."

* * *

The months passed quickly. I took a day off work so that I could accompany her and her boyfriend to her first ultrasound. I was afraid to ask her if she wanted me to be at the birth. Our relationship had healed in ways I had never thought possible during the writing of my memoir. She now knew all the sordid little crannies of my past, things I thought I would never tell anyone, let alone my daughter. Yet shame still held me back from asking her. I wondered how much of a part she would want me to play in her baby's life. She knew that I battled an eating disorder when she was a baby, and problems with alcohol and drugs when Sam was a baby. I wasn't sure if she would be able to trust me with her most precious gift in the world. The life of her child.

As Katie's pregnancy progressed she made it very clear that not only did she want me to be present at the birth, but she also asked if I would take two weeks off work to stay with her and help her look after the baby.

The birth was brutal and shocking for all of us and totally unexpected for Katie, who was hoping for a natural delivery. Sam joined us after ten long hours, bringing added support and encouragement to her sister, as Barry slept on a couch in the waiting room. I relived the trauma of giving birth to Katie because there were so many similarities between our two labors, except I had been alone and she wasn't. Through the long hours of night into morning, I never left her side. After her heroic attempt to give birth naturally, she went through an emergency C-section in order to deliver a healthy nine-pound-and-eleven-ounce baby boy.

I called my mother on the way home, elated and exhausted at the same time. She was now a great-grandmother. She loved to brag how she was outliving all her siblings; of the original six, three had passed on. We joked about her living until she was a hundred.

The two weeks I stayed at Katie's house brought even more healing between us, if that could be possible. The trauma of the delivery and subsequent complications interfered with what should have been her joyful experience of new motherhood. I was so grateful to be there for her.

It wasn't until the end of the second week that I happened to notice a liquor shelf in her kitchen I must have walked by ten times a day. The shelf held an assortment of wines and hard alcohol collected over the years. As I looked at the bottles, I wondered about the woman who needed alcohol more than she cared for her children? How does one explain that to people who don't understand the tragic soul death of alcoholism? It now felt as if the choice to drink had been removed, it just didn't exist anymore. I felt free to be who I was meant to be, my own person, a mother, a wife, a friend, an employee. Not a prisoner of my addictions with an inability to tolerate my feelings and cope with life.

I can't even explain exactly how the relapses stopped almost fourteen years ago, or why that last drink was my last drink. I think I just gave up fighting and allowed the good to come into my life. If you feel good about yourself, you don't try to harm yourself. I also completed the Twelve Steps and then sponsored women, which was something I had never done previously. I had left the main ingredient out of the recipe of sobriety. As for the almost impossible struggle to stay sober, to paraphrase Churchill, "Success is the ability to move from one failure to another without loss of enthusiasm."

I realized now, I had never given up; I never quit trying.

* * *

In February of 2016, Barry and I were in Philadelphia celebrating his mother's eighty-fifth birthday when Sam called me. "Hi, Mum," she said, "Grandma's back in the hospital." I could hear the stress in her voice.

I had been in the hospital with her the week before on the day of her eighty-fifth birthday. She had endured a twelve-hour wait in the emergency room before being given a bed. I had arrived after work and traded places with her caretaker Nan. By then my mother was delusional and suffering dehydration. She was given fluids intravenously, but fifteen minutes later she pulled the IV out of the back of her hand, and no one returned to replace it despite my pleas for help.

After three days the in the hospital doctors had deemed her well enough to go home. Now she was back in the hospital with what appeared to be internal bleeding and Sam was getting calls asking her to make life-and-death decisions.

"I can't do it Mum! I don't know what to do." She sounded panicked.

"It's okay Sam, I'm flying back in the morning and I'll take all the calls now."

I felt Sam might be suffering post-traumatic stress disorder flashbacks from her father's death. She had also experienced the recent suicide death of an ex-boyfriend with whom she had had a long and tumultuous relationship. My mother's health crisis was too much for her to handle.

Barry and I drove straight to the hospital from Los Angeles International Airport. By then my mother was in intensive care and intubated. As I looked at her small and shrunken frame surrounded by technology that was keeping her alive, I realized she had seen me the same way after the horse accident so many years before.

I realized how helpless she must have felt.

Barry went home to relieve our dog sitter, promising that he'd be back as soon as he could. I donned the oversized gown and gloves that were too tight and settled into an uncomfortable plastic armchair. I had no idea how long I would be there.

I started texting friends and emailing my two aunts in England. I also texted Pete, letting him know that our mother was hospitalized with complications from internal bleeding. I told him she was in critical condition and I would keep him updated.

Within the next hour both her primary care physician and the doctor on shift stopped by the room to talk to me. They let me know that my mother was bleeding from her small intestine. She had also contracted Clostridium difficile and her blood pressure was rapidly dropping. They were able to stabilize her temporarily with intravenous blood pressure medication and keep her sedated with Dilaudid and Propofol.

Her doctor looked at me gently as he explained the facts.

"Your mother is not going to be able to recover from the extent of her organ damage. Her kidneys have stopped working and we can see from lab work that her liver is also compromised."

I turned and looked at my mother's grotesquely swollen and discolored hands resting on top of the hospital sheet and wondered if she could hear what we were saying.

"If we stop the blood pressure medication she will pass fairly quickly," he continued.

Both physicians concurred there was no bringing my mother back. They said they would leave me to process the information and spend some time with her. Sam arrived and gowned up, and Barry shortly thereafter. I had told Katie not to come, it wasn't worth the risk of exposing her three-month old baby to C. Diff. Sam sat on my lap and I held her, just as I had when she was a child. The room was cold, and we were all tired.

"Mom, I feel so bad for always making fun of Grandma and not being kinder to her," Sam whispered as she lay her head on my shoulder.

"I do too Sam, but it was hard not to as she was so inappropriate and said such crazy stuff. Let's get up and talk to her."

I led Sam by the hand to my mother's bedside.

"Mum," I said, my voice suddenly catching in my throat. "I'm sorry for not being kinder and more understanding."

Sam's arm was around my waist and her other hand stroking the bangs off my mother's forehead. "Grandma, I'm sorry I always made fun of you. Please forgive me."

"Please forgive me Mum," I added, also caressing her head.

Sam turned to me with tears in her eyes. "Mom, I have to go. I can't stay and watch her die."

"I understand. You don't have to stay. I'll be here and so will Barry."

As she left, the nurse came back into the room.

"I've made the decision." Now crying, I told the nurse, "You can stop the medication and let her go."

She reached out and gently touched my arm, and then walked over to an IV tower, turned a knob, and flipped a switch.

Was it that easy?

I stayed by my mother's head and rested my hand on her shoulder.

"Mum, can you hear me? Can you hear me? Mum?" I said raising my voice desperately trying to elicit a response, a last connection.

"Just tell her you love her," Barry said softly.

I told her I loved her and stroked her forehead as I watched her heart rate on the screen drop from eighty-eight beats per minutes to fifty within ten minutes. I told her to relax and not worry. As I touched her, I sadly realized that I never hugged or held my mother and I felt a deep sense of sadness that our relationship had lacked that physical component.

I was caught off guard when her heart rate dropped from fifty to zero. I didn't expect it to happen so fast. She hadn't moved or taken a visible last breath during that time. This was nothing like my father's passing. I could hear Barry softly weeping behind me, his hand resting on my shoulder. In that moment, on that day, I felt like I had lost a perfect mother. All the craziness and dysfunction were eradicated. I knew she loved me and that was all that mattered. All the years I had hated her and blamed her for all my problems melted away like a sheet of ice on a lake warmed by the sunshine.

Goodbye, Mum. I love you and I'll miss you.

The Hidden Power

"Strange as it may seem to you, there exists a mystic power that is able to transform your life so thoroughly, so radically, so completely, that when the process is completed, your own friends would hardly recognize you, and, in fact, you would scarcely be able to recognize yourself. You would sit down and ask yourself: 'Can I really be the man or woman that I vaguely remember, who went about under my name six months or six years ago? Was I really that person? Could that person have possibly been me?' And the truth will be that while in one sense you are indeed the same person, yet in another sense you will be someone utterly different."

Emmet Fox, *The Wonder Child*

Acknowledgements

I would like to thank, Victor Wilson, Mikey and Adam Reid, Steven Karash, Sherry Robb and the Robb Company, Robin Krieger M.F.T., Gail Garbutt, Allie Levy Akoka M.F.T., and Gina Trikonis for all your support and feedback.

Amanda, Samantha, William, and Richard, for making me feel part of your family.

Fox Huntington and Nick Huntington for their creative input.

My daughter Katie Fox, without whose critical eye and talented writing, this memoir would never have birthed into the world. My daughter, Sam Fox for her creative talent, feedback, and myriad concepts for a cover.

Jean-William and David Claxton, thank you for accepting me as your stepmother and I love you both very much.

Thank you to the program of Alcoholics Anonymous, my sober brothers and sisters, and the women I sponsor and have sponsored in the past. I cannot name you due to anonymity. You have all made me realize we cannot walk this sobriety journey alone.

Dr. Walter Thomas, who believed in me and gave me the opportunity to run a successful community treatment facility. My amazing coworkers, who I probably bored to death, endlessly talking about the challenges of writing a memoir.

The Claxton family who became my surrogate family and showed me a healthy family system.

Barry Claxton, the love of my life. Thank you for your patience and understanding as I struggled through thirteen years of writing, editing, and re-writing this memoir.

About the Authors

Janine (left) and Katie Fox

Janine Fox survived an extraordinary life. From a childhood of abuse, neglect, abandonment, and British boarding schools interspersed with summer vacations on Corsican nudist beaches. She came to the US in 1985 with her young daughter Katie. Following years of a severe eating disorder and brutal addictions, she emerged a survivor. Janine has run treatment facilities since 2004, helping hundreds recover from their life-threatening addictions. She lives in Agoura Hills, California with her husband Barry. They share a blended family of four, including several animals.

Katie Fox lives with her partner and son, surrounded by nature in a peaceful canyon. She teaches at a private school and enjoys sharing her passion for reading and writing with her students.

Made in the USA
Monee, IL
22 December 2023

48156150R00178